# DISCIPLE'S PRAYER LIFE

## Walking in Fellowship with God

# T. W. Hunt &
# Catherine Walker

LifeWay Press
Nashville, Tennessee

© Copyright 1997 • LifeWay Press
6th reprint 2002

Originally published 1988
© Copyright The Sunday School Board of the Southern Baptist Convention

ISBN 0-7673-3494-9

This book is a resource in the Prayer category of the Christian Growth Study Plan.
Course CG-0001

Dewey Decimal Classification: 248.3
Subject Heading: PRAYER

Unless otherwise indicated, biblical quotations are from the *King James Version*.

Quotations marked NASB are from the NEW AMERICAN STANDARD BIBLE,
© Copyright The Lockman Foundation, 1960, 1962, 1963, 1968, 1971, 1972, 1973, 1975, 1977, 1995.
Used by permission.

Quotations marked NIV are from the Holy Bible, *New International Version*,
copyright © 1973, 1978, 1984 by International Bible Society.

To order additional copies of this resource: WRITE LifeWay Church Resources Customer Service,
One LifeWay Plaza, Nashville, TN 37234-0113; FAX order to (615) 251-5933; PHONE 1-800-458-2772;
EMAIL to *CustomerService@lifeway.com*; ONLINE at *www.lifeway.com*; or visit the LifeWay Christian Store serving you.

"In 1974 God called Glaphré to a life of prayer. What began as a private ministry of prayer developed into a nondenominational teaching ministry called *Prayerlife*. *Prayerlife* helps people around the world, from children to adult, develop intimate fellowship with God. There are audio and video seminars for all ages and other devotional materials available."

Design: Edward Crawford
Cover illustration: Richard Tuschman

*Printed in the United States of America*

Adult Ministry Publishing
LifeWay Church Resources
One LifeWay Plaza
Nashville, TN 37234-0175

# CONTENTS

The Authors. . . . . . . . . . . . . . . . . . . . . . . . . . . . . . . . . . . . . . . . . . . . . . . . . . . . . . . . . . 4

Week 1: Developing a Life of Prayer . . . . . . . . . . . . . . . . . . . . . . . . . . . . . . . . 5

Week 2: Knowing God. . . . . . . . . . . . . . . . . . . . . . . . . . . . . . . . . . . . . . . . . . . . 21

Week 3: Walking in Personal Fellowship with God. . . . . . . . . . . . . . . . . . . . 35

Week 4: Using the Bible in Prayer . . . . . . . . . . . . . . . . . . . . . . . . . . . . . . . . . 48

Week 5: Expressing Gratitude in Prayer . . . . . . . . . . . . . . . . . . . . . . . . . . . . 63

Week 6: Worshiping God in Prayer . . . . . . . . . . . . . . . . . . . . . . . . . . . . . . . . 79

Week 7: Praying Together . . . . . . . . . . . . . . . . . . . . . . . . . . . . . . . . . . . . . . . . 95

Week 8: Agreeing with God. . . . . . . . . . . . . . . . . . . . . . . . . . . . . . . . . . . . . . 109

Week 9: Applying the Principles of Asking . . . . . . . . . . . . . . . . . . . . . . . . . 125

Week 10: Dealing with Hindrances and Delays. . . . . . . . . . . . . . . . . . . . . . 141

Week 11: Asking for Yourself and Others. . . . . . . . . . . . . . . . . . . . . . . . . . . 158

Week 12: Praying for Missions . . . . . . . . . . . . . . . . . . . . . . . . . . . . . . . . . . . 173

Week 13: Establishing a Ministry of Prayer . . . . . . . . . . . . . . . . . . . . . . . . 187


Prayer Guides . . . . . . . . . . . . . . . . . . . . . . . . . . . . . . . . . . . . . . . . . . . . . . . . 205
How to Memorize Scripture . . . . . . . . . . . . . . . . . . . . . . . . . . . . . . . . . . . . 218
How to Have a Quiet Time . . . . . . . . . . . . . . . . . . . . . . . . . . . . . . . . . . . . . 218
Bible Promises . . . . . . . . . . . . . . . . . . . . . . . . . . . . . . . . . . . . . . . . . . . . . . . 220
Praise and Thanksgiving List . . . . . . . . . . . . . . . . . . . . . . . . . . . . . . . . . . . 222
Daily Intercession . . . . . . . . . . . . . . . . . . . . . . . . . . . . . . . . . . . . . . . . . . . . 223
Weekly Intercession. . . . . . . . . . . . . . . . . . . . . . . . . . . . . . . . . . . . . . . . . . . 223
Daily Prayer List . . . . . . . . . . . . . . . . . . . . . . . . . . . . . . . . . . . . . . . . . . . . . 224
Weekly Prayer List . . . . . . . . . . . . . . . . . . . . . . . . . . . . . . . . . . . . . . . . . . . 225
Leader Guide. . . . . . . . . . . . . . . . . . . . . . . . . . . . . . . . . . . . . . . . . . . . . . . . 226
Christian Growth Study Plan . . . . . . . . . . . . . . . . . . . . . . . . . . . . . . . . . . . 243

# THE AUTHORS

T. W. HUNT, who wrote the content for *Disciple's Prayer Life*, has given much of his life to teaching others the ways of the Lord. For 24 years he taught music and missions at Southwestern Baptist Theological Seminary in Forth Worth, Texas. For 7 years prior to his retirement T.W. served as a prayer consultant for The Sunday School Board of the Southern Baptist Convention. He was a member of the Bold Mission Prayer Thrust Team that issued a Call to Prayer and Solemn Assembly on September 17, 1989.

T. W. is a graduate of Ouachita Baptist College and holds master of music and doctor of philosophy degrees from North Texas State University. In addition to *Disciple's Prayer Life: Walking in Fellowship with God*, T. W. has written numerous articles and several other books, including *Music in Missions: Discipling Through Music*, *The Life-Changing Power of Prayer* (previously published as *The Doctrine of Prayer*), *The Mind of Christ*, and *From Heaven's View*. T. W. also compiled and wrote portions of *Church Prayer Ministry Manual*.

T. W. is married to his childhood sweetheart, Laverne. They have one daughter, Melana, and five grandchildren. T. W. and Laverne make their home in Spring, Texas.

CATHERINE WALKER, the writer of the learning activities for this course, served as a missionary in China and Indonesia from 1946 until 1980. During this 34-year period she taught Bible and wrote seven seminary textbooks for the Indonesia Seminary. Her *Bible Workbook and Study Guide*, volumes 1 and 2, has been used by Bible students for more than 40 years. After retiring from the mission field, Catherine served as special assistant to the president for intercessory prayer at the International Mission Board of the Southern Baptist Convention. A native of Georgia, she attended Wheaton College, Columbia Bible College, and WMU Training School (now a part of Southern Baptist Theological Seminary). She received her doctor of education degree from Southwestern Baptist Theological Seminary. Catherine resides in Richmond, Virginia.

## [ *week 1* ]
# DEVELOPING A LIFE OF PRAYER

**Giving God a Reason**

On the outskirts of Longview, Texas, I realized with horror that the clutch on our car had gone out! In only two hours I was to be in Shreveport, Louisiana, to begin the first session of a Bible conference on the mind of Christ. To get to the foreign-car repair shop without a clutch, I had to put the car into second gear with the engine off, then hold tightly while the car bucked like a horse as I started the motor. Every stop sign or light required us to buck to a stop and buck to a start again.

I prayed and my wife prayed with me: "Father, I am going to teach the very work and character of Jesus. That itself is a legitimate basis for asking You to get us to Shreveport in time. Paul prayed that You would fulfill every desire for goodness and the work of faith with power in the lives of the Thessalonians, 'that the name of our Lord Jesus Christ may be glorified in you, and ye in him, according to the grace of our God and the Lord Jesus Christ' (2 Thess. 1:11-12). That is what I am on my way to do—glorify the Lord Jesus. It is Your work I am doing, Your Word I am teaching, and Your Son I am glorifying. On these bases we ask that You get this car fixed in time for us to arrive before the conference begins."

The shop owner gave me the bad news that the hydraulic brake valve had gone out. He began to call parts shops, finally locating the part in a shop that was about to close for the day! The man jumped in his car and raced off to get the part. More than a half hour later, he returned obviously worn-out, pointed his finger in my face, and exclaimed: "Mister, you're not living right! Just after I left here, I had a flat. After I got the flat fixed, I got stopped by a train. Then in downtown traffic at a left-hand turn, the car ahead of me stalled, the driver threw up the hood, and I could not pull right into the heavy traffic."

By that time he had the attention of everyone in the shop. The mechanics were staring at me. I told him: "Let me give you another view of these troubles. I am on my way to lead a Bible conference, and you have just informed me that Satan doesn't want me to get there. Now I am more excited about what God wants to do in that church!" The whole shop stared open-mouthed at my pronouncement, so I finally broke the silence. "Did you get the part?" Well, yes, he did.

After handing the valve to the mechanics, he told me of his own faith in the Lord and volunteered to lend me a car. However, my prayer had not been for another car. I had prayed for God to fix our car. I told the man I believed that the mechanics would finish quickly. In a few minutes the mechanic brought me the key. I had been concerned about the expense, because we do not travel with much money. When I asked about the charges, the mechanic grinned as he replied: "Mr. B. [the owner] told us not to charge the preacher for the part; he wants to give it to you. We mechanics decided that you were different from anyone we had ever met before. We would also like to give you our labor!"

We sang and praised the Lord all the way to Shreveport—and arrived in time!

# Day 1

## Introduction to *Disciple's Prayer Life*

Welcome to a study of *Disciple's Prayer Life: Walking in Fellowship with God*. You are beginning the study of one of the most exciting subjects of your life, one you can study for the rest of your life. You were created for fellowship with God, your Creator. As you learn about and practice the ways men and women of the Bible walked in fellowship with God, you will discover that your own relationship with God will become a fresher experience every day.

This book is not one to be skimmed in an eager search to find new ideas about prayer. The teachings presented must be experienced if they are to be learned. The unique feature of this course is constant interaction between information about prayer and practice based on that information. The teaching in your workbook is highly experiential. You will learn much in prayer by following the instructions given throughout each week's study. Only God knows what He plans to do in your life as you seek to have continuous fellowship with Him in prayer. We have a very ambitious learning goal for this course:

> ### COURSE LEARNING GOAL
> After completing the study of *Disciple's Prayer Life: Walking in Fellowship with God*, you will understand and be able to apply biblical principles that develop intimacy with God and effectiveness in prayer. You will demonstrate your commitment to God's leadership about your involvement in a personal or church prayer ministry.

 Read the course learning goal again and circle the key words that describe the kind of prayer life you can expect to develop. Write those key words here:

You may have written other words, but at least three concepts will characterize your prayer life after you complete this course: greater *intimacy* with God, *effectiveness* in prayer, and a *commitment* to become involved in a personal or church prayer ministry. Read more about this course.

### *Disciple's Prayer Life* Is a LIFE Course

*Disciple's Prayer Life* is a course in the Lay Institute for Equipping (LIFE) learning system. LIFE provides a variety of courses designed to equip laypersons for ministry in the church and in the world. *Disciple's Prayer Life* is designed to equip you for a ministry of worship and intercession, or praying for others.

*MasterLife* by Avery T. Willis, Jr., is the foundational LIFE course. Though *MasterLife* is not a prerequisite for this course, it provides spiritual preparation for the basic disciplines and ministries of the Christian life. If you have not experienced *MasterLife*, you may want to consider it for your next course of study.[1]

All LIFE courses share common characteristics:

• You will interact with this self-paced workbook for 30 to 60 minutes each day.

- You will meet once each week for a group session to process and practice what you have learned during the week.
- Practical exercises will help you make learning life-related and life-changing.

## Getting Started

*Resources you will need.* You are reading your primary resource—your *Disciple's Prayer Life* workbook. In addition, if your leader has not already done so, he or she needs to secure for you a copy of *The Life-Changing Power of Prayer* by T. W. Hunt.[2] You will also need a Bible, a pencil, and extra paper.

*Get acquainted with your workbook.* Check the following steps as you complete them.

❑ Using the contents page (p. 3), turn to the first page of each week's study. Read the key idea and the learning goal for each week. Which week's topic are you most anxious to study? _____

❑ Locate the 12 prayer guides beginning on page 205. These prayer guides are practical resources you will use throughout the course to learn to pray more effectively. After you study a prayer guide as directed in your workbook, regularly review the guide so that you can use the concepts and principles in your daily prayer life. You may photocopy the charts in these prayer guides for your personal use in prayer.

❑ Find the prayer articles and charts on pages 218–25. These are additional tools you will use during your daily quiet time. You may photocopy the charts in these sections for your personal use in prayer.

❑ Cut out the Scripture-memory cards that follow page 244 and carry them with you to review often.

❑ If you plan to lead a group study of this course, overview the leader guide on pages 226–42.

❑ Turn to page 243 and read about the Christian Growth Study Plan. What must you do to earn a *Disciple's Prayer Life* diploma?

_____

_____

*The most important thing you will do in this course is to pray.*

You should have written five things: (1) read this book, (2) complete the learning activities, (3) attend group sessions, (4) show your work to a church leader, and (5) complete and return the form on page 243.

## Your Daily Quiet Time

The most important thing you will do in this course is to pray. Therefore, you will be asked to have a daily quiet time with God. To keep notes of your communication with the Father, you will use the Daily Master Communication Guide in the margin of each day's lesson to record what God says to you and what you say to God. Each day you will need to select a Scripture verse to focus on during your quiet time. You may choose one of the verses from the day's lesson, or you may choose your own verse.

**Examine today's Daily Master Communication Guide on page 9.**

After you have completed this course, plan to continue the important practice of a daily quiet time. You can create your own prayer journal by recording in a blank journal or notebook your daily communication with God. You may also want to duplicate and insert in a three-ring notebook the prayer guides on pages 205–17, as well as the prayer articles and charts on pages 218–25. Feel free to photocopy the charts in these sections of your workbook for your personal use in prayer. Another option for your quiet times after this study is to use *Day by Day in God's Kingdom: A Discipleship Journal*, which provides an easy-to-use format for your daily quiet time. This 13-week journal provides room for you to write entries about your Bible reading and prayer five days each week.[3]

## Study Tips

Five days a week you will be expected to study a segment of material. Thirty minutes to one hour of study time will be needed each day. Throughout this course you will be asked to answer questions, reflect on problems, pray, or complete other assignments. To gain the most from this course, pause in your reading to complete each assignment as you come to it. If you do not follow this approach, you will miss significant opportunities to learn and apply teachings that will change your life. Look on *Disciple's Prayer Life* as a teacher who is working with you one-to-one. When he asks a question or gives an assignment, he awaits your response. Then, in most cases, he gives you feedback on the correctness of your response.

Each week's study recommends two "Verses to Memorize." You may choose to memorize one or both. Work on your memory verses every day and *review, review, review*. At the end of each week you will be asked to write your verse(s) from memory. You will also share your memory verses in the group sessions.

 **Turn to page 218 and read "How to Memorize Scripture." Select one of your memory verses for this week on page 5 and study it according to the instructions you read.**

Decide on a definite, quiet place for study where you will be reasonably uninterrupted. A table or a desk will enable you to spread out your books and have all of your resources at your fingertips.

Begin each day's study with a brief prayer. God is concerned that you learn to pray. He wants to fellowship with you in prayer. His Holy Spirit will be your special Teacher, so welcome His activity in your study times.

Each day ends with an assignment called "Walking in Fellowship with God Today." This section gives you a specific suggestion for your prayers during the next 24 hours. It usually helps you focus on and apply concepts or principles you have studied that day. Take these assignments very seriously. Our primary desire and prayer is that you develop intimate fellowship with God. Walk and talk with Him every day. You may want to jot the suggestions on a card or in your daily schedule planner to remind you of the assignment as you go through the day.

*Disciple's Prayer Life* will require faithfulness and commitment to the task. If you will spend time in God's Word and in prayer as suggested in this workbook,

*To gain the most from this course, pause in your reading to complete each assignment as you come to it.*

your life will be changed forever after these 13 weeks. If you are serious about learning to pray more effectively, prayerfully consider making the *Disciple's Prayer Life* Covenant that follows.

---

### DISCIPLE'S PRAYER LIFE COVENANT

Because I want to learn to pray more effectively, I covenant with God and my *Disciple's Prayer Life* group to study faithfully *Disciple's Prayer Life* between sessions and to contribute openly during our small-group sessions. Furthermore, I will seek to attend every session, to have a daily quiet time, and to pray daily for those in my *Disciple's Prayer Life* group between sessions.

Signed: _____ Date: _____

Group members:

_____     _____

_____     _____

_____     _____

_____     _____

_____     _____

_____     _____

---

### ❧ Walking in Fellowship with God Today ❧

1. If you signed the *Disciple's Prayer Life* Covenant, you made a significant commitment of yourself to God and to your *Disciple's Prayer Life* group. Throughout the next 24 hours, reflect on your commitment and pray this prayer: "Lord, teach me to pray."
2. Read "How to Have a Quiet Time" on page 218. Then have your quiet time, focusing on the verse you memorized today. Complete the Daily Master Communication Guide in the margin.

---

[1] To order MasterLife: WRITE LifeWay Church Resources Customer Service; One LifeWay Plaza; Nashville, TN 37234-0113; FAX order to (615) 251-5933; PHONE 1-800-458-2772; EMAIL to *CustomerService@lifeway.com*; order ONLINE at *www.lifeway.com*; or visit the LifeWay Christian Store serving you.
[2] Order *The Life-Changing Power of Prayer* (item 0-6330-1980-1) from one of the sources in footnote 1.
[3] Order *Day by Day in God's Kingdom: A Discipleship Journal* (item 0-7673-2577-X) from one of the sources in footnote 1.

---

## Daily Master Communication Guide

SCRIPTURE REFERENCE:

_____

*What God said to me:*

_____

_____

_____

_____

_____

_____

*What I said to God:*

_____

_____

_____

_____

_____

_____

_____

# Day 2
# Acknowledging God's Honor and Character

## A Reason to Answer

All answered prayer begins in God. God calls His children to prayer. God Himself is the great Initiator. Prayer serves God's purposes before it serves humanity's. The prayers in the Bible are records of men and women who recognized God's initiative and sought the divine mind about His directions for their lives.

Whenever men and women of the Bible presented requests to God, they presented bases for asking. Those bases always reflected divine purposes. The particular bases that biblical characters used varied with the persons asking and the circumstances of their requests. If we look carefully, however, we always find a reason for God's granting the request. Looking closely at the wording of prayers in the Bible, we sense that the men and women of the Bible had heard God ask them, "Why should I grant this request?" In other words, they approached prayer seeking God's viewpoint. They wanted to pray for what God wanted to do. Then they offered God a reason to grant their requests.

As you develop your prayer life, keep in mind that God's perspective must always be considered. Each time you prepare to make a request of God, ask yourself, *Why should God answer this prayer?* Give God a reason to answer.

This week you will study four reasons God answers prayer. Learn these four reasons, which appear in the box below, and practice using them in your prayers this week. Prayer guide 1, "Giving God a Reason," on page 205 also lists the four reasons. Refer to that tool in your prayer times each day as you practice basing your prayers on these reasons.

> ### REASONS GOD ANSWERS PRAYER
> 1. The prayer acknowledges God.
> 2. The prayer is supported by the intercession of Jesus through His priesthood.
> 3. The prayer is supported by the intercession of the Holy Spirit.
> 4. The prayer comes from one who is related to God and Christ.

Begin now to develop a prayer life that is properly based on sound biblical principles of prayer.

Read in the margin terms you will encounter over the next two days' studies.

## Acknowledging God

God answers prayer when that prayer takes into account who He is. The great pray-ers of the Bible did that by reviewing His attributes, characteristics, or qualities and His identity. When a person recognizes God for who He is, when a person demonstrates reverence for Him, when a person shows genuine concern for God's reputation in the world, he is acknowledging God.

 **In the list on the following page, write an *S* beside the words that have a similar meaning to the word *acknowledge*. Write a *D* beside words that have a different or an opposite meaning.**

## Glossary
*Acknowledge*—to recognize, avow, disclose, or agree with
*Character*—traits; qualities; main or essential nature
*Glory*—something that elicits worshipful praise; magnificence; great beauty or splendor; the outshining of God's attributes
*Honor*—good name; reputation; integrity
*Sovereignty*—supreme excellence; power; authority; rule

| | | |
|---|---|---|
| _____ recognize | _____ announce | _____ reject |
| _____ disallow | _____ avow | _____ proclaim |
| _____ declare | _____ contradict | _____ deny |
| _____ confess | _____ negate | _____ agree with |

Have you completed this exercise? In interactive learning it is important that you respond to assignments when requested. Then you will generally receive feedback on your responses in the paragraphs that follow. When you take advantage of these opportunities to learn, you will be surprised by how much you remember.

In the exercise above you should have placed an S beside the following words: *recognize, declare, confess, announce, avow, proclaim,* and *agree with*. The other words have a different or opposite meaning from *acknowledge*.

One reason God answers prayer is that the one praying acknowledges God. This means recognizing—

    • His honor    • His glory    • His character    • His sovereignty

Today we will examine acknowledging God's honor and character. Tomorrow we will study His glory and sovereignty.

### Acknowledging God's Honor

Many Bible prayers concern God's honor. Those who offered the prayers wanted to protect God's reputation or integrity. God's honor is His good name, His reputation. Specifically, it is the integrity of His character and His name. We acknowledge God's honor by seeking to maintain the integrity of His character and His name. Let's examine two Bible prayers in which men acknowledged God's honor.

*Ezra.* A scribe and the leader of the exiles in Babylon, Ezra asked King Artaxerxes for permission to return to Jerusalem and rebuild the temple. The king granted his request (see Ezra 7). Ezra was concerned about the safety of the people as they traveled to Jerusalem carrying a large quantity of gold and silver for the temple.

Read Ezra 8:21-23. How was God's honor involved in this request?

> EZRA HAD TOLD KING - THE HAND OF
> OUR GOD IS ON EVERYONE WHO LOOKS
> TO HIM

Why would God want to grant Ezra's request?

> GOD WAS GOING WITH THEM TO JERUSALEM
> AND IT WOULD NOT LOOK GOOD TO HAVE
> HIS PEOPLE INJURED DURING THE JOURNEY

Ezra had "spoken unto the king, saying, The hand of our God is upon all them for good that seek him." If Ezra had asked the king for soldiers to protect them on their journey, he would have dishonored God with his distrust or disbelief.

Read Ezra 8:31-32. God answered Ezra's prayer by providing the people with safe passage to Jerusalem. God answered this prayer because it was offered to protect His reputation as One who protects those who seek Him.

---

*Daily Master Communication Guide*

SCRIPTURE REFERENCE:

_____

*What God said to me:*

_____

_____

_____

_____

_____

*What I said to God:*

_____

_____

_____

_____

_____

*"Now if thou shalt kill all this people as one man, then the nations which have heard the fame of thee will speak, saying, Because the Lord was not able to bring this people into the land which he sware unto them, therefore he hath slain them in the wilderness"* (Num. 14:15-16).

*"Now, I beseech thee, let the power of my Lord be great, according as thou hast spoken, saying, The Lord is longsuffering, and of great mercy, forgiving iniquity and transgression … Pardon, I beseech thee, the iniquity of this people according unto the greatness of thy mercy, and as thou hast forgiven this people, from Egypt even until now"* (Num. 14:17-19).

*"I beseech thee, O Lord God of heaven, the great and terrible God, that <u>keepeth covenant</u> and <u>mercy for them that love him</u> and <u>observe his commandments</u>: Let thine ear now be attentive, and thine eyes open, that thou mayest hear the prayer of thy servant"* (Neh. 1:5-6).

*Moses.* After the faithless report of the spies who were sent into the promised land, God threatened to slay the Israelites. Moses prayed on behalf of God's honor. In Numbers 14:15-16, in the margin, Moses expressed a desire to protect God's honor and reputation among the surrounding nations.

## Acknowledging God's Character

Our prayers may be based on God's character. In the passage that follows the one we just studied, Moses continued his request by appealing to the character of the Lord. In his prayer in the margin (Num. 14:17-19) Moses identified several qualities of God's character, and he asked God to respond to his request on the basis of those qualities. He believed that God's power would be magnified in the eyes of the people when they experienced these qualities of God.

 **List three qualities of God's character that Moses felt would be reasons for God not to destroy the people of Israel.**

SLOW TO ANGER    ABOUNDING IN LOVE    FORGIVING OF SIN + REBELLION

The three qualities Moses identified are listed on the chart "Character Traits of God" in prayer guide 1. Turn to page 205 and check your answers.

Because qualities of God's character can serve as bases for your requests, begin keeping a list of God's character traits to refer to in your prayers. Use the remaining space on the chart "Character Traits of God" to continue a list of God's character traits. You have permission to reproduce the chart for your personal use.

*Nehemiah.* As Nehemiah heard about the tragic situation of the Jews in Jerusalem, the breaking down of the walls, and the breaking down of the gates, he prayed. Read in the margin his prayer in Nehemiah 1:5-6.

 **Reread Nehemiah's prayer in the margin and circle the qualities of God Nehemiah mentioned in his prayer. Stop and list these on the chart "Character Traits of God" in prayer guide 1, page 205.**

Nehemiah acknowledged God as heavenly, great, terrible or awesome, and a keeper of His covenant or promise. God is also One who hears the prayers of His servants.

*Hannah.* Hannah, the mother of Samuel, also included important qualities of God in her prayer of praise for her son: "There is none holy as the Lord: for there is none beside thee: neither is there any rock like our God" (1 Sam. 2:2). In the next verse she called the Lord a "God of knowledge."

 **Underline God's qualities in Hannah's prayer and list these on the chart "Character Traits of God" in prayer guide 1, page 205.**

We discover from Hannah's prayer that she acknowledged God's holiness, uniqueness, and knowledge or wisdom.

1. Reflect on the integrity of God's character. Has His perfection ever been diminished or blemished in any way? If not, His integrity has been maintained. Praise Him for the honor His integrity points to.

2. Ask God to reveal to you any areas or activities of your life that dishonor Him. Pledge to Him a determination to maintain His honor and integrity in every area of your life.

3. Think of something you are praying for. Ask yourself: *Why would God want to grant this request? What quality would God demonstrate if He granted that request?* Acknowledge that quality of God as a basis for your request.

4. Referring to the four reasons in prayer guide 1, try to base your requests today on God's honor or character. Record each request, the basis of the request, and the answer in "Prayer-Request Log" in prayer guide 1 (p. 206).

5. As you have your quiet time, complete the Daily Master Communication Guide in the margin on page 11.

# Day 3
# Acknowledging God's Glory and Sovereignty

## Acknowledging God's Glory

Prayer can be based on God's glory. God's glory is the outshining of His attributes. God is not like any other; His attributes set Him apart from all others. His glory must be acknowledged. We dare not give His glory to another or take it for ourselves. Read in the margin God's declaration about Himself in Isaiah 42:8.

The Lord required Gideon to reduce an army of 32,000 men to 300 so that the glory could not go to humanity but to God (see Judg. 7:1-25). When David pridefully numbered Israel, he was glorying in his own strength. God required of him a choice of punishments (see 2 Sam. 24:10-17). God's standards are very strict about the assignment of glory.

 Review the definition of *glory* in the glossary on page 10. Write your own definition here.

_____

The men and women of the Bible were always diligent to ensure that divine work was recognized as truly from God—they gave God the glory. Daniel was careful to credit the Lord when summoned before King Nebuchadnezzar to interpret his dream: "There is a God in heaven that revealeth secrets" (Dan. 2:28). Daniel's caution yielded a confession from the king himself about the glory of the Lord. Read his words in the margin (Dan. 2:47). Simon Peter, after he had been God's instrument in healing the crippled man at the temple gate, carefully pointed out that the glory went to God.

*Today's Learning Goal*
You will understand ways to acknowledge God's glory and sovereignty in your prayers. You will demonstrate your reverence for His glory and sovereignty.

*"I am the Lord: that is my name: and my glory will I not give to another"* (Isa. 42:8).

*"The king answered unto Daniel, and said, Of a truth it is, that your God is a God of gods, and a Lord of kings, and a revealer of secrets, seeing thou couldest reveal this secret"* (Dan. 2:47).

## Daily Master Communication Guide

SCRIPTURE REFERENCE:

_____

*What God said to me:*

_____

_____

_____

_____

_____

*What I said to God:*

_____

_____

_____

_____

_____

🌿 **Read Acts 3:11-13. How did Peter turn the attention away from himself and to Jesus?**

_____

Peter redirected the admiration and wonder of the people away from himself and to God. He explained that the healing was an evidence of God's glorifying His Son, Jesus Christ.

🌿 **Read the following passages. One is an instance in which God was given the glory due Him. The other is an example of a person's trying to assume glory he was not entitled to. Identify the person(s) involved and draw a star beside the one in which the glory went to God.**

Read Acts 12:21-23. Person(s) involved: _____

Read Acts 14:8-18. Person(s) involved: _____

We acknowledge God's glory when we worship Him for who He is or for what He has done. We acknowledge God's glory when we tell others about His marvelous works. We rob God of His glory when we claim credit for something He has done.

In the first passage in the activity, Herod refused to give God glory for giving him the ability of effective public speaking. God is jealous of His glory and does not tolerate our taking it for ourselves. In Acts 14:8-18 Paul and Barnabas went to great extremes to refuse for themselves glory that was due God.

🌿 **Assume that God has answered a request you have been praying about for years. With joy you tell others about the answered prayer. What are some things you might say that would take the glory away from God?**

_____

_____

**What are some things you could say that would correctly give God the glory?**

_____

_____

Be prepared to discuss these questions in your group session this week.

### Acknowledging God's Sovereignty

God's sovereignty is another basis for our prayers. God's sovereignty means His supreme power, rank, or authority over all else.

Sennacherib was gathering his Assyrian army against Hezekiah. In Hezekiah's prayer in the margin (2 Kings 19:15-19) Hezekiah acknowledged God's sovereignty over all kingdoms of the earth. He realized that a positive answer to his request would cause all kingdoms of the earth to recognize that truth as well.

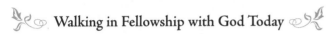 Read Matthew 8:5-13. Look for the way the centurion acknowledged his belief in Jesus' sovereignty, or authority. What were the results of the centurion's expressing his faith in Jesus' authority?

_____

_____

The centurion based his petition to Christ for healing his servant on Christ's sovereignty. He did not expect Jesus to come to his home physically. Jesus' word was enough. The centurion was correct, and Jesus healed his servant.

Many of David's prayer requests were granted. His remarkable prayer when presenting the offerings of the people for the temple gives insight into the reason. He recognized the imperial rank of the one true God as being above all creation. Read in the margin his prayer in 1 Chronicles 29:11-12.

## Walking in Fellowship with God Today

1. You'll need a vivid imagination to try this one. Imagine that you are in the enormous throne room of the mightiest monarch who ever lived—the royal King of kings, Jesus. Picture the reverent fear and respect on the faces of the courtiers, or attendants. Their eyes are on the King. Immediate access to the throne is available only through the strictest protocol. You receive instructions from an imaginary expert in protocol on titles to use when you speak to Jesus, on subjects you may talk about or must avoid, and on the various courtesies that must be observed because of His office. Now approach Him and say what you would say if you were looking at royalty—as though you could see royal robes, a many-tiered crown, and an array of royal angels ready to execute any word He gives. Live this day as a courtier of the King. Intentionally acknowledge His glory. Avoid violating His sovereignty, as you would if you were serving an earthly king.

2. Reflect on which of God's attributes or character traits are most meaningful in your thinking. Name those attributes to Him in adoration. Thank Him for showing you His glories. Today consciously and actively seek an opportunity to credit God with one of His glories in an encounter with another person.

3. Use "Prayer-Request Log" in prayer guide 1 (p. 206) to record each prayer request, the basis of the request, and the answer.

4. As you have your quiet time, complete the Daily Master Communication Guide in the margin on page 14.

*"Hezekiah prayed before the Lord, and said, O Lord God of Israel, which dwellest between the cherubims, thou art the God, even thou alone, of all the kingdoms of the earth. … Now therefore, O Lord our God, I beseech thee, save thou us out of his hand, that all the kingdoms of the earth may know that thou art the Lord God, even thou only" (2 Kings 19:15-19).*

*"Thine, O Lord, is the greatness, and the power, and the glory, and the victory, and the majesty: for all that is in the heaven and in the earth is thine; thine is the kingdom, O Lord, and thou art exalted as head above all. Both riches and honour come of thee, and thou reignest over all; and in thine hand is power and might; and in thine hand it is to make great, and to give strength unto all" (1 Chron. 29:11-12).*

# Day 4
## Jesus and the Holy Spirit—Intercessors

*Today's Learning Goal*
You will demonstrate an
appreciation for the roles of
Jesus and the Holy Spirit as
your intercessors. You will be
able to pray with the assurance
that Jesus presents your prayers
to the Father to be answered.

*Glossary*
*Intercede*—to seek to reconcile
differences between two parties;
to mediate; to pray to God
for another
*Intercession*—prayer in the
interest of another or as a
representative of another

*"Seeing then that we have a great
high priest, that is passed into the
heavens, Jesus the Son of God, let us
hold fast our profession. For we have
not an high priest which cannot be
touched with the feeling of our
infirmities; but was in all points
tempted like as we are, yet without
sin. Let us therefore come boldly unto
the throne of grace, that we may
obtain mercy, and find grace to help
in time of need" (Heb. 4:14-16).*

*"Since we have a great priest over the
house of God, let us draw near with
a sincere heart in full assurance of
faith, having our hearts sprinkled
clean from an evil conscience and
our bodies washed with pure water"
(Heb. 10:21-22).*

Today you will study the second and third reasons God answers prayer. Turn to "Reasons God Answers Prayer" in prayer guide 1 on page 205 and read the four reasons. Are you learning to use these reasons as the bases for your prayers? You should be using prayer guide 1 in your prayer time each day this week.

### Jesus' Priesthood
In all religions a priest is someone who has special, direct access to Deity. The high priest in Judaism was especially important. He had duties no other priest could perform. He alone was allowed into the holiest room of the temple, where God dwelled. This priesthood was especially valuable to the Jews in the Old Covenant.

Read Hebrews 4:14-16 in the margin and answer the following questions.

Who is our High Priest? _____

Where is He? _____

How is He like the people He represents? _____

How does He differ from His people? _____

For what purpose do we approach God's throne and our High Priest?

_____

What is our attitude to be toward approaching God's throne?

_____

God's own Son, Jesus, is our High Priest. We know that God attends to Him, for He is God's beloved Son (see Matt. 3:17). We can be assured that Jesus attends to us. He is in heaven, standing before God representing us. He is like us in that He was tempted in every way we are tempted. He is unlike us, however, in that He never sinned. We are taught to approach God's throne to obtain mercy and find grace. We should approach God's throne with confidence and boldness.

The writer of Hebrews also enjoined us to remember through whom we present our requests when we draw near to God in prayer. Read Hebrews 10:21-22 in the margin. We have no reason to be tentative or timid with our requests.

### Jesus Intercedes for You
An immeasurable assurance comes when we understand that Jesus Himself is our High Priest and that He intercedes for us. If you could choose only *one* person to pray for you, could you possibly choose a better one than Jesus Himself? You do not pray alone. You pray jointly with Jesus Himself.

Jesus' intercessory work must be especially important for our cause, because at least three New Testament writers emphasize it. Notice what each one said about Jesus and His praying. Paul asked: "Who is he that condemneth? It is Christ that died, yea rather, that is risen again, who is even at the right hand of God, who also maketh intercession for us" (Rom. 8:34). The writer of Hebrews assures us that "he is able also to save them to the uttermost that come unto God by him, seeing he ever liveth to make intercession for them" (Heb. 7:25). Later that writer gave us a lovely picture of Christ's work of intercession: "Christ is not entered into the holy places made with hands, which are the figures of the true; but into heaven itself, now to appear in the presence of God for us" (Heb. 9:24). John tells us, "If any man sin, we have an advocate with the Father, Jesus Christ the righteous" (1 John 2:1). Jesus prays for you. Every prayer you utter has Jesus supporting you, interested in you, seeking God's very best for you.

 Imagine once again that you are in the throne room of heaven. Jesus is there praying to the Father in your behalf. Stop now and thank Jesus for being your intercessor.

### The Holy Spirit Intercedes for You

Just as astonishing as the remarkable work of Christ on our behalf is the work of the Holy Spirit. Because of the Holy Spirit's intercession, we cannot plead our weakness or our ignorance; God anticipated our excuses. Romans 8:26-27, in the margin on page 18, states that He whose name is Holy is ceaselessly interpreting our prayers to the Father in light of God's will.

 This is your first assignment from the supplementary text *The Life-Changing Power of Prayer* by T. W. Hunt. Read "The Holy Spirit Helps Us Know God's Will" on pages 43–46. How would you summarize the work of the Holy Spirit in helping you know God's will?

_____

The Holy Spirit helps you understand God's will. He is both teacher and revealer of God's will.

Think of what this means: The Holy Spirit, who indwells you, is your advocate here on earth. Jesus Christ, the One who gave His life to save you, is your Advocate in heaven. You have two great, high, and holy advocates constantly working together to bring you to a position of glory before God. They both, with one mind, are faultlessly pleading and interceding for you to God. The highest motives possible from the highest Beings possible are constantly reaching on our behalf the highest throne possible.

 Read in Acts 7:54-60 Stephen's experience just before being stoned to death. Besides the angry mob on earth, who else was aware of Stephen's plight? Who else certainly prayed for Stephen? Answer on the next page.

---

*Daily Master*
*Communication Guide*

Scripture reference:

_____

*What God said to me:*

_____
_____
_____
_____
_____
_____

*What I said to God:*

_____
_____
_____
_____
_____
_____

*"The Spirit also helpeth our infirmities: for we know not what we should pray for as we ought: but the Spirit itself maketh intercession for us with groanings which cannot be uttered. And he that searcheth the hearts knoweth what is the mind of the Spirit, because he maketh intercession for the saints according to the will of God" (Rom. 8:26-27).*

Respond to the following.

What would your life and prayer life be like if Jesus and the Holy Spirit stopped interceding for you?

Describe an instance when the intercession of Jesus and the Holy Spirit may have influenced circumstances even though you may not have been aware of their intercession at the time.

 Walking in Fellowship with God Today

1. Make one statement of praise, petition, or thanksgiving to God. Now picture Jesus saying that same thing to the Father. If your prayer was not one that Jesus would present to the Father—even on your behalf—then it is not acceptable for you to pray, either.
2. If Jesus Himself were walking in your shoes today, what would He say to God? Throughout your times of prayer today, think of presenting your prayers to God through Jesus.
3. Use "Prayer-Request Log" in prayer guide 1 (p. 206) to record each prayer request, the basis of the request, and the answer.
4. As you have your quiet time, complete the Daily Master Communication Guide in the margin on page 17.

## Day 5
# Children and Servants

*Today's Learning Goal*
You will understand how you relate to God as child and servant, and you will learn to base your prayers on these relationships.

Believers relate to God as children and as servants. Both of these relationships are bases for expecting answers from the Father and the Master.

### Father and Child

God answers prayer because of who we are in relationship to Him. We frequently reject telephone sales solicitations. But if the voice in the receiver calls out "Dad" or "Mom," we usually take time, even if our schedule is pressed. After His resurrection Jesus told Mary Magdalene, "I ascend unto My Father, and your Father" (John 20:17). Including Mary in His own family relationship to the Father must have astounded her. Yet Jesus commanded us to pray to God as Father (see Matt. 6:9). This relationship as a child of God ought to influence the way we pray. God hears us because we are His children.

 Read Romans 8:14-17 and write words or phrases that indicate your family relationship to God the Father.

_____

If your list is not like ours, that's OK. We listed: *sons of God; adoption; we cry, Abba, Father; children of God; heirs of God; joint-heirs with Christ.*

Sons and daughters trust their fathers. Trust is an aspect of the family relationship, and scripturally, it is a basis for prayer. Read in 1 Chronicles 5:20, in the margin, what happened when the sons of Reuben, Gad, and Manassah were facing the Hagarites.

 Read Luke 11:2-13, focusing your attention especially on verses 11-13. List ways God is like a human father in answering a child's requests. Then list ways God is unlike a human father.

| Like | Unlike |
|------|--------|
| _____ | _____ |
| _____ | _____ |
| _____ | _____ |
| _____ | _____ |

## Master and Servant

We can also pray on the basis of being God's servants. Elijah was one of the mightiest prayer champions of all time. His prayer on Mount Carmel to demonstrate to Israel who is the true God is well known. False prophets, using the influence of Queen Jezebel, had led Israel to worship the false god Baal. Elijah challenged these false leaders to pray for their god to send fire on their sacrifices, and of course, they failed to get a response from Baal. When Elijah prayed to Jehovah, the Lord sent fire to devour his sacrifice. His prayer (1 Kings 18:36), in the margin, was made in his role as a servant of the Lord.

 Read 2 Kings 19:34 in the margin to see what God did for Hezekiah for the sake of His servant David.

_____

God often acted on behalf of Jerusalem for the sake of David, whom He called His servant.

*"They were helped against them, and the Hagarites were delivered into their hand, and all that were with them: for they cried to God in the battle, and he was entreated of them; because they put their trust in him"* (1 Chron. 5:20).

*"It came to pass at the time of the offering of the evening sacrifice, that Elijah the prophet came near, and said, Lord God of Abraham, Isaac, and of Israel, let it be known this day that thou art God in Israel, and that I am Thy servant, and that I have done all these things at thy word"* (1 Kings 18:36).

*"I will defend this city, to save it, for mine own sake, and for my servant David's sake"* (2 Kings 19:34).

*"Let these my words, wherewith I have made supplication before the Lord, be nigh unto the Lord our God day and night, that he maintain the cause of his servant, and the cause of his people Israel at all times, as the matter shall require: That all the people of the earth may know that the Lord is God, and that there is none else"* (1 Kings 8:59-60).

Read in the margin on page 19 Solomon's prayer after the dedication of the temple (1 Kings 8:59-60).

The outstanding example of servanthood in the Bible is Jesus, the Righteous Servant (see Isa. 53:11), and the greatest prayers in the Bible are His. Just as we cannot separate an employer's cause from that of his employees, we cannot separate God's cause from that of His servants. If we are His servants, it is His work that is touched by our prayers. His work is important to Him, and both in Bible days and in the present day, servanthood secures His interest in our prayers.

**Scripture reference:**

 **As a servant of God, you have tasks to complete that are His work. List some of your tasks as a servant of God.**

_____

**What God said to me:**

Both the prayers of children and the prayers of servants are important to God. When we pray as His children, our prayers most likely emphasize our spiritual growth. We call Him Father as we talk to Him. We are likely to pray for resemblance to Him and for a life that represents Him well. On His behalf we emphasize our Father's reputation and things that maintain the honor of the family name.

When we pray as servants, our prayers emphasize work. On our behalf we are likely to pray for guidance and help in our work. We call Him Master as we talk to Him. On the Lord's behalf we must pray for the spread of His kingdom and for correlation with other servants. We should pray that His blessings will demonstrate in all of His various enterprises how right His way is.

Being God's children and being His servants secure His interest in our work. Both demonstrate the richness of our relationship with Him and the many things He wants to accomplish through the power of the prayers He leads us to pray. It all begins in God and ends in God.

**What I said to God:**

 **As you pray daily, check your prayers to see that they have the right bases. Regularly review the four reasons God answers prayer (see prayer guide 1, p. 205) until you have learned to use these concepts naturally.**

Write this week's memory verse(s) on a separate sheet of paper.

### Walking in Fellowship with God Today

1. Present to the Heavenly Father one aspect of your character that you would like to be more like Him. Call Him Father as you ask Him to perfect this character trait. Pray about your relationships in the family of God.
2. Pray about your work for the Master. Ask Him to show you as His servant what is most important to Him. Praise Him for His masterfulness in creation, in revelation, and in your life. Call Him Master as you pray about your work for Him today. Use "Prayer-Request Log" in prayer guide 1 (p. 206) to record each prayer request, the basis of the request, and the answer.
3. As you have your quiet time, complete the Daily Master Communication Guide in the margin.

# [week 2]
# KNOWING GOD

## All-Powerful God

I was flying in stormy weather in a small plane to speak at a retreat in South Texas. When we landed at College Station to refuel, authorities warned us that we should not fly farther south because of the storm's severity. The pilot ignored them. As we continued south, the ceiling got lower. Eight miles out of Lake Jackson, the tower radioed: "Turn back. We are fogged in. No one can land here." By now we were too low to bank and turn back. The pilot had no choice but to pull up into the "soup" and try to turn back. He would have to try it blind, without vision.

When the pilot felt that we were headed back north, he began to ease down to try to get below the lowest layer of clouds. I looked at the swirling mists and thought, *My all-powerful Lord controls those winds!* He was also all-present—right there in the grey tumbling clouds and with us in the little tossing plane. As we cleared the mistiness of the bottom layer, our plane zoomed beside a radio-broadcasting antenna, barely missing it!

By now we were lost. We began searching for a landmark, but we were flying in open country. Night came. We had no place to land, and no airport was expecting us. Then the pilot told me that he was not instrument-rated!

For the next hour we flew in the dark searching for a landing strip. I thought of the intercessors at Southcliff Baptist Church in Fort Worth who were praying for me. Much intercessory prayer depends on <u>God's qualities</u> of being <u>all-knowing</u>, <u>all-powerful</u>, and <u>all-present</u>. My heart eased at the thought.

Suddenly we spotted a landing field illuminated for cotton dusters. The pilot brought the plane to a safe landing. We had strayed 60 miles off course, and I missed the first session of the retreat. I knew, however, that my Lord had answered prayer mightily. Since that demonstration of His all-power, my prayer life has never been the same.

## Prayer Begins with Awe and Reverence

Most mornings I begin my quiet time by pausing, before I say anything, to contemplate whom I am addressing. <u>Successful prayer begins with God's identity</u>. We are not equals with Him. <u>He is God.</u> We are the work of His hands and the product of His redemption.

Concepts about God are so great that we are forced to describe some aspects of His character with negative words. Obviously, none of us understand all that is implied by words like *infinite* or *immortal*. The *in-* in *infinite* and the *im-* in *immortal* mean *un-*. *Infinite* means *not finite*, and *immortal* means *not mortal*. God is not finite (we understand being <u>finite</u>, or <u>limited</u>) and not mortal (we understand being mortal). We cannot know how much beyond finiteness or how much beyond mortality God is. Our limitations keep us from understanding God's lack of limitations.

God is also transcendent—He is other than what we are. He is beyond our comprehension. We cannot even understand all that is implied in words like *holy* or *gracious*. All this tells us that prayer should begin in awe and reverence for who God is. Genuine awe and reverence produce humility.

### Key Idea
Knowing God is the most important element in learning to fellowship with Him through prayer.

### This Week's Learning Goal
You will know some of the qualities and names of God and will understand how they affect your relationship with Him. You will learn to base your prayers on these different aspects of your relationship with God.

### Verses to Memorize
*"That which we have seen and heard declare we unto you, that ye also may have fellowship with us: and truly our fellowship is with the Father, and with his Son Jesus Christ"* (1 John 1:3).

*"Now therefore, I pray thee, if I have found grace in thy sight, shew me now thy way, that I may know thee, that I may find grace in thy sight"* (Ex. 33:13).

### Related Prayer Guide
Prayer guide 2, "Knowing God," page 207

# Day 1
# Names of God

**Today's Learning Goal**
You will understand names of God and ways His characteristics affect your personal relationship with Him.

Two persons cannot know each other unless they tell each other about themselves. One way we can be sure God wants us to know Him is that He has revealed Himself to us in so many ways. One of those ways is through His many names in the Bible.

I have many names—Daddy, Teacher, Honey. The way people use my names reveals something about their relationships with me. Likewise, each name of God gives us a different perspective on our relationship with Him. As you read about various names of God today, consider what they indicate about your relationship with Him.

## God *(Elohim)*

The Bible begins with the words "In the beginning God." The Hebrew word for *God* here is *Elohim*, the word most frequently translated as *God* in the Old Testament. All the power of creation in Genesis 1 (and in the rest of the Bible) is implied in this word. God is first. The foremost commandment is to love God above all (see Mark 12:29-30). We are to seek first the kingdom of God and His righteousness (see Matt. 6:33). The name *Elohim* means that God is the source; all we have comes from Him. Whatever might, strength, power, and glory are visible in the created universe are infinitely less than the One who created it. *Elohim* causes us to reflect on the sum of all divine power. Through the name *Elohim* we learn that God is Sovereign over His own domain.

*"They shall teach no more every man his neighbour, and every man his brother, saying, Know the LORD: for they shall all know me, from the least of them unto the greatest of them, saith the LORD: for I will forgive their iniquity, and I will remember their sin no more" (Jer. 31:34).*

*"God remembered Noah, and every living thing, and all the cattle that was with him in the ark: and God made a wind to pass over the earth, and the waters assuaged" (Gen. 8:1).*

## Lord *(Adonai)*

The title *Adonai*, usually translated *Lord*, is used to refer to God as Master or Owner. Its first occurrence in Scripture is in a prayer: Abraham asks God (*Elohim*) as Lord or Master (*Adonai*—thus the compound name *Lord God*) about his heir (see Gen. 15:2). The title implies dominion on God's part and submission on our part. Abraham saw God as Master or even Ruler. *Elohim* and *Adonai* imply creation and dominion, power and authority. Used together in English, they form the majestic name *Lord God*.

*"He said unto him, Oh my Lord, wherewith shall I save Israel? Behold, my family is poor in Manasseh, and I am the least in my father's house" (Judg. 6:15).*

*"Moses said unto the LORD, O my LORD, I am not eloquent, neither heretofore, nor since thou hast spoken unto thy servant: but I am slow of speech, and of a slow tongue" (Ex. 4:10).*

## LORD *(Jehovah)*

The name *Jehovah* is from a verb form God used as a name for Himself that means *Self-Existent*. Although it occurs as early as Genesis 2:4, it became the covenant name for God in the Old Testament, the name God used to send Moses to Israel (see Ex. 3:13-15). It carried with it such reverence that the Israelites would not pronounce it. As the most frequently used personal name for God, *Jehovah* implies many things about Him:

+ He existed before creation.
+ He cannot cease to exist.
+ He is utterly faithful to His own nature.
+ He never changes.

God is the great I AM (see Ex. 3:14). This is one way to express the name *Jehovah* in English. If God says, "I AM," we must say to Him, "You are" and to others, "He is." This is the best news anyone can ever hear!

Most Bible translations render this name as LORD (capital L with small capitals for ORD). Thus, in most Bible translations Lord translates *Adonai* and means *Master* or *Ruler*, while LORD translates *Jehovah* and means something like *Self-Existent One*.

 **Read the Scriptures in the margin on page 22 and match them with the name or names of God used.**

     \_\_\_\_\_ 1. Jeremiah 31:34    **a. God** (*Elohim*)
     \_\_\_\_\_ 2. Genesis 8:1        **b. Lord** (*Adonai*)
     \_\_\_\_\_ 3. Judges 6:15        **c. LORD** (*Jehovah*)
     \_\_\_\_\_ 4. Exodus 4:10        **d. Both Lord and LORD**

Answers are at the end of today's assignment.

## Compound Names

God's process of revealing Himself led to using the name for God's self-existence, *Jehovah*, in compound forms with other words. Read Genesis 22:14 in the margin on page 24. When God supplied a ram in place of Isaac for Abraham to offer as a sacrifice, Abraham called God *Jehovah-Jireh—the Lord our Provider*.

 **Find and list other compound names using *Jehovah* with additional words.**

Exodus 15:26: _____

Exodus 17:15: _____

Leviticus 20:8: _____

Judges 6:24: _____

Psalm 23:1: _____

Jeremiah 23:6: _____

Ezekiel 48:35: _____

You may use these compound names in direct address in English: the Lord our Provider (*Jehovah-Jireh*), the Lord our Healer (*Jehovah-Rophe*), the Lord our Banner (*Jehovah-Nissi*), the Lord who sanctifies (*Jehovah-M'Kaddesh*), the Lord our Peace (*Jehovah-Shalom*), the Lord our Shepherd (*Jehovah-Rohi*), the Lord our Righteousness (*Jehovah-Tsidkenu*), the Lord who is there (*Jehovah-Shammah*).

This last title, *Jehovah-Shammah* (the Lord who is there), is especially promising for Christians looking forward to that final city Ezekiel described, where His presence will be manifested. It is also comforting to think of the Lord who is there as the protection of Daniel in the lion's den; of Shadrach, Meshech, and Abednego in the fiery furnace; and of Paul and Silas in the Philippian prison.

*Daily Master Communication Guide*

*"Abraham called the name of that place Jehovah-Jireh: as it is said to this day, In the mount of the Lord it shall be seen" (Gen. 22:14).*

 Take a few moments to think about and praise the Lord who is there. Write a summary of your prayer.

_____

_____

## God Almighty

Significantly, many of these names were given by God Himself. When the time came for God to change Abraham's name, establish His covenant with Abraham, and institute circumcision, God called Himself *El Shaddai—God Almighty*. The *El* is God's name in power (the singular form of *Elohim*), and *Shaddai* suggests inexhaustible resource or bounty. *El Shaddai* is one of the most powerful names in the Bible. As a matter of fact, almightiness is itself suggested in the name *El*, and *Shaddai* suggests the Almighty's willingness to supply perfectly. The idea is of pouring out blessing. You need not know Hebrew to understand that these powerfully suggestive ideas can be expressed in many ways. For example, the idea of all-might and all-supply might be expressed in names like *Powerful Bounty*, *God Who Supplies*, or *Great Bestower of Blessings*.

Answers to the matching activity completed earlier: 1. c, 2. a, 3. b, 4. d.

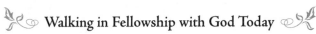 Walking in Fellowship with God Today

1. Before you begin to pray, spend a brief time contemplating who God is. Use the chart "Names of God" in prayer guide 2, "Knowing God" (p. 207), to reflect on God's names and character. Choose one of the names as your own special name for God for today. Pause and use the name in prayer on the following occasions:
   • At mealtimes    • As you begin your day    • As you get into bed tonight
2. Remember to use the name at other times in prayer (which may be silent). Focus your attention on how God's character, as revealed in that name, can meet your needs at this time of your life.
3. As you have your quiet time, complete the Daily Master Communication Guide in the margin on page 23.

# Day 2
# God Is Love

## God's Love

 As you read the following paragraph, circle words or phrases that describe God's love.

Various kinds of love are described in the Bible. One kind, a holy and sacred love, is in a class by itself. God's love is so big and so grand that it cannot be

*Today's Learning Goal*
You will be able to respond to God's love for you, His creation, by following Mary's pattern of prayer and adoration.

contained; it demands an outlet. Love must find satisfaction in reaching for another. It requires fellowship in order to be what it is. The greater the love, the greater the volume of its expression. A magnificent love reaches for a magnificent expression. God's love is so great that God Himself reached out for a wider expression—even beyond the borders of the perfect love within the Trinity. God made the human race to have more to love.

## Fellowship with God

Beings of different natures cannot fellowship, because fellowship demands that those involved share some things in common—common interests, common outlooks, common speech, and common character qualities. When God decided to create humanity for fellowship with Him, He created a race of beings in His own image. In the course of time, the ravages of sin required a further step to redeem humans after they fell and spoiled the Godlike image they were created with. God, through Christ's death on the cross of Calvary, created, or re-created, a new person. The purpose of this new creation was specifically to bring human beings into the image of God's Son. Redeemed humans are restored to a condition in which intimate fellowship with God is possible.

 **What is the reason God created human beings?**

_____

*Prayer is fellowship between the highest Being in the universe and the highest and noblest of His creation.*

God does not need us or our prayers, but He wants to have fellowship with us. Fellowship comes through our prayers. The level of the fellowship that exists in true prayer is so awesome that it is difficult to comprehend. Prayer is fellowship between the highest Being in the universe and the highest and noblest of His creation. Prayer is a joint work (see 2 Cor. 6:1 in the margin), a divine work. Prayer is the divine use of human faculties and the human use of divine faculties. The trade-off is marvelously unequal, and yet that is exactly what God wants—the fellowship of those He does not need but desires.

*"We then, as workers together with him, beseech you also that ye receive not the grace of God in vain" (2 Cor. 6:1).*

 **Read "If God Already Knows Everything, Why Should We Pray?" in** *The Life-Changing Power of Prayer* **(pp. 73–76) and complete the personal learning activity on page 76 in that book.**

**Close your eyes for a moment and think of the God of creation creating you because He wanted to love you, to have fellowship with you, and to have you reign with Him. What words or phrases describe your feelings as you think of this truth?**

_____

_____

Prepare to share some of your thoughts in your group session this week.

## Daily Master Communication Guide

SCRIPTURE REFERENCE:

_____

*What God said to me:*

_____

_____

_____

_____

_____

_____

*What I said to God:*

_____

_____

_____

_____

_____

_____

## Mary's Prayer Example

A personal knowledge of God is the most important element in learning to pray. That is why we are studying "Knowing God" this week. Mary, the mother of Jesus, had a personal knowledge of God. After Mary learned that God was going to give her a Son, she beautifully expressed her feelings about God to her cousin, Elisabeth. Mary's prayer of adoration and praise can become an example for you to follow in your own prayers of praise. Mary's prayer in Luke 1:47-55 is called the Magnificat.

Prayerfully read Luke 1:39-58, paying attention to Mary's statements about God. Now read her praise again in verses 47-55 and list the things she stated about God.

Verse 47: _____

Verse 48: _____

Verse 49: _____

Verse 50: _____

Verse 51: _____

Verse 52: _____

Verse 53: _____

Verse 54: _____

Refer to "The Magnificat" in prayer guide 2 (p. 207) to check your work.

### Walking in Fellowship with God Today

1. As you begin your prayer time today, use Mary's prayer as a guide to praise God for each of His qualities mentioned. Refer to "The Magnificat" in prayer guide 2, page 207.
2. Name some things you have in common with God (a common nature, a common outlook, common desires, a common future in eternity, and so on). Ask God to give you more things in common with Him as you grow more completely into the image of His Son.
3. Concentrate a few minutes on the person of Christ. Mentally compare the qualities in your life to those you observe in His character. Ask God to make you conscious of any un-Christlike qualities in your life. Confess and repent of those and seek His help in replacing them with Christlike qualities.
4. As you have your quiet time, complete the Daily Master Communication Guide in the margin.

# Day 3
# God Is All in All

Fellowship with God becomes more personal when we know what He is like. Today let's examine three magnificent characteristics of God.

**All-Knowing**

*Omniscient* means *all-knowing*. When we come to pray, we are touching Someone who knows everything that can be known. God knows all aspects of every case, but He welcomes the fellowship of those who are ignorant, uninformed, and unlearned. God is omniscient; yet His eyes seek a certain kind of heart for fellowship. Read 2 Chronicles 16:9 in the margin.

 **In the following verses, in the margin, what characteristics of God are mentioned?**

Psalm 139:1-4: _____

Psalm 147:5: _____

Romans 11:33: _____

1 John 3:20: _____

Some of these verses describe more than one characteristic. However, each tells us that God's knowledge and understanding have no limits.

 **How does the fact that God knows everything affect your praying?**

_____

**In light of God's omniscience (all-knowing), decide how you would pray for each of the following needs.**

1. Seriously ill, Mary is going into the hospital for tests.

_____

2. William is struggling with a job offer that will require him to move to another state.

_____

3. Having moved to a new city, Lenzie needs a trustworthy child-care center to care for her preschooler while she works.

_____

*"The eyes of the Lord run to and fro throughout the whole earth, to shew himself strong in the behalf of them whose heart is perfect toward him"* (2 Chron. 16:9).

*"O Lord, thou hast searched me, and known me. Thou knowest my downsitting and mine uprising, thou understandest my thought afar off. Thou compassest my path and my lying down, and art acquainted with all my ways. For there is not a word in my tongue, but, lo, O Lord, thou knowest it altogether"* (Ps. 139:1-4).

*"Great is our Lord, and of great power: his understanding is infinite"* (Ps. 147:5).

*"O the depth of the riches both of the wisdom and knowledge of God! How unsearchable are his judgments, and his ways past finding out!"* (Rom. 11:33).

*"If our heart condemn us, God is greater than our heart, and knoweth all things"* (1 John 3:20).

4. Patrick is experiencing marital difficulties. Neither he nor his wife can identify exactly what is wrong.

_____

Bring your responses to your next group session.

## All-Present

As well as knowing all things, God is in all places. *Omnipresent* means *all-present*, or *always present*. When we pray, we appeal to Someone who is everywhere—in all places. He is in the midst of those gathered in His name in a very special way. Although He is omnipresent, we have access to Him in only one way—through Christ.

 God's presence in all places affects our praying. For example, a missionary in Africa receives word that his mother is greatly distraught over the failing health of his father in Georgia. How do you think that the missionary's prayer for his father and mother would be affected by the knowledge that God is omnipresent?

_____

How do you think that the missionary's feelings would be changed if he believed that God was limited in the number of places He could be at one time?

_____

*"Am I a God at hand, saith the Lord, and not a God afar off? Can any hide himself in secret places that I shall not see him? saith the Lord. Do not I fill heaven and earth? saith the Lord"* ( Jer. 23:23-24).

*"Whither shall I go from thy spirit? or whither shall I flee from thy presence? If I ascend up into heaven, thou art there: if I make my bed in hell, behold, thou art there. If I take the wings of the morning, and dwell in the uttermost parts of the sea; even there shall thy hand lead me, and they right hand shall hold me. If I say, Surely the darkness shall cover me; even the night shall be light about me. Yea, the darkness hideth not from thee; but the night shineth as the day: the darkness and the light are both alike to thee"* (Ps. 139:7-12).

Do you think the missionary would feel rather helpless if God were not omnipresent? The knowledge that God is omnipresent should be a comfort and an encouragement to us as we pray.

Many Scriptures speak of God's omnipresence. Read Jeremiah 23:23-24 and Psalm 139:7-12 in the margin.

 **God's omnipresence can be a comfort but also a deterrent to sin. Why?**

_____

Daylight or dark, near or far away, we cannot hide from the watchful eye of God's Spirit. That is good news for the righteous. It is bad news for the sinner.

## All-Powerful

In addition to being all-knowing and all-present, God is all-powerful. *Omnipotent* means *all-powerful*. When we pray, we ask Someone who can do anything to act for us. He can do all things, but He wants us to do some things. We are becoming like Him by fellowshipping in His company, thinking His thoughts, observing His actions, absorbing His wonders.

List some Bible events that gave testimony of God's power. Start with these: Matthew 8:23-27; Joshua 6:1-21; Joshua 10:7-14; Acts 3:1-16.

_____

_____

Have you had an experience in which you were keenly aware that God answered prayer by using His great power? Briefly describe what happened.

_____

_____

To help you remember these three qualities of God when you pray, write them at the three corners of this triangle.

OMNI
TRIANGLE

Now briefly describe each quality. Review today's lesson if you need help.

_____

_____

_____

🌿 Walking in Fellowship with God Today 🌿

1. Concentrate on the meaning of God's presence in your life today. Is it your will to allow His omniscience, omnipresence, and omnipotence to have complete control of you in personal holiness?
2. All-knowledge is also perfect knowledge. Is there any change that perfect knowledge would introduce in your life?
3. All-presence implies personal presence. If Jesus were to do your tasks today, which would He emphasize or de-emphasize?
4. By definition, all-power controls every area of your life. One area in which most of us deny the Lord's power is His control of our tongue. Commit to the Lord your willingness for Him to control your tongue.
5. As you have your quiet time, complete the Daily Master Communication Guide in the margin.

*Daily Master Communication Guide*

SCRIPTURE REFERENCE:

_____

*What God said to me:*

_____

_____

_____

_____

_____

_____

_____

*What I said to God:*

_____

_____

_____

_____

_____

_____

# Day 4
# God Is

Today we will examine three other characteristics of God: God is Spirit, God is holy, and God is loving. (For convenience we will consider His essential nature—Spirit—together with His qualities of holiness and love.)

## Spirit

Our fellowship with God becomes greater as we know more about Him. The Bible tells us more about God's nature in John 4:24: "God is Spirit." We must have spiritual life in order to fellowship with God, who is Spirit.

In John 3:5-6 Nicodemus was told that in order to enter the kingdom of God and to have fellowship with God, he must be born of the Spirit: "That which is born of the Spirit is spirit." Do you already have spiritual life?

 **A natural person does not know the things of God and can never learn them. Read 1 Corinthians 2:14-16 in the margin and write why he or she cannot.**

_____

*"The natural man receiveth not the things of the Spirit of God: for they are foolishness unto him: neither can he know them, because they are spiritually discerned. But he that is spiritual judgeth all things, yet he himself is judged of no man. For who hath known the mind of the Lord, that he may instruct him? But we have the mind of Christ" (1 Cor. 2:14-16).*

Without a new nature and the mind of Christ, a natural person cannot understand the things of God. They can only be spiritually discerned.

We must learn to distinguish our natural inclinations from those prompted by our new nature—our spiritual nature as a new creation in Christ. We must pray spiritually if we are to pray to God, who is Himself Spirit.

 **Spend time in prayer thanking God for your new nature. Listen to what He may want to say to you about your natural inclinations. Record your dialogue here.**

_____

_____

## Holy

Holiness is another characteristic or moral attribute of God that affects our relationship with Him in prayer. If we are to fellowship with God, we must be holy, and our prayer must be holy. Holiness cannot fellowship with sin.

 **In** *The Life-Changing Power of Prayer* **read "Prayer Is Based on God's Nature" (pp. 16–18). Describe the relationship between God's holiness and His mercy.**

_____

_____

God's holiness separates Him from sinners, but His tender mercy provides for forgiveness and a restored relationship.

**Loving**

God's attribute of lovingkindness also affects our prayers. God's mercy is only one indication of His love. Knowing that God is love reminds us that He cares about our needs and that He provides for His own. Our Heavenly Father is a loving Father.

 God is Spirit, holy, and loving. On the double triangle shown, fill in the three characteristics of God we have just studied.

OMNISCIENT (ALL-KNOWING)

OMNIPRESENT (ALL-PRESENT)

OMNIPOTENT (ALL-POWERFUL)

Now briefly describe what each characteristic means.

_____

_____

_____

This Star of David may help you think of God's great qualities when you approach Him in prayer. Refer to this star in prayer guide 2 (p. 207) as you pray.

 Walking in Fellowship with God Today

Even natural things can be done in spiritual ways. Jesus had to do those "natural" things, but all of His actions were touched by the Holy Spirit.

1. Today as you eat, try to imagine how Jesus ate. He gratefully recognized His food as being from God. He also knew when the next bite would be sin!
2. As you talk with friends, try to visualize Jesus as being with you. Ask Him to speak to your friends through you—to express His holiness and His love.
3. As you work, think of Jesus in His carpenter's shop. What quality of job would He do? Ask Him to work beside you and with you today.
4. As you have your quiet time, complete the Daily Master Communication Guide in the margin.

*Daily Master Communication Guide*

SCRIPTURE REFERENCE:

_____

*What God said to me:*

_____

_____

_____

_____

_____

_____

*What I said to God:*

_____

_____

_____

_____

_____

_____

# Day 5
# Names of Jesus

**Today's Learning Goal**
By studying names of Jesus, you will understand the different relationships you have with Him. You will learn to call on these relationships as needed when you pray.

The clearest revelation of God is in the person of Jesus Christ. Fellowship with God is made even more personal by knowing the names of Jesus and His names for us.

## The "I Ams" of John
Seven times in John's Gospel Jesus gave Himself a name.

 Read each passage and briefly describe the meaning that name has for you. You will discuss these meanings with your *Disciple's Prayer Life* group.

I am the Bread of life (John 6:25-58): _____

_____

I am the Light of the world (John 8:12): _____

_____

I am the Door for the sheep (John 10:1-10): _____

_____

I am the Good Shepherd (John 10:11-18): _____

_____

I am the Resurrection and the Life (John 11:17-44): _____

_____

I am the Way, the Truth, and the Life (John 14:5-14): _____

_____

I am the true Vine (John 15:1-17): _____

_____

*The many names of Jesus indicate a variety of human needs He can meet.*

The many names of Jesus indicate a variety of human needs He can meet. As your circumstances change, your needs and desires vary.

 Think about each name of Jesus listed on the following page. Briefly describe a situation or a condition in which that aspect of Jesus' character would help you in your prayer.

Bread of life: _____

Light of the world: _____

Door for the sheep: _____

Good Shepherd: _____

Resurrection and Life: _____

Way, Truth, and Life: _____

Vine: _____

I hope you have discovered an exciting list of opportunities to call on your relationships with Jesus in prayer. Do you need guidance? Go to the Good Shepherd. Do you need spiritual resources to bear much fruit? Talk to the true Vine. Do you need comfort for your grieving heart because a loved one died? Ask the Resurrection and the Life for a shoulder to lean on. We can be thankful that Jesus gave us such clear descriptions of Himself!

Select one of the names of Jesus and pray to Him through the relationship that name portrays. Write about the name you selected here.

_____

_____

## Other Titles for Jesus

Other titles for Jesus reveal additional aspects of His character or role, deepening the way we can relate to Him.

Read the following verses in the margin. What names are given to Jesus?

John 3:2: _____

Acts 10:42: _____

Hebrews 3:1: _____

Revelation 19:16: _____

## Other Relationships with Jesus

Jesus also gave names to His followers that indicated His relationships with them. As modern-day followers, we too may have these relationships with Jesus.

*Friend.* Read John 15:12-17 in the margin for Jesus' beautiful description of this relationship.

"The same came to Jesus by night, and said unto him, Rabbi, we know that thou art a teacher come from God: for no man can do these miracles that thou doest, except God be with him" (John 3:2).

"He commanded us to preach unto the people, and to testify that it is he which was ordained of God to be the Judge of quick and dead" (Acts 10:42).

"Holy brethren, partakers of the heavenly calling, consider the Apostle and High Priest of our profession, Christ Jesus" (Heb. 3:1).

"He hath on his vesture and on his thigh a name written, KING OF KINGS, AND LORD OF LORDS" (Rev. 19:16).

"This is my commandment, That ye love one another, as I have loved you. Greater love hath no man than this, that a man lay down his life for his friends. Ye are my friends, if ye do whatsoever I command you. Henceforth I call you not servants; for the servant knoweth not what his lord doeth: but I have called you friends; for all things that I have heard of my Father I have made known unto you. Ye have not chosen me, but I have chosen you, and ordained you, that ye should go and bring forth fruit, and that your fruit should remain: that whatsoever ye shall ask of the Father in my name, he may give it you. These things I command you, that ye love one another" (John 15:12-17).

"Both he that sanctifieth and they who are sanctified are all of one: for which cause he is not ashamed to call them brethren" (Heb. 2:11).

## Daily Master Communication Guide

SCRIPTURE REFERENCE:

_____

*What God said to me:*

_____

_____

_____

_____

_____

*What I said to God:*

_____

_____

_____

_____

_____

Describe Jesus' work in the relationship and the friend's responsibilities in the relationship.

Jesus' work: _____

_____

Friend's responsibilities: _____

_____

Jesus established the friend relationship with His disciples. If you are His disciple, you learn that Jesus loved you, laid down His life for you, made known all that the Father told Him, chose you, ordained you, and gave commands to you. As His friend, you are to love one another, do what He has commanded, and bring forth fruit. Did you notice the tremendous prayer promise that grows from that kind of relationship? He has established this relationship so "that whatsoever ye shall ask of the Father in my name, he may give it you."

If He called His disciples friends, then you, as His disciple, may call Him Friend in prayer.

*Brother.* Read Hebrews 2:11 in the margin on page 33. Jesus was not ashamed to call those He sanctified brethren, or brothers. When we are adopted into God's family as His children, we indeed become brothers and sisters to Jesus, God's only begotten Son. Since Jesus called us brothers, we can consider Him our Brother. This title may seem audacious or arrogant to you. I prefer to call Him High and Holy Brother.

Write this week's memory verse(s) on a separate sheet of paper.

### Walking in Fellowship with God Today

1. In the section "Names of Jesus" in prayer guide 2 (p. 207) you will find the names of Jesus you have studied today. Use several of them today in expressing your needs, as well as in praising Him. Thank Him that He is Bread (nourishment) for your spirit, that He is your Rabbi, and so forth. Also thank Him for considering you His brother and friend. Actually say these things to God in prayer. This kind of prayer is a way to walk in fellowship with God. Refer to prayer guide 2 during coming weeks when you pray. Get to know God better through His names revealed in Scripture.

2. As you have your quiet time, complete the Daily Master Communication Guide in the margin.

# WALKING IN PERSONAL FELLOWSHIP WITH GOD

## The Lord Is My Professor

Many years ago I discovered a lovely promise in Isaiah 50:4:

> He awakens Me morning by morning.
> He awakens My ear to listen as a disciple (NASB).

Although the passage is about the Messiah, we are to realize the Messiah's character. So one night I prayed: "Lord, You know how much sleep my body needs, and You also know how much You want to say to me. I ask You to wake me up tomorrow morning at the time that will balance my need for sleep and Your desire for my fellowship."

I woke up at 5:30 the next morning, even though at that time I was a night person who had a hard time waking up in the morning. For all of these years since, that pattern has produced some interesting "awakenings" from the Lord. I have found that if I wake up at 5:00 or 5:30, the morning yields a blessed prayer time. If I awaken at 4:30, I receive an abundance of new insights into my relationship with the Lord. One morning I woke up at 3:00. With excitement I entered the prayer room in my home, dropped to my knees, and exclaimed, "The Lord is really my Shepherd!" But I suddenly realized that I knew very little about shepherds and sheep. Most of my life I have been in institutions of higher learning. So I wrote a highly personal version of Psalm 23:

> The Lord is my Professor;
> I shall not lack knowledge of God.
> He makes me understand His ways;
> He leads me into refreshing new insights.
> He restores my mind;
> He leads me in an understanding of holiness for the sake of His glory.
> Yes, though I walk in an age of dangerous untruth,
> I will fear no evil; for You are with me;
> Your Spirit and Your Book, they reassure me.
> You prepare a curriculum before me in the presence of my detractors;
> You anoint my mind with glory;
> My notebook overflows!
> Surely wisdom and knowledge shall fill me all the days of my life,
> And I shall sit at the feet of my Teacher forever!

David was a shepherd, and his prayer fit his life peculiarly. I was a professor. Now I have my own prayer identity and pattern that is pleasing to God and exciting to me!

---

### Key Idea
Knowing who you are before God is the second most important element in learning to fellowship with Him through prayer.

### This Week's Learning Goal
You will understand the way your personal identity before God can enhance your fellowship with Him. You will discover your personal identity before God and will begin using it in your fellowship with Him.

### Verses to Memorize
"My voice shalt thou hear in the morning, O Lord: in the morning will I direct my prayer unto thee, and will look up" (Ps. 5:3).

"O God, thou art my God; early will I seek thee; my soul thirsteth for thee, my flesh longeth for thee in a dry and thirsty land, where no water is" (Ps. 63:1).

### Related Prayer Guide
Prayer guide 3, "Prayer Identities," page 208

# Day 1
# Your 23rd Psalm

Last week you learned the first great secret of fellowship with God: knowing God enhances your fellowship with Him. This week we will look at the second great secret: knowing and understanding your personal and unique identity before God strengthens your fellowship with Him.

## A Unique Relationship

An individual's unique relationship with God is sometimes revealed by the names the person uses in speaking of God or to God. In week 2 you studied many different names of God.

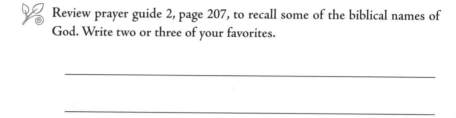 Review prayer guide 2, page 207, to recall some of the biblical names of God. Write two or three of your favorites.

_____

_____

A name used for God should be in keeping with the attitude of your heart. When you think of your relationship with God, is it as a child to a father, a worker to a boss, a pupil to a teacher, a hiker to a guide, a team member to a coach, a crew member to a captain, a musician to a conductor, a servant to a master, a subject to a king, a citizen to a president, an employee to an employer? Think about the way you relate to God most frequently.

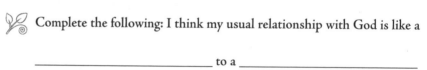 Complete the following: I think my usual relationship with God is like a

_____ to a _____

Do not continue until you have given special thought to this relationship.

With the writing of my personal 23rd Psalm, I found a way to express my own individuality with God in prayer. My prayer life, like that of the prayer champions of the Bible, was peculiar to me. My prayer identity became that of a disciple or a student, and God was especially for me the great Teacher or Professor. Prayer became learning from God. That prayer identity has deepened my sense of personal fellowship with God.

## Your 23rd Psalm

Every person has a special relationship with God that can be expressed in prayer. You have an identity with God that no other person has. God wants to be for you a special Person with an identity that can be assigned one or more titles or names. You can develop a better understanding of your identity in Him by writing your own 23rd Psalm.

Psalm 23 has six verses. Read the psalm in your Bible and notice how each verse expresses the following:

*You have an identity with God that no other person has.*

- Verse 1: who God is in relation to you—two phrases
- Verse 2: where He puts you—two phrases
- Verse 3: the walk you have with Him—two phrases
- Verse 4: potential danger and His protection—three phrases
- Verse 5: God's provision—three phrases
- Verse 6: your future in this special relationship with God—two phrases

 Using the outline above, write six verses to compose your own 23rd Psalm, expressing who God is in your life and how He has cared for you. Your psalm should describe the relationship you identified earlier in today's lesson. Use a separate sheet of paper for your work.

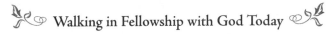 Walking in Fellowship with God Today

1. During your time of praise and thanksgiving today, use the title you chose for God in your psalm. Your choice of that title indicates that you have experienced a need or a situation in which God was adequate to meet your needs or to be Master. Thank and praise God for His adequacy.
2. Throughout your times of prayer today, think of ways God relates to you in this personal way.
3. As you have your quiet time, complete the Daily Master Communication Guide in the margin.

## Day 2
## Your Personal Identity, Part 1

### A Unique Relationship
Each person's relationship with God is unique. The way one person views God and prays to Him is different from that of another. Just as one fingerprint is different from all others, a person's prayer identity is unique.

Your uniqueness, your special circumstances, and your understanding of God all contribute to making your prayer fellowship with God special and unlike any other. Your circumstances shape how you perceive God. Your perception of God affects your fellowship with Him in prayer.

During the next two days' studies, seek to discover and understand your primary identity with God in prayer. Seek a clear understanding of how you perceive God. Seek to identify and develop your prayer activity. You will start by looking at the examples of several Bible characters.

### Bible Pray-ers
The Bible is not only the story of God's plan of redemption but also a record of the prayer fellowship of men and women with their God. They walked with God in their daily experiences.

Each Bible pray-er had a specific type of prayer life. Each was created different,

*Daily Master Communication Guide*

Scripture reference:

_____

*What God said to me:*

_____
_____
_____
_____
_____
_____
_____

*What I said to God:*

_____
_____
_____
_____
_____
_____

You will understand the way your personal identity and prayer activity enrich your prayer life. You will discover and learn to appreciate the uniqueness of your primary personal identity with God in prayer.

lived in different circumstances, and faced different problems. Each viewed God from a different perspective and therefore prayed differently.

Most likely the great men and women of prayer in Bible times did not consciously pursue a unique path or purposefully intend to be different. They simply followed God as He led. The result was a contribution to the stream of God's history unlike any other. God was able to meet their special needs as they walked their individual paths.

A survey of the prayers of the Bible reveals three very important aspects of Bible pray-ers:

1. Each pray-er had a special prayer identity (how he or she related to God).
2. Each pray-er had a particular prayer activity.
3. Each pray-er saw God in a special way (as seen in God's activity, name, or title).
   Let's take a look at two examples.

### Cornelius

 Study Acts 10:1-8,30-33. See if you can write a response to each of the following questions.

What was the prayer identity of Cornelius? _____

What was his most important prayer activity? _____

Who was God for Cornelius? _____

This assignment may have required a great deal of thought. Do not be discouraged if you did not find all of the clues. In looking for these factors, try to put yourself in the person's place. You sometimes have to read between the lines. You may not have worded your response just like ours; that is OK. Luke described the Gentile Cornelius with four phrases: he was a devout man, he feared God, he gave many alms to the Jewish people, and he prayed to God continually. Cornelius established an identity for himself: he was a *God-fearer* (see v. 2). He was not a Jew, but he sought the God of the Jews by praying to Him always (see v. 2). Thus, he pursued an important prayer activity—*seeking God*. He had already claimed an allegiance to the God of the Jews. God was for him the *True God*. Cornelius's prayers must have been very effective with God, because the angel declared, "Thy prayers and thine alms are come up for a memorial before God" (v. 4). God moved in a way that was to change the history of the world. Cornelius's prayers effectively opened the door of Christianity to the Gentile world.

### Daniel

Daniel's enemies wanted to get rid of the "competition." Knowing of his consistency in prayer, they decided that this was the one area in which they could trap him (see Dan. 6:5). They obtained a declaration that no person should pray to anyone but the king for 30 days.

*"When Daniel knew that the writing was signed, he went into his house; and his windows being open in his chamber toward Jerusalem, he kneeled upon his knees three times a day, and prayed, and gave thanks before his God, as he did aforetime" (Dan. 6:10).*

 Read Daniel 6:10 in the margin. What word would you use to describe Daniel? _____

Daniel believed that God was Most High (see Dan. 4:17; 5:18 in the margin) and above all authority, including the king. Daniel continued praying to God, so King Darius cast him into the lion's den. God proved that He really was (and still is) above earthly authority by delivering Daniel from the animals. You may have described Daniel as courageous, faithful, or loyal. This reveals his prayer identity—that of a *loyal follower*. Prayer was for him *being faithful to God*. God was for him the *Most High God*.

*"This matter is by the decree of the watchers, and the demand by the word of the holy ones: to the intent that the living may know that the most High ruleth in the kingdom of men, and giveth it to whomsoever he will, and setteth up over it the basest of men"* (Dan. 4:17).

*"O thou king, the most high God gave Nebuchadnezzar thy father a kingdom, and majesty, and glory, and honour"* (Dan. 5:18).

## Applications

Cornelius desired a relationship with the one True God. Renouncing the gods of his homeland, he sought the True God. Perhaps he claimed a prayer promise like Jeremiah 29:13.

 **Read Jeremiah 29:13 in the margin. What are some times when you might want to seek the True God?**

_____

*"Ye shall seek me, and find me, when ye shall search for me with all your heart"* (Jer. 29:13).

God rewarded Cornelius's searching by revealing Himself as Savior through Peter's preaching. You may want to become a God-fearer like Cornelius to get to know God better. If members of your household are lost, you might assume this identity before God in praying for their salvation.

 **What are some occasions in which you might want to assume an identity and prayer activity like Daniel's?**

_____

Daniel's loyalty was commendable. God protected His loyal follower from harm and received glory as Most High God. Have you ever faced situations in which you were pressured to compromise your faithfulness to God? Daniel's identity and prayer activity would be worth imitating always but especially when God can receive glory in the world through your faithfulness.

## Describe Yourself

You have examined two examples of how someone's prayer identity affected the person's relationship to God. Yesterday I shared with you how I discovered my own identity. Your 23rd Psalm may already describe your identity that is most characteristic of your relationship with God.

 **At this point in time, how would you describe the following?**

Your primary prayer identity: _____

Your most important prayer activity: _____

Who God is for you: _____

## Daily Master Communication Guide

SCRIPTURE REFERENCE:

_____

*What God said to me:*

_____

_____

_____

_____

_____

_____

*What I said to God:*

_____

_____

_____

_____

_____

_____

Keep in mind as we continue our study that these are descriptions most characteristic of your relationship with God in prayer. Your identity may change from time to time when circumstances, needs, or concerns change.

 On a separate sheet of paper write a paragraph describing how your prayer life is affected by your primary relationship with God. Consider the following questions as you write.
+ How do your needs or circumstances affect your identity?
+ What are the strengths of your prayer activity?
+ Does your main prayer activity keep you from other types of prayer that are important?
+ What feelings do you have when you think of who God is for you?

 Walking in Fellowship with God Today

Today you observed men who looked to God in specific ways. Cornelius was a seeker who looked to the True God. Daniel was a loyal follower whose eyes were on the Most High God.
1. Choose one of these titles—True God or Most High God—for your prayers today. Use the title repeatedly in your prayers throughout the day.
2. As you have your quiet time, complete the Daily Master Communication Guide in the margin.

## Day 3
## Your Personal Identity, Part 2

**More Bible Pray-ers**
Find the chart "Bible Pray-ers" in prayer guide 3, "Prayer Identities," on page 208. This chart lists the prayer relationships of some of the great pray-ers of the Bible. They came to God in their peculiar circumstances. They recognized an identity God was opening to them. They established an identity for themselves—an identity God wanted them to establish. They perceived God in a role that He chose to reveal to them according to His nature and according to who they were.

 For each person below, read the passage(s) indicated. Find on the chart "Bible Pray-ers" (p. 208) the three facts about his or her prayer relationship with God. On the line beside each name, describe circumstances, needs, or concerns that may have prompted the person to assume the prayer identity and activity he or she developed. You may want or need to read additional verses before or after those listed to learn more about the person's circumstances. If you see a different perspective of their relationship, write it on the chart.

Enoch (Gen. 5:22-24): _____

Abraham (Gen. 15:1-6; 18:23-33; Jas. 2:23): _____

Jacob (Gen. 32:9-12,24-30): _____

Moses (Ex. 3:5; 4:10-15; 32:11-14; 33:12-13): _____

Gideon (Judg. 7:1-7): _____

On the chart "Bible Pray-ers" in prayer guide 3 (p. 208) read the relationships each of the following persons had with God in prayer. You may want to study about their prayer lives as time permits.

- Hannah (1 Sam. 1:10,15-18; 2:1-10)
- Elijah (1 Kings 18:36-37)
- Elisha (2 Kings 6:15-17)
- Hezekiah (2 Kings 19:14-19)
- Nehemiah (Neh. 1:4-11)
- Isaiah (Isa. 26:7-9; 33:2)
- Jeremiah (Jer. 14:7-9,20-22)
- Ezekiel (Ezek. 3:17-21; 11:13-21)
- Mary (Luke 1:46-55)
- Peter (Acts 4:23-31)
- Paul (Eph. 1:15-21; 3:14-21)
- John (1 John 1:3; 4:16)
- Jesus (John 17:1-26)

In your group session this week you will have an opportunity to discuss some of these relationships. You will want to discover circumstances when the example of the Bible pray-er would be instructive for you. Let's examine a few right now.

## Applications

*Enoch.* Not much is said about Enoch in the Bible. Yet being a companion of God is an appealing relationship. You may be studying *Disciple's Prayer Life* because you too want this kind of relationship—walking in fellowship with God. When you are lonely, when you need someone who will listen, when you need a friend, Enoch is an example to follow. Select God as your Companion.

*Jacob.* Jacob was at a significant turning point in his life. The next day he was to face his brother, Esau, whom he had cheated out of his birthright. Jacob feared for his life and the lives of his family. With his future in the balance he recalled some promises of God. Jacob was persistent in clinging to these promises as his source of hope. God blessed him and kept His promises.

When you reach points of hopelessness, helplessness, or uncertainty, clinging to God's promises can provide you strength to face tomorrow with hope. Jacob is a good example of persistence in prayer.

*Gideon.* God enlisted Gideon to lead Israel's army against their enemy. Earlier Gideon had put out his fleece to make sure he clearly understood God's will (see Judg. 6:36-40). With confidence he accepted the task. God, as we have already learned, is jealous of His glory. He did not want Israel to claim victory by its own strength. Therefore, God drastically reduced Gideon's resources from 32,000 men to 300. Obediently, Gideon went to battle, and God won the victory through Gideon's band.

*When you reach points of hopelessness, helplessness, or uncertainty, clinging to God's promises can provide you strength to face tomorrow with hope.*

Many times our prosperity, strength, and personal resources keep us from placing our full dependence on God. When something good happens, we have a tendency to pat ourselves on the back for a job well done. When God calls us to a task and does not provide (or even takes away) resources we think are necessary, we cannot shrink from the task. We must follow Gideon's example and obediently follow God's will. He is our great Commander. He gets greater glory through our weakness (see 1 Cor. 1:26-31).

### Selecting an Identity According to Need

You, like the Bible characters we have studied, have a primary relationship with God in prayer. This identity is how you relate to Him most of the time. At times, however, a different prayer identity or activity will be more appropriate to your circumstances. By learning from the examples of Bible pray-ers, you can select an identity and a prayer activity more appropriate for your present circumstances. David is an example of someone who did just that.

 Perhaps more than any other person in the Bible, David demonstrated the greatest variety of relationships with God in prayer. The chart "David's Prayer Relationships" in prayer guide 3 summarizes David's relationships. Examine the chart on page 208. Which relationship can you best relate to today?

_____

**Read the related passage of Scripture on the chart.**

David approached God in different ways and through different relationships according to his needs at the time. David's primary prayer identity was his *humanity*. He was human in all of the senses in which we understand that word. Prayer for him was *acknowledging God*. God for him was *Lord*.

David's heart was on course even when his performance was off course. Sin or purity, victory or defeat, persecution or rulership, success or failure—all were occasions for acknowledging God. God's lordship in David's life demonstrates that human sins and misjudgments need not deter us from prayer.

### ❧ Walking in Fellowship with God Today ❧

1. Review the different prayer relationships on the chart "Bible Pray-ers" in prayer guide 3, p. 208. Select one that seems most appropriate for your situation today. Adapt it to make it uniquely yours.
2. During your times of prayer, come to God from the perspective of the relationship you have selected as appropriate for your situation today. Practice the prayer activity of the Bible pray-er.
3. As you have your quiet time, complete the Daily Master Communication Guide in the margin.

# Day 4
## Unique Praise and Thanksgiving

God created you different from anyone else. You are physically unique—one of a kind. God also works in your life in a unique way. His purpose and plan for your life are different from His plan for anyone else. God gives each of His children individual glories. Only when each of us reflects God's peculiar work in his or her life does God receive the glory that is rightfully His.

Your personal relationship with God is unique because you are uniquely created. Another way to enrich your personal fellowship with God is through the praise you give Him for your uniqueness. Each unique factor or quality in your life is a reason for praise and thanksgiving.

### Physical Traits

Are you aware that your heart pumps about 72 times each minute to carry oxygen-rich blood to every cell in your body? God created a marvelous body just for you. Your eyes provide sight, your tongue gives the pleasure of taste, your digestive system provides you with nourishment, your bone marrow produces new blood cells, your lungs provide your blood with oxygen and remove carbon dioxide, and your brain controls all this without your having to give it a single conscious thought.

 **Pause now to praise God for the wonder of His creation, particularly for your body. Perhaps you would like to begin by using the psalmist's praise that appears in the margin.**

Have you paused to pray? Consider assignments like the one above as fresh opportunities to walk with God. If you are not memorizing Psalm 63:1, I want to challenge you to do so. Begin to pray daily that God will create in your spirit the kind of desire for Him that the psalmist expressed. Continue to pray until your request is answered.

### Disabilities and Overcoming

**Do you have any physical, mental, or emotional disabilities? Do you believe you have disadvantages due to your background, education, or current circumstances? List them below.**

_____

Have you ever thought that a disability or another disadvantage could become a means of glorifying God? If you are not careful, you can let disabilities or other disadvantages keep you from achieving your full potential with what you have. This requires overcoming. God does not delight in your looks or your intelligence but rather in your growth and your overcoming. God loves you just as you are, but He also wants you to become all you can be through His help. He can get glory through your life that He cannot get from any other source. Look on your disability as a challenge to excel in a different area of your life.

*"I will praise thee; for I am fearfully and wonderfully made: marvellous are thy works; and that my soul knoweth right well" (Ps. 139:14).*

*My Prayer of Praise and Thanksgiving*

_____

_____

_____

_____

_____

_____

_____

_____

_____

_____

_____

_____

_____

_____

🌱 Reflect on any disabilities or disadvantages you listed. In what areas are you not disabled or disadvantaged? Pause and ask God to reveal to you ways He wants to get glory through your life. Write your response here.

_____

## Natural Abilities

🌱 List some of your natural abilities, such as mechanical, mathematical, reasoning, or singing.

_____

God is the source of every good and perfect gift (see Jas. 1:17 in the margin). Acknowledging God as the source of your abilities is important. Being a good steward of your abilities—using them in honorable ways—is also important. Think about a time when you used your natural abilities to help someone.

🌱 Thank and praise God for your natural abilities. Thank Him for the privilege of using them to serve others. Check each one in your list above as you thank God for it.

## Praise for New Birth

When I was saved at the age of 10, my parents sought all of the people who might have influenced my decision and thanked them for their work and witness in my life. Above all, they thanked God for my salvation and made me aware of their purposeful praise.

🌱 Describe a circumstance that helped bring you to Christ.

_____

Name the persons who were most influential in your decision.

_____

In the margin write a brief prayer of thanksgiving and praise to God for His work in your new birth.

## Spiritual Gifts

Much more important than our natural abilities are our spiritual abilities, or gifts. Do you know what your spiritual gifts are? If so, think of some ways God has used these gifts. Bless the Lord because He has given you the gifts and because He has used them.

🌱 In the margin write a prayer of thanksgiving and praise for these gifts and their use.

If you do not know what your spiritual gifts are, ask God to reveal to you the gifts He has given you. Promise to begin using them for Him as He reveals them.

## Your Kingdom Purpose

Every Christian is brought into the Kingdom for a purpose.

 **Name a way God has used you for Kingdom purposes.**

_____

What immediate opportunities for the advancement of the Kingdom lie before you at this time?

_____

What is the most far-reaching goal toward which God seems to be leading you?

_____

The three previous questions relate to God's calling for your life. In the margin on page 44 write a prayer thanking and praising the Master for His purpose for you as His servant.

### Walking in Fellowship with God Today

1. Make this a day for examining your uniqueness before God. Throughout the day celebrate with Him His purposes for your life. Ask Him also to help you appreciate His private and holy work in each person you meet. You may want to meditate on Psalm 139 or to pray the psalm to God.
2. As you have your quiet time, complete the Daily Master Communication Guide in the margin.

## Day 5
## Review

You have now been studying *Disciple's Prayer Life* for three weeks. I know that you are already experiencing a deeper fellowship with God in prayer. You have been studying important concepts this week. Let's spend this day reviewing and applying them to your prayer life.

## Two Secrets

At the beginning of this week you learned two great secrets of fellowship with God. Turn to page 36 and find them.

---

*Daily Master Communication Guide*

SCRIPTURE REFERENCE:

_____

*What God said to me:*

_____
_____
_____
_____
_____
_____
_____

*What I said to God:*

_____
_____
_____
_____
_____
_____
_____

You will be able to apply the ideas you have studied this week to your daily walk with God.

 Write your understanding of how your fellowship with God is improved by applying each secret.

Secret 1: _____

_____

Secret 2: _____

_____

*The more you know about God, the deeper your fellowship with Him becomes.*

As you get to know a friend better, your friendship can grow stronger. The more you know about God—His qualities, His character, His attributes, His names—the deeper your fellowship with Him becomes. Your fellowship grows richer as you discover more about the breadth, length, depth, and height of God's person. Likewise, the more you know about yourself, the better you are able to relate to God in ways that please Him and benefit your fellowship.

## 23rd Psalm

 Read the 23rd Psalm you wrote (see p. 37). What new insights have you gained about your relationship with God through your psalm?

_____

_____

An optional idea is to write another 23rd Psalm, using a different identity before God. If you do, bring your psalm to your next group session.

## Selecting an Identity According to Need

Referring to prayer guide 3 on page 208, read the following list of needs, concerns, or circumstances. If you were in this situation, which identity and prayer activity would you want to use in your prayers? Write the name of the Bible pray-er (or in David's case, his prayer identity).

1. Your nation is suffering from staggering sinfulness. Sin is rampant. People give no thought to God or His will for their lives.

_____

2. You observe a believer in a restaurant acting overly familiar with a person who is not his or her spouse. During your prayer time you sense that God wants you to confront your brother and challenge him to right living.

_____

3. Your employer suffered a great loss because of wrong decisions. A fellow employee has falsely accused you to cover up his own guilt. Unfortunately, you have only your word to defend yourself.

_____

4. This has been a terrific day! Your quiet time this morning was especially meaningful. On the job you got several compliments for the quality of your work. Family time this evening was a rich, quality time of abundant love. When you reflect on the day, you think, *Hasn't God richly blessed me today?*

_____

Since this is almost an opinion activity, your answers may differ from ours; that is OK. You should be able, however, to explain how your response relates to the situation. For number 1 we chose Moses. In this situation you could become your nation's intercessor, seeking mercy from the Holy One. For number 2 we selected Ezekiel as a model to follow. This is not a pleasant task. It must be done only after much prayer; yet it must be done obediently. In number 3 you are a victim who needs a righteous Judge. David faced unjust enemies in Psalm 7. That psalm and his example could become your model for prayer in this case. How would you like number 4 to be true more often? Several Bible pray-ers could be your examples here—David's worship in Psalm 103, Mary's exultation, Paul's looking to God as his glorious Source, or John's recognizing God's gracious love.

Make a habit of using prayer guide 3 when your needs, concerns, or circumstances change and you sense a need to approach God through an appropriate relationship. Study the lives of these and other Bible pray-ers. Watch for opportunities to enrich your personal fellowship with God by following their examples.

### Unique Praise and Thanksgiving

Review day 4 by glancing at your responses to the activities. Reread your prayer of praise and thanksgiving in the margin on page 44.

 On a separate sheet of paper write two or three paragraphs on the topic "My Personal Fellowship with God." Or if you prefer, write or talk to a friend and explain how this week's study has enriched your prayer life.

Write this week's memory verse(s) on a separate sheet of paper.

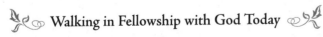 Walking in Fellowship with God Today

1. Imagine today is an anniversary celebration of your relationship with God. Spend the day celebrating your unique relationship with Him. Be as creative as you like. At the end of the day, write reflections from the celebration.
2. As you have your quiet time, complete the Daily Master Communication Guide in the margin.

---

## Daily Master Communication Guide

_____

*What God said to me:*

_____

_____

_____

_____

_____

_____

*What I said to God:*

_____

_____

_____

_____

_____

_____

# USING THE BIBLE IN PRAYER

## Key Idea
The Bible provides us models for our prayers, content for our prayers, and promises God makes to those who pray.

## This Week's Learning Goal
You will learn to approach prayer with a knowledge of Scripture and to respond by praying in the spirit and words of Scripture.

## Verses to Memorize
"I will hasten my word to perform it" (Jer. 1:12).

"If ye abide in me, and my words abide in you, ye shall ask what ye will, and it shall be done unto you" (John 15:7).

## Related Prayer Guide
Prayer guide 4, "Using the Bible in Prayer," page 209

### Applying a Bible Promise

The voice on the phone was urgent: "Dad, we need a powerful Bible promise, and we need it quickly!" We had taught our daughter, Melana, to understand and appropriate Bible promises. She explained that her husband, Steve, through no fault of his own, had not submitted an application for his navy commissioning. Six weeks prior to graduation all cadets were to submit an application for the commissioning in preparation for a ceremony on graduation day. But the authority over him had failed to notify Steve to submit the application. Now the commissioning was only two days away.

I asked her, "Why not submit it tomorrow morning?" She explained that it could not be processed within the university. It should have been submitted in quadruplicate to the Pentagon for processing. With military red tape being involved, that process required the full six weeks. She told me: "We have no way to get it to Washington, and if we did, the Pentagon could not possibly telescope such complicated bureaucratic processing into one day. I guess what we need is a verse that says that God is the God of the Pentagon!" I laughed and told her: "I can give you one better than that. Listen to Jeremiah 32:27: 'Behold, I am the Lord, the God of all flesh: is there anything too hard for me?'" She remembered the verse but asked, "Do you think that could apply to us now in this situation?"

I suggested that we pray on the telephone. We presented to the Lord the fact that Steve had been innocent in the oversight. He was trapped through no fault of his own. They had begun their marriage in the Lord and were learning the meaning of prayer. As we prayed, I sensed that a Bible promise fulfilled early in their marriage could be instructive and memorable for the new home they were establishing. Faith grew as we prayed. We were certain that even the Pentagon was under God's sovereignty! We confidently asked God to provide a means of getting the application to Washington, then to cut red tape, and finally to get the orders back—in one day.

The next afternoon my wife and I had to decide whether we believed our prayer enough to make the three-hour drive for the commissioning. We went. Steve and Melana had found an oil company that had been willing to let them use its telex machine that morning; the orders had been completely processed and telexed back to College Station—all before 2:30 in the afternoon!

This experience greatly influenced Steve and Melana's family prayer life. It did the same for us!

# Day 1
## The Value of Scripture in Prayer

If we spent all of our quiet time verbalizing our own prayer, our fellowship with God would become one-sided. Hearing from God is more important than speaking to Him. The psalmist's attitude is expressed in Psalm 85:8, in the margin. The clearest, most accurate way to hear God's voice is to hear what He says in His Word.

Paul described the value of Scripture in 2 Timothy 3:16-17. Read those verses in the margin. The phrase "all good works" tells us there is no activity in our Christian life that cannot profit from Scripture—whether witnessing, growing, or praying. The word *inspiration* is literally *God-breathed*. Our spiritual lives need the God-breathed Word. God's Word equips us for the "good work" of prayer. Four qualities of Scripture make it valuable for prayer:

> ### SCRIPTURE'S VALUE IN PRAYER
> 1. The Bible is holy; it provides preparation for prayer.
> 2 The Bible is trustworthy; it provides guidance.
> 3. The Bible is enlightening; it provides wisdom.
> 4. The Bible is true; it provides subjects for prayer.

### Scripture Provides Preparation for Prayer

The Bible is holy. Anything from the Holy Spirit is holy. Read 2 Peter 1:20-21 in the margin. Bible study is worthy preparation for prayer because it brings holiness into our thinking.

Example: Fred is reading through the Book of Psalms this month. He reads five chapters each morning before his prayer time. This practice helps him focus his thoughts on the character and nature of God in relationship to His people. Fred finds that the psalms help prepare his mind for his prayer time.

### Scripture Provides Guidance

The Bible is trustworthy. Read Psalm 12:6 in the margin. The Bible is pure. Whatever we learn from Scripture is reliable; Scripture is a trustworthy guide for living.

Example: Myrtle desires to be the kind of wife God wants her to be. This morning she read about the virtuous woman described in Proverbs 31:10-31. She read a verse, prayed, applied it to her life, and then read the next verse. Myrtle used Scripture to guide her to be the kind of wife God wants her to be.

### Scripture Provides Wisdom

The Bible is enlightening. Read Psalm 119:130 in the margin. God's wisdom need not be hidden; any of His children can understand as much as is necessary for their prayers. Scripture is a source of God's wisdom.

Example: In his quiet time John read Ephesians 5:18—6:9. When he read Ephesians 6:4, "Fathers, provoke not your children to wrath: but bring them up in the nurture and admonition of the Lord," this passage caused him to reflect on the arguments he had had with his daughter lately. He realized that his daughter's poor self-esteem may be caused, in part, by his harshness and stubbornness. He

*Today's Learning Goal*
You will understand the value of Scripture in prayer and will allow it to become an important part of your prayer time.

*"I will hear what God the Lord will speak: for he will speak peace unto his people, and to his saints"* (Ps. 85:8).

*"All scripture is given by inspiration of God, and is profitable for doctrine [teaching], for reproof, for correction, for instruction in righteousness: that the man of God may be perfect, thoroughly furnished unto all good works"* (2 Tim. 3:16-17).

*"Knowing this first, that no prophecy of the scripture is of any private interpretation. For the prophecy came not in old time by the will of man: but holy men of God spake as they were moved by the Holy Ghost"* (2 Pet. 1:20-21).

*"The words of the Lord are pure words: as silver tried in a furnace of earth, purified seven times"* (Ps. 12:6).

*"The entrance of thy words giveth light; it giveth understanding unto the simple"* (Ps. 119:130).

SCRIPTURE REFERENCE:

_____

_____

*What God said to me:*

_____

_____

_____

_____

_____

_____

*What I said to God:*

_____

_____

_____

_____

_____

_____

_____

turned to God in prayer for forgiveness and help. John used Scripture as a source of wisdom, gaining new insight into a problem he had with his daughter.

## Scripture Provides Subjects for Prayer

The Bible is truth. The Holy Spirit is the "Spirit of truth" (John 15:26). Jesus prayed, "Thy word is truth" (John 17:17). God cannot lie (see Num. 23:19; Heb. 6:18). The words of the Bible are acceptable to God in our prayers.

Example: Adele read Ephesians 3 during her quiet time. She thought that the prayer of Paul in verses 14-21 was a powerful and meaningful prayer that she could pray for her Christian friends. She began, "Father, I pray that Susan will be strengthened with might by your Spirit." Adele let those verses provide the subject matter for her prayer.

 Describe in your own words the four qualities of Scripture that make it valuable for prayer. Use these key words to get you started.

1. *Preparation:* _____

2. *Guidance:* _____

3. *Wisdom:* _____

4. *Subjects:* _____

## Jesus' Example

Scriptural words were constantly in Jesus' mind, affecting the way He spoke and prayed. He had memorized much Scripture, so it was available to Him at any time. He countered temptations with Scripture.

Read Matthew 4:1-11 and the passages listed below. Draw a line between each temptation on the left and the passage on the right that Jesus quoted to counter that temptation.

Turn stones into bread.                    Deuteronomy 6:13

Throw yourself down.                    Deuteronomy 6:16

Bow down and worship me.            Deuteronomy 8:3

If you have read the Scriptures listed, you should have the correct answers. Jesus used Scripture to refuse to yield to temptation. He taught us to pray, "Lead us not into temptation, but deliver us from evil" (Matt. 6:13). He prepared His heart and mind to resist temptation with Scripture.

Jesus also used the words of Scripture in some of His prayers. Two prayers He uttered on the cross were direct quotations of Scripture. His cry "My God, my God, why hast thou forsaken me?" (Matt. 27:46) is the beginning of the great messianic psalm on crucifixion, Psalm 22. His final prayer, "Father, into thy hands I commend my spirit" (Luke 23:46), quoted Psalm 31:5. Jesus' mind was saturated with Scripture. In the extremities of life He had access in His memory to inspired words to express prayers of an intensity we cannot imagine.

1. Select one or more of the following ways to use Scripture in your prayer time today. Place a check mark beside the one(s) you use. You may want to use all of these suggestions by setting aside several times for prayer today. As a reminder as you pray, refer to "Scripture's Value in Prayer" in prayer guide 4, "Using the Bible in Prayer," on page 209.

   ❑ Use Scripture to prepare your mind and heart for prayer (as Fred used the Book of Psalms).

   ❑ Read Scripture as a trustworthy guide for living (as Myrtle read Prov. 31:10-31).

   ❑ Seek wisdom for your relationships today by reading and praying through Ephesians 5:18—6:9 (as John did).

   ❑ Use Paul's prayer in Ephesians 3:14-21 as the subject matter for your prayers for fellow Christians (as Adele did).

   ❑ Use meaningful statements from Psalms to express your praise, thanksgiving, confession, or petition to the Lord.

2. As you have your quiet time, complete the Daily Master Communication Guide in the margin on page 50.

# Day 2
# Ways to Use Scripture in Prayer

The Bible prayers we will examine today show how men of God used Scripture in their prayers. They quoted Scripture in various ways and for several purposes. You will learn to use Scripture in these same ways. Actually, you began during your prayer time yesterday. Here are five ways to use Scripture in prayer.

*Today's Learning Goal*
You will understand ways to use Scripture in prayer and will respond by using Scripture in prayer.

> ### WAYS TO USE SCRIPTURE IN PRAYER
> 1. Quote a promise as assurance of an answer.
> 2. Quote a fulfilled promise as a reason for praise.
> 3. Apply Bible verses to a current situation.
> 4. Use Bible verses as a prayer or a praise.
> 5. Use Bible phrases in prayer.

As you read the following biblical examples of prayer, decide which of the above five ways was used. Some examples may use more than one way. On the line in each activity, write the way(s) the Bible pray-er(s) used Scripture in prayer.

**Jerusalem Believers**

Read Acts 4:24-30; Exodus 20:11; and Psalm 2:1-2. The way(s) Scripture was used in prayer:

_____

In Acts 4:24 the disciples seemed to use a phrase from Exodus 20:11 as part of their prayer. They also quoted Psalm 2:1-2 as a prophecy fulfilled by Herod, Pilate, the Gentiles, and the people of Israel in their response to Christ. The disciples also applied this prophecy about rulers being against Christ to the persecution they were receiving. They applied Scripture to their own situation.

Today as we read Scripture, we often relate verses to our present situation. For example, a believer may apply to himself the Scripture describing the storm on Galilee by praying, "Lord, say to the turmoil in my heart, 'Peace be still.'"

*Today as we read Scripture, we often relate verses to our present situation.*

### Nehemiah

 Read Nehemiah 1:4-11; Leviticus 26:33; and Deuteronomy 30:1-4. The way(s) Scripture was used in prayer:

_____

In Leviticus 26:33 God promised to punish and scatter Israel if the people were disobedient. That punishment had happened. In Nehemiah 1:9 Nehemiah recalled a promise from Deuteronomy 30:1-4. As Nehemiah prayed, he did not use the exact words of Scripture, but he used the main ideas of these promises. He quoted the essence of a Bible promise as the assurance of an answer. Quoting God's promise in prayer strengthened Nehemiah's faith. Later this week you will learn how to use Bible promises in your prayers.

### Simeon

 Read Matthew 12:18-21; Luke 2:25-32; and Isaiah 42:1-7, especially verse 6. The way(s) Scripture was used in prayer:

_____

Isaiah 42 prophesies the coming Messiah. Matthew quoted from this passage as a prophecy fulfilled in Jesus Christ. Simeon quoted from verse 6 as he met the Christ child in the temple.

Bible promises are used in prayer in two ways. As we saw in Nehemiah's prayer, a promise can be used as assurance of an answer. Simeon used a Bible promise in a different way. He saw that in Jesus the promise of the Messiah had been fulfilled. He quoted the fulfilled promise as a reason for praise.

As you read Scripture and see Old Testament prophecies fulfilled, praise the Lord. As you claim a Bible promise and God grants your request, quote the fulfilled promise as a reason for praise.

*As you claim a Bible promise and God grants your request, quote the fulfilled promise as a reason for praise.*

### Jeremiah

 Read Jeremiah 32:17-19; Deuteronomy 9:29; Genesis 18:14a; and Exodus 34:7. The way(s) Scripture was used in prayer:

_____

Jeremiah's mind was full of Scripture. God's "great power and stretched out arm" reflect "mighty hand" or "mighty power" and "stretched out arm" found in Deuteronomy 4:34; 5:15; 7:19; 9:29; 11:2. "There is nothing too hard for thee" comes from Genesis 18:14. Verse 18 reflects the teaching in Exodus 34:7. It is obvious that Jeremiah used phrases from Scripture in his prayers.

As you study and memorize Scripture, you will find yourself using phrases from Scripture in your prayers. You already use names and descriptions of God in your prayers. You may already use statements of praise in your prayers. Reflecting Scripture in prayers enriches their meaning.

Go back to the box at the beginning of today's study and underline the key words in the five ways to use Scripture in prayer.

In your own words describe five ways to use Scripture in prayer.

1. _____

2. _____

3. _____

4. _____

5. _____

In the following prayers identify the primary ways Scripture is used by writing the numbers that correspond to the ways you listed in the previous activity.

_____ a. "Father, I claim Your promise 'My presence shall go with you.' I thank You in advance for giving me courage to go."

_____ b. "Lamb of God, which was slain for us, we offer our praise for Your glory, dominion, riches, power, wisdom, and love. You are worthy."

_____ c. "Father, Paul said that You do not allow us to be tempted beyond what we are able and that You provide the way of escape. Thank You for removing my worldly roommate and for giving me a Christian roommate. You provided. I praise You."

_____ d. "'Bless the Lord, O my soul: and all that is within me, bless his holy name.'"

_____ e. "Father, guide me in preparing to teach this Bible study. You have said, "Feed my sheep," and that is what I want to do with Your aid."

You may have found some overlap, but this is how we matched these examples: a. 1, b. 5, c. 2, d. 4, e. 3.

*Daily Master Communication Guide*

SCRIPTURE REFERENCE:

_____

*What God said to me:*

_____

_____

_____

_____

_____

_____

_____

*What I said to God:*

_____

_____

_____

_____

_____

_____

1. Jeremiah 1:12, one of your Scripture-memory verses this week, tells you that God is watching over His Word to perform it, or to fulfill it. Name any Scripture that has been significant in your life—one that has influenced you; comforted you; provided hope; offered the solution for a problem; or guided you through decisions, hard times, or everyday living. Likely, God was fulfilling His Word in your life by applying that Scripture to your situation. Thank God for fulfilling His Word in your life. Review that verse or those verses as you pray and as you go through the day.

2. In your times of prayer today try to use three or more of the ways to use Scripture in prayer. As you pray, refer to the five ways listed in "Ways to Use Scripture in Prayer" in prayer guide 4, page 209.

3. As you have your quiet time, complete the Daily Master Communication Guide in the margin on page 53.

## Day 3
# Responding to God's Word

*Today's Learning Goal*
You will understand and demonstrate a willingness to practice the proper ways of responding to God's Word.

God expects us to respond to Him and to His Word. Our response to God's Word should be:

• Immediate    • Obedient    • Continuing

### Immediate
In the Bible the response of God's people when He spoke was usually immediate. The most amazing records of biblical obedience are those of the people who knew Jesus. They never questioned Him. They obeyed instantly and unquestioningly when He told them to lower their nets (see Luke 5:4-5), to leave their nets (see Matt. 4:19-20), or to leave profitable professions (see Matt. 9:9). The readiness of their responsive spirit may have played a part in the choosing of Jesus' disciples and friends. One trait He saw in them was their ability to recognize spiritual authority.

The readiness of Jesus' intimate circle to respond to Him stands in stark contrast to the unresponsiveness of the Jewish officials He dealt with. If there is no response to God, there is no fellowship, for fellowship is two-way. Jesus had two-way fellowship with Peter, James, and John. If He asked a question, they answered (see Matt. 16:13-16). But He accused the council of elders in Jerusalem, "If I also ask you, ye will not answer" (Luke 22:68). *If we do not respond to God's Word, we can have no fellowship with God.* If we have no fellowship with God, our prayers are not truly prayers.

*If we do not respond to God's Word, we can have no fellowship with God.*

🌿 Circle the words on the following page that describe immediate responses. Mark out the words that do not describe immediate responses.

| | | | |
|---|---|---|---|
| later | now | instantaneous | quickly |
| ready | delayed | meander | pronto |
| today | tomorrow | defer | hurry |
| lickety-split | hasten | prompt | avoid |
| postpone | expedite | capitulate | timely |

This exercise was not intended to be a vocabulary test. Rather, it should help you get a better understanding of what an immediate response to God's Word means. You should have marked out *later, delayed, meander, tomorrow, defer, avoid, postpone,* and *capitulate.*

## Obedient

The primary response to the Bible (and to God) must be obedience to the known commands. Some Christians may object that they are not familiar with Bible commands, but most Christians are more familiar with them than they realize. How serious have we been with the most famous of all commandments: to love God with all our heart, soul, and mind and to love our neighbor in the same way we love ourselves (see Matt. 22:37-39)? Other commandments, perhaps not so well known, require an intention of the will to obey. Examples are John 13:34 and Galatians 6:2, in the margin.

*"A new commandment I give unto you, that ye love one another; even as I have loved you"* (John 13:34).

The appropriate response to God's Word is obedience. The only alternative is disobedience. There is no middle ground. Disobedience destroys fellowship and thus prayer.

*"Bear ye one another's burdens, and so fulfil the law of Christ"* (Gal. 6:2).

Remember that a command from God is also a promise. God does not command you to do something that you cannot do. He enables you to be obedient if you choose to be obedient. Thus, a command from God is also a promise of the power, ability, skill, or opportunity needed to obey.

 **Read Philippians 2:13 in the margin and record this verse on the chart "Bible Promises" on page 221.**

*"It is God which worketh in you both to will and to do of his good pleasure"* (Phil. 2:13).

**Write a brief summary of why obedience to God's Word is important to prayer.**

_____

_____

## Continuing

Read in the margin Jesus' words in John 8:31 about continuing, or abiding, in His Word. Abiding in His Word implies that fellowship is not occasional. You cannot properly say, "I abided yesterday afternoon." Obedience is not occasional. All godly relationships in the Bible are permanent. There are no occasional fathers, occasional children, or occasional friends. If you are truly abiding in Christ, your thoughts and your prayers are shaped 24 hours a day, 365 days a year by His Word. This can happen only if His Word becomes a vital part of your being.

*"If ye continue in my word, then are ye my disciples indeed"* (John 8:31).

## Daily Master Communication Guide

SCRIPTURE REFERENCE:

_____

### What God said to me:

_____

_____

_____

_____

_____

_____

_____

### What I said to God:

_____

_____

_____

_____

_____

_____

_____

🌿 List activities you can do that would help you continue or abide in God's Word.

_____

_____

You may have listed things like spending more time in Bible study, memorizing Scripture, finding and making lists of commands and promises from the Bible, and talking with friends about the way the Word applies to your life.

### Kinds of Responses

The kinds of prayer responses made to God's Word vary. The combination of a person's situation and the Word received from God determines the suitable prayer response.

*Confession.* A prayer of confession is an appropriate response to an awareness of sin. A failure to be obedient in any area requires confession in prayer. If you feel inadequate in a difficult area of obedience, you may ask God for help.

*Commitment.* A prayer of commitment to obedience is an appropriate response to God's authority and commands. You respond to His authority by submission. Jesus' statements about anger, lust, divorce, vows, recrimination, and loving our enemy (see Matt. 5:22,28,32,34-37,38-41,44-47) are authoritative for a Christian. These matters are best dealt with in prayer. Settle the issue of obedience at the moment you discover a command in the Bible. The very reading of the Bible should be done in an attitude of constant prayer.

*Praise.* A prayer of praise is an appropriate response to knowledge of God's characteristics or attributes. Almost every time you open the Bible, an attribute of God is revealed that you can respond to in prayer. You can rejoice simply to be in His presence (see Ps. 16:11). You can respond with gratitude to the Lord's lovingkindness (see 1 Chron. 16:34). You can respond to His beauty with adoring contemplation (see Ps. 27:4). You can respond to the Lord's law (or principles) with delight (see Ps. 1:1-2). You can respond to His great power by glorifying Him (see Eph. 3:20-21), or you can respond to His power by accepting His help (see Ps. 121:2). You can respond to God's love by loving Him (see 1 John 4:19). The Bible can be a constant stimulant to a rich interchange between Creator and created, Redeemer and redeemed, Teacher and disciple, and many other relationships.

*Thanksgiving.* A prayer of thanksgiving is an appropriate response to an awareness of God's blessings and benefits. James 1:17, in the margin on page 57, reminds us of God's good gifts. The prayer response for good gifts is to offer prayers of thanksgiving.

🌿 Match the appropriate prayer response on the right with the stimulus on the left.

_____ 1. commands and authority       a. confession

_____ 2. blessings and benefits       b. commitment

_____ 3. sin       c. praise

_____ 4. God's characteristics and attributes       d. thanksgiving

Check your answers by reviewing the preceding paragraphs. The prayer responses of different people to the same Bible verse often vary.

"Every good gift and every perfect gift is from above, and cometh down from the Father" (Jas. 1:17).

Read Philippians 2:14 in the margin. Check the responses that might be appropriate in your life today.

❑ Lord, help me today to do all my work without grumbling or disputing.

❑ Father, forgive me for the awful way I have been grumbling. Change me.

❑ Thank You so much, Lord, for enabling me yesterday to do my work without grumbling and arguing as I used to. Thank You for Your power You give me to obey Your will.

❑ Lord, I commit myself in the future to do all my work with joy and thanksgiving.

*"Do all things without murmurings and disputings" (Phil. 2:14).*

### Walking in Fellowship with God Today

1. Commit yourself to immediate and continuing obedience in response to God's Word today. Read Matthew 5:22,28,32,34-37,38-41,44-47.

2. Respond to God's Word in prayer, using an appropriate kind of response (confession, commitment, praise, thanksgiving). You might say: "You said that if I look on the opposite sex to entertain lust, I have committed adultery. I commit myself to obedience with my eyes today."

3. What has God said to you through these passages? What are your prayer responses?

4. As you have your quiet time, complete the Daily Master Communication Guide in the margin on page 56.

# Day 4
# Seeking, Knocking, and Making Decisions

## Seeking

Modern novels and movies picture people seeking and searching for many things; most of them are unworthy things. The biblical character Abraham sought something worthy. Read in Hebrews 11:10, in the margin, what he sought.

If your life for the past five years were written in story form, what are two or three main goals the reader would think you were seeking in your life?

*Today's Learning Goal*
You will understand and be able to apply the principles of seeking and knocking in prayer. You will learn ways to base decisions on Bible principles.

_____

_____

Read the Scriptures on page 58 and write what each says about seeking.

*"He looked for a city which hath foundations, whose builder and maker is God" (Heb. 11:10).*

1 Chronicles 16:11: _____

Amos 5:4,6: _____

1 Chronicles 28:8-9: _____

Psalm 34:10: _____

Proverbs 28:5: _____

Psalm 27:8: _____

Colossians 3:1-2: _____

Matthew 6:33: _____

*Seek God.* God desires and commands that we seek Him, His strength, His face (see 1 Chron. 16:11). He makes several promises to those who seek Him. Those who seek Him will—

- live (see Amos 5:4,6);
- find Him (see 1 Chron. 28:9);
- not want (lack) any good thing (see Ps. 34:10);
- understand all things (see Prov. 28:5).

David is an example for you to follow in seeking God. Read in the margin his response to God in Psalm 27:8.

The face is where all of the organs of communication are lodged—eyes, ears, and mouth. Seeking God's face indicated a desire to communicate and fellowship with Him. Seeking implies importunity, or persistence. Persistent prayer to know Him better is one way to seek His face.

*Seek God's commandments.* We are also told to seek God's commandments and keep them (see 1 Chron. 28:8-9). You will find God's commandments throughout Scripture. As you find His commands, write them on the chart "God's Commands" in prayer guide 4, page 209. Do not take the chance of forgetting them. The diligence implied by seeking means that the commandments should become part of your thinking.

*Seek things above.* Colossians 3:1-2 gives us a high goal for our seeking. Read those verses in the margin, as well as Jesus' words in Matthew 6:33.

The way of the world is to seek "things below"—money, fame, power, position, or getting even with someone who hurt you. "Things above" might include the qualities described in Philippians 4:8, which appears in the margin.

## Knocking

Knocking in Scripture is associated both with entrance and with opportunities. Knocking speaks of admission. Jesus said, "Knock and it shall be opened unto you" (Matt. 7:7). God wants us to feel welcome in His presence. Jesus said, "I am the door" (John 10:9). Hezekiah invited Israel, "Yield yourselves unto the Lord, and enter into his sanctuary" (2 Chron. 30:8). The writer of Hebrews invited us to

*"When thou saidst, Seek ye my face; my heart said unto thee, Thy face, Lord, will I seek" (Ps. 27:8).*

*"Seek those things which are above, where Christ sitteth on the right hand of God. Set your affection on things above, not on things on the earth" (Col. 3:1-2).*

*"Seek ye first the kingdom of God, and his righteousness" (Matt. 6:33).*

*"Whatsoever things are true, whatsoever things are honest, whatsoever things are just, whatsoever things are pure, whatsoever things are lovely, whatsoever things are of good report [whatever is excellent]" (Phil. 4:8).*

"come boldly unto the throne of grace" (Heb. 4:16). Later he spoke of "boldness to enter into the holiest by the blood of Jesus" (Heb. 10:19).

Knocking can also imply the opening of opportunities. Missionaries often knock in their prayers about their work. The directions of Paul's journeys came as he sought God's will. Although Gentiles had been admitted to the church, Paul's first missionary journey brought a sweeping Gentile (and European) movement of major proportions. The call of Paul and Barnabas came in prayer (see Acts 13:2-3). Paul quoted Isaiah 49:6 (see Acts 13:47) as he unceasingly witnessed to the Gentiles. He could test his direction by the prophecies that one day Gentiles would come to the Lord (see Jer. 16:19; Mal. 1:11).

Which of the following describe a biblical meaning of *knocking*? Check each correct answer.
_____ Asking God to open doors of opportunity
_____ Desiring entrance into God's presence
_____ Desiring admission into countries presently closed

The previous section indicates that all three are correct meanings of *knocking*.

### Basing Decisions on Bible Principles

Seeking and knocking in prayer and using Scripture guide you in decision making. These activities, using God's Word, acquaint you with God's principles and leadership. Read Psalm 119:105 in the margin, page 60. We seek, using God's Word as a lamp. This does not mean that you can ask, "Should I take that job?" and expect God to make the Bible fall open to a passage that says, "This is the way; walk ye in it." Rather, it means that if God's Word has saturated your mind and your prayers, the Holy Spirit will help you recognize good and evil in the paths you might take. Knowing God's principles, you will more easily discern if that job, for example, would damage your Christian name, cause you to compromise God's name or His ways, or present legitimate opportunities for witnessing. The Spirit will guide you in all truth (see John 16:13). Read Psalm 37:23-24 in the margin, page 60.

A gifted musician was offered a lucrative job playing the piano in nightclubs. He needed the money. He prayed and searched the Scriptures to find God's will. Would he be right in meeting his financial needs by playing in the nightclubs only long enough to pay his current bills? His prayers and his searches led him to 2 Corinthians 6:17: "Wherefore come out from among them, and be ye separate, saith the Lord, and touch not the unclean thing; and I will receive you."

We can use the Bible as a touchstone for the Spirit to test our own genuineness or the genuineness of principles presented to us. The musician had enough understanding of God to make his decision. He said no to the job.

Luke said that the Bereans "received the word with all readiness of mind and searched the scriptures daily, whether those things were so" (Acts 17:11). The Bereans were familiar with the prophecies of the coming Messiah. When they tested Paul's account of Jesus against the biblical record, the account measured up. It passed the test. Many teachings today would not pass the test of Scripture. Scripture reveals to you error and truth. A prayer life is incomplete without the use of Scripture in it.

*Daily Master Communication Guide*

SCRIPTURE REFERENCE:

_____

*What God said to me:*

_____

_____

_____

_____

_____

_____

*What I said to God:*

_____

_____

_____

_____

_____

_____

*"Thy word is a lamp unto my feet, and a light unto my path"* (Ps. 119:105).

*"The steps of a good man are ordered by the Lord: and he delighteth in his way. Though he fall, he shall not be utterly cast down: for the Lord upholdeth him with his hand"* (Ps. 37:23-24).

1. Prayerfully consider the following commitments you feel God has quickened you to pursue. Check those you desire to make.
   ❑ A commitment to seek God in prayer and in the Bible
   ❑ A commitment to seek God's commandments
   ❑ A commitment to seek things above
   ❑ A commitment to knock daily on the door of prayer in order to be with God and to maintain an open door for Him to enter your heart at any time
   ❑ A commitment to knock on the door of opportunities to advance God's kingdom
   ❑ A commitment to base your decisions on biblical principles
   ❑ A commitment to use the Bible to test truth and error
2. Select one of the commitments you checked. Spend time with God and His Word in prayer.
3. As you have your quiet time, complete the Daily Master Communication Guide in the margin on page 59.

# Day 5
# Using Bible Promises

*Today's Learning Goal*
You will learn to use Bible promises in your prayers.

Jesus was so steeped in Scripture that His prayers and everything He did were shaped by Scripture. He is our model. Jesus met temptation with Scripture. He answered His critics with Scripture. He approached prayer with a knowledge of Scripture. In the course of His prayers He used the spirit of Scripture and the very words of Scripture. This should be our pattern.

Scripture should become such a part of your mind that you use it in life situations. A prayer journal can be most helpful. Keep a list of commands that are important to you, like the one on page 209. Note Scriptures that would be useful in meeting particular temptations. Also keep a list of Bible promises, like the one on page 221. If you memorize these, they are likely to surface when needed.

## Jesus and Bible Promises
The Old Testament prophecies of the Messiah were actually Bible promises fulfilled in Christ. Jesus found encouragement through His knowledge of scriptural promises about Himself. Jesus felt that the very course of His life was outlined in Scripture. His circumstances in Jerusalem during the last week of His life were hardly conducive to faith in the words of Psalm 118:22: "The stone which the builders refused is become the head stone of the corner." Yet that was Scripture. Facing the cross, Jesus quoted it in Matthew 21:42, in the margin. It was what today we might call a prayer promise. Jesus' life was in God's hands, and the Word of God cannot be broken.

*"Jesus saith unto them, Did ye never read in the scriptures, The stone which the builders rejected, the same is become the head of the corner: this is the Lord's doing, and it is marvellous in our eyes?"* (Matt. 21:42).

## Bible Promises

In a sense, any statement by God is a promise. An invitation is a promise. If Jesus says, "Come unto Me," He is assuring us that He will receive us. A command is a promise. If God commands, "Be ye holy," we can be confident that in Christ we can indeed be holy. A prayer promise is a statement by God about how He will act in a certain situation or, in some cases, in all situations.

 **Read in the margin the promise in 2 Chronicles 7:14. Describe the promises and the conditions for fulfillment.**

Promises: _____

Conditions: _____

*"If my people, who are called by my name, shall humble themselves, and pray, and seek my face, and turn from their wicked ways; then will I hear from heaven, and will forgive their sin, and will heal their land"* (2 Chron. 7:14).

God promised to hear prayer, forgive sin, and heal the land (people). However, He gave conditions for fulfillment. The people had to humble themselves, pray, seek God's face, and repent (turn from their wicked ways).

 **Now read 2 Chronicles 34:27 in the margin. Did Josiah fulfill the conditions?** ❑ Yes ❑ No **Did God keep His promise?** ❑ Yes ❑ No **Turn to page 221 and record this promise on the chart "Bible Promises."**

**Read in the margin the promise in Isaiah 43:1-2. What were the promises, and what, if any, were the conditions?**

Promises: _____

Conditions: _____

*"Because thine heart was tender, and thou didst humble thyself before God, when thou heardest his words against this place, and against the inhabitants thereof, and humbledst thyself before me, and dist rend thy clothes, and weep before me; I have even heard thee also, saith the Lord"* (2 Chron. 34:27).

Later, Shadrach, Meshach, and Abednego were thrown into Nebuchadnezzar's fiery furnace for refusing to worship the king's idol. Daniel recorded that the king said, "Lo, I see four men loose, walking in the midst of the fire, and they have no hurt; and the form of the fourth is like the Son of God" (Dan. 3:25). God was faithful to His promise made earlier through Isaiah.

Two kinds of promises are in the Bible. The first is a statement God makes of something He intends to do at some future point. The second is a promise that is intended for all times. Some promises have conditions, and others do not.

*Special promises for a future time.* Solomon thanked the Lord for keeping His promises to Israel. Read his words in the margin (1 Kings 8:56). God had promised to bring Israel out of Egypt and to give the people the land of Canaan. God kept His promise, and Solomon thanked Him for it.

*Promises for all times.* Some promises are valid for all times and circumstances. For example, Hanani's word to Asa when Asa relied on Syria instead of the Lord was "The eyes of the Lord run to and fro throughout the whole earth, to shew himself strong in the behalf of them whose heart is perfect toward him" (2 Chron. 16:9). This is a statement about how God always acts.

*"Now thus saith the Lord that created thee, O Jacob, and he that formed thee, O Israel, Fear not: for I have redeemed thee, I have called thee by thy name; thou art mine. When thou passest through the waters, I will be with thee; and through the rivers, they shall not overflow thee: when thou walkest through the fire, thou shalt not be burned; neither shall the flame kindle upon thee"* (Isa. 43:1-2).

*"Blessed be the Lord, that hath given rest unto his people Israel, according to all that he promised: there hath not failed one word of all his good promise, which he promised by the hand of Moses his servant"* (1 Kings 8:56).

## Daily Master Communication Guide

SCRIPTURE REFERENCE:

_____

*What God said to me:*

_____

_____

_____

_____

_____

_____

_____

*What I said to God:*

_____

_____

_____

_____

_____

_____

_____

Jesus made a conditional promise in Matthew 6:33: "Seek ye first the kingdom of God, and his righteousness; and all these things shall be added unto you." The things Jesus said that God would take care of are mentioned in verses 25-31—food, drink, and clothing. God is concerned about our needs, and He wants us to be concerned about His kingdom and His righteousness. When we are concerned with His affairs first, He promises to provide for our needs.

### Keeping a List of Bible Promises

We have already suggested that you add certain promises to the chart "Bible Promises" on page 221. As you study the Bible, watch for ways God says He will act. What God says He will do is a promise. Keep listing those statements and His conditions on the chart. This list will become a valuable tool as you pray. Hundreds of promises are in the Bible. Let's look at some samples.

 Read these Scripture passages and record them on the chart "Bible Promises," page 221.

| Psalm 138:8 | Proverbs 3:5-6 | Jeremiah 32:27 |
| Jeremiah 33:3 | James 1:5 | |

The Bible does not predict the details of your life as it described Jesus' life. However, "we are his workmanship, created in Christ Jesus unto good works, which God hath before ordained that we should walk in them" (Eph. 2:10). The principles in the Bible are eternal, and God always keeps His promises. God knows our lives, and He has prepared for our lives here on earth. He gave us His principles in His Word to guide us in our walk. He gave us His promises. Our job is to learn His principles and to meet His conditions. God's promises are gifts to you. Use them in your prayers. Keep records of your specific requests, the dates requested, the dates answered, and how God answered (see pp. 223–25).

When we are faithful to Him, we arrive at a point at which we can say, as Solomon did, "Blessed be the Lord … there hath not failed one word of all his good promise, which he promised" (1 Kings 8:56).

 Write this week's memory verse(s) on a separate sheet of paper.

 Walking in Fellowship with God Today

1. Review the many promises you have recorded on the chart "Bible Promises," page 221. Remember the two ways to use promises in prayer: (1) Quote one as an assurance of an answer. (2) Quote a fulfilled promise as a reason for praise.
2. During your prayer times today, claim appropriate promises of God with the assurance of an answer. Praise God for promises fulfilled.
3. As you have your quiet time, complete the Daily Master Communication Guide in the margin.

# EXPRESSING GRATITUDE IN PRAYER

## God Is My Source

I was squeezing my toothpaste onto the toothbrush one morning when I realized that I had never thanked the Lord for toothpaste. Come to think of it, I had never thanked Him for my teeth. I wondered: *What if tomorrow everything I received depended on my acknowledging its being from God today? If I did not thank God for air and lungs today, there would be no air tomorrow, and my lungs would collapse.* Few of us realize how totally dependent on God we are. We do not acknowledge God as the source of *everything* we have.

One day I was reviewing Psalm 20:7, "Some trust in chariots, and some in horses: but we will remember the name of the Lord our God." Translated into modern English, that might read, "Some trust in brains and some in scheming (or education or hard work), but we will trust in the name of the Lord our God." I resolved that I would trust God not only for life's necessities but also for everything—things I thought I had earned or provided for myself in the past. I would not tell anyone if I had a need, but I would tell God.

The time had come to have the syllabi printed for a course I teach called *The Mind of Christ.* However, our checkbook showed that we had only $37 in the bank. With the assurance that it was God's will that I teach *The Mind of Christ,* we prayed for God to provide the money for the printing. We felt strongly that we should tell no one but God about the need. The treasurer of our church called and informed me that someone had given him a check for my ministry. When I opened the envelope, a check was enclosed for $1,000—about right for printing the syllabi.

When the printing bill came three weeks later, it was for $1,097. I was dismayed. But another envelope in my mail that morning had a Little Rock postmark. The letter read: "I heard you speak in North Little Rock and have been praying for your ministry. This morning as I prayed, the Lord told me you had a need. Then He impressed me to fulfill that need, so here is the check." Enclosed was a check for $100!

God is the Source who can supply all of our needs, big and small. After that day I became aware of benefits I had not been thanking Him for—water, bed sheets, vitamin supplements, air-conditioning and heating—everything in my life. Just as I *depend* on Him for all of them, I also *thank* Him for all of them.

*Key Idea*
A continuous and permanent attitude of gratitude is a Christian's natural response to God's goodness.

*This Week's Learning Goal*
You will understand biblical teachings about gratitude to God and will begin to practice an attitude of gratitude.

*Verses to Memorize*
"I will praise thee, O Lord my God, with all my heart: and I will glorify thy name for evermore" (Ps. 86:12).

"In every thing give thanks: for this is the will of God in Christ Jesus concerning you" (1 Thess. 5:18).

*Related Prayer Guide*
Prayer guide 5, "Expressing Gratitude in Prayer," page 210

# Day 1
# The Attitude of Gratitude, Part 1

*Today's Learning Goal*
You will understand the attitude of gratitude and will demonstrate your gratitude to God in prayer.

*"Bless the Lord, O my soul: and all that is within me, bless his holy name. Bless the Lord, O my soul, and forget not all his benefits: who forgiveth all thine iniquities; who healeth all thy diseases; who redeemeth thy life from destruction; who crowneth thee with lovingkindness and tender mercies; who satisfieth thy mouth with good things; so that thy youth is renewed like the eagle's. The Lord hath prepared his throne in the heavens; and his kingdom ruleth over all. Bless the Lord, ye his angels, that excel in strength, that do his commandments, hearkening unto the voice of his word. Bless ye the Lord, all ye his hosts; ye ministers of his, that do his pleasure. Bless the Lord, all his works in all places of his dominion: bless the Lord, O my soul"* (Ps. 103:1-5,19-22).

*"Now unto him that is able to do exceeding abundantly above all that we ask or think, according to the power that worketh in us, unto him be glory in the church by Christ Jesus throughout all ages, world without end. Amen"* (Eph. 3:20-21).

To begin thinking about gratitude, describe one occasion when you recall having a strong feeling of gratitude for something.

_____

_____

Toward which of the following was your feeling of gratitude directed? Check one.
❑ things and happenings     ❑ people     ❑ God

Check all of the following ways you have expressed gratitude to a person who befriended you.
❑ Said "thank you"          ❑ Wrote a thank-you letter
❑ Phoned                    ❑ Sent a gift

## Bless the Lord
Many times in our lives gratitude is an appropriate and expected response. We can express gratitude in many ways. The Bible is full of prayers that express a believer's gratitude to God, especially in the Psalms.

Read Psalm 103:1-5,19-22 in the margin and try to imagine the feelings in the writer's heart. The word *bless* in these verses implies *to adore God for His goodness and return thanks.* Read the verses with that meaning in mind.

Rewrite Psalm 103:1 in your own words.

_____

_____

Personalize the list of wonderful benefits from God mentioned in Psalm 103:3-5. Use *me* and *my* in recording your benefits.

_____

_____

Thank God for His benefits you listed from Psalm 103:3-5. Check here when finished: ❑

## To Him Be Glory
Now examine a New Testament expression of gratitude toward God. Read Ephesians 3:20-21 in the margin and see if you can feel the gratitude expressed.

In verse 20 what ability of God did Paul mention with adoration or gratitude?

_____

Do these verses thank God for ❑ the good He has already done or ❑ His capacity to do good? Check one.

True or false? "Unto him be glory" is an expression of gratitude. _____

According to verse 21, how often or for how long should believers have an attitude of heart that glorifies God?

_____

Paul acknowledged in Ephesians 3:20-21 that God is able to do everything we ask or dream of (think). Paul stated his confidence in God's capacity to do good. "Unto him be glory" can be seen as an expression of gratitude for who God is and for what He can do. Christians should ascribe glory to God throughout the ages.

 On a separate sheet of paper rewrite Ephesians 3:20-21 as your personal prayer directed toward God. Instead of using _Him_ in each verse, use _to You, Father_ and change _that is_ to _who is._ Then pray your prayer to God.

Now let's study gratitude more carefully.

## A Relationship Between Source and Receiver

Gratitude indicates a relationship between source and receiver. In our prayers gratitude indicates one of the most important aspects of our relationship with God. Gratitude acknowledges a specific kind of relationship. Part of Israel's failure in the desert was its failure to acknowledge God. Moses cried, "Do ye thus requite [repay] the Lord, O foolish people and unwise?" (Deut. 32:6). Only when the particular relationship of giver to receiver is acknowledged properly can the relationship grow.

Gratitude indicates a relationship between the source of good—God—and the receiver of good—people.

 In the drawing below, indicate God's feeling or attitude toward you and your attitude toward God. Write one word in His heart and one in yours.

My Heart          His Heart

## Daily Master Communication Guide

SCRIPTURE REFERENCE:

_____

_What God said to me:_

_____
_____
_____
_____
_____
_____
_____

_What I said to God:_

_____
_____
_____
_____
_____
_____
_____
_____

*"Giving thanks always for all things unto God and the Father in the name of our Lord Jesus Christ" (Eph. 5:20).*

*"Be careful for nothing; but in every thing by prayer and supplication with thanksgiving let your requests be made known unto God" (Phil. 4:6).*

Read the following verses in the margin. What does Paul say about gratitude in each verse?

Ephesians 5:20: _____

_____

Philippians 4:6: _____

_____

Paul repeatedly tells us *always* to be thankful for *all* things. He teaches us to include thanksgiving (gratitude) with our prayers and supplications. This is difficult, if not impossible, for most of us. We think of gratitude merely as a reaction to a good favor, not for all things.

True gratitude is not a reaction; it is a response. Reaction can be negative or positive. Reaction waits for an event. Response to God in gratitude can be a continuous attitude of your heart. The response of gratitude is one of the courtesies that characterize a continuing relationship.

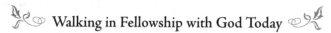 Walking in Fellowship with God Today

1. Consider the staggering list of benefits in Psalm 103:1-5. Name each benefit to the Lord from your personal perspective. That is, apply each one to your history. Consider how far-reaching the work of God is in your life, especially as your Source.
   + After you read "who forgiveth all thine iniquities," consider the enormous work of the cross.
   + After you read "who healeth all thy diseases," consider the sicknesses you have experienced and the healing God has given.
   + After you read "who redeemeth thy life from destruction," thank the Lord for your preservation. Name to Him one or more of the rescues He has effected in dangerous circumstances in your past—spiritual danger, moral danger, physical danger, or mental danger.
   + When you thank Him for crowning you with lovingkindness and tender mercies, thank Him especially for the joys of His company.
   + When you read verse 5, review the past several years of your life spiritually. Thank Him for spiritual nourishment that has helped you grow—the meat of His will (see John 4:34), the Bread of life (see John 6:35), the Water of life (see John 4:14), and the milk of His Word (see 1 Pet. 2:2).
2. As you go through the day, continue to bless God for His benefits—your job, salary, food, friends, church, transportation, shelter, and so forth. Thank Him for everything today that you would like to have tomorrow—water, clothing, conveniences, tools (such as telephones and appliances), and so forth.
3. As you have your quiet time, complete the Daily Master Communication Guide in the margin on page 65.

# Day 2
# The Attitude of Gratitude, Part 2

Look at the points in the box below. As you study each point today, try to think of a mental picture that will help you remember it. You will be asked to draw or describe your pictures at the end of today's study.

| A CHRISTIAN'S ATTITUDE OF GRATITUDE | |
| --- | --- |
| • Permeates life | • Believes that God is good |
| • Produces trust | • Glorifies God |

## Permeates Life

Gratitude is more than an acknowledgment. It is also more than a set of words. Gratitude is an attitude of life.

 Compare Colossians 4:2 in the following two versions: "Devote yourselves to prayer, keeping alert in it with an attitude of thanksgiving" (NASB). "Continue in prayer, and watch in the same with thanksgiving" (KJV). What idea do you see in the *New American Standard Bible* **that is not as clear in the** *King James Version?*

_____

Paul said for us to keep alert or watchful in prayer with thanksgiving. True gratitude cannot be contained in words alone, although our words are important. Gratitude is a continuing attitude about our relationship with the One who continuously gives to us, supplies our needs, and brings us joy. Gratitude is a response not only to what God does but also to what God is. Gratitude is the heart's response to God's goodness—not merely to the fruit of His goodness in giving but also to His quality of goodness.

 What is the opposite of gratitude?  _____

What are some ways you demonstrate a lack of gratitude? _____

_____

You may have stated that the opposite of gratitude is indifference or ingratitude. Think about how much gratitude permeates your life. Read again Colossians 4:2 and spend time in prayer speaking to God and letting God speak to you about your attitude of gratitude.

## Believes That God Is Good

Our attitude of gratitude shows that we believe that God is good. This conviction must cover every aspect of God's dealing with us: His gifts are good; His will is good. God is consistent with His own nature; He has nothing to give except good gifts.

---

## Daily Master Communication Guide

SCRIPTURE REFERENCE:

_____

*What God said to me:*

_____

_____

_____

_____

_____

_____

_____

*What I said to God:*

_____

_____

_____

_____

_____

_____

*"Every good gift and every perfect gift is from above, and cometh down from the Father of lights, with whom is no variableness, neither shadow of turning" (Jas. 1:17).*

*"What man is there of you, whom if his son ask bread, will he give him a stone? Or if he ask a fish, will he give him a serpent? If ye then, being evil, know how to give good gifts unto your children, how much more shall your Father which is in heaven give good things to them that ask him?" (Matt. 7:9-11).*

 **Read James 1:17 and Matthew 7:9-11 in the margin. What do these verses say about God's goodness?**

_____

_____

_____

God is good. Every good gift comes from Him. Although we are evil in our nature, we know how to give good gifts to our children. In a much more abundant way, God gives good things to those who ask Him.

 **Write on these gifts six things in your life for which you are grateful.**

Express your gratitude. God hears and appreciates this. Record the more significant things on "Praise and Thanksgiving List," page 222.

Not everything that happens is from God, but God can use everything for your good and His glory (see Rom. 8:28 in the margin). One memory verse for this week, "In every thing give thanks: for this is the will of God in Christ Jesus concerning you" (1 Thess. 5:18), tells us in the midst of difficulties and disasters to look to God with an attitude of gratitude. God is still in charge of His universe and our lives. Giving thanks in all things forces us to remember that God is still alive; He is still in control.

The trivial grievances of life annoy us because so many of us make our goals day by day without reference to the greater goal God has in His mind for us—His glory demonstrated in us and His character realized in us and in others. Day-by-day satisfactions too often become our measuring stick for the degree of our gratitude. The little things may be good and sometimes important, but they are not all-important. Gratitude is based on the belief that God is painting a picture that will turn out for His glory regardless of our present circumstances.

*"We know that all things work together for good to them that love God, to them who are the called according to his purpose" (Rom. 8:28).*

Usually, the "good" in our everyday lives is that which pleases us. What we call needs are oftentimes self-centered greeds. Our "needs" sometimes have to do with comfort, with glorifying ourselves, with fulfilling personal wishes that are foreign to and even hostile to greatness of spirit.

God sees a greater good, more grand in scope than we can realize. The canvas of His great story is stretched wide. What God sees as good for us fits into a cosmic picture that brings good to many others as well as ourselves. His good will ultimately be seen to be better for us than we could have chosen for ourselves.

*God's good will ultimately be seen to be better for us than we could have chosen for ourselves.*

 On a separate sheet of paper make a list of some "bad" things that have happened to you. Write down as many as you can think of in three minutes. Now write beside each one, if possible, ways God may have used that experience for your good. Remember, sometimes we may not even understand His work in a particular situation. In many cases, however, we can see His fingerprints in our lives. Bring your list to this week's group session.

## Produces Trust

Belief in God's goodness not only produces gratitude but also stimulates faith or trust. Sometimes (perhaps unconsciously) we are merely grateful for the satisfactions of the moment. If that becomes our habit, our faith bobbles up and down like a cork in water. Circumstances are poor indicators of what God is up to. God's kind of happiness comes partly from relating all of the little things, pleasant and unpleasant, to an ultimate goal not perceptible to us in single events. Forming an attitude of trust in God's goodness is aided by understanding what God purposes to do in the lives of His children.

 Read Ephesians 4:13-15 in the margin. Write a summary of what God wants to do in your life.

_____

_____

_____

*"… till we all come in the unity of the faith, and of the knowledge of the Son of God, unto a perfect man, unto the measure of the stature of the fulness of Christ: that we henceforth be no more children, tossed to and fro, and carried about with every wind of doctrine, by the sleight of men, and cunning craftiness, whereby they lie in wait to deceive; but speaking the truth in love, may grow up into him in all things, which is the head, even Christ" (Eph. 4:13-15).*

The final goal stated in Ephesians 4:15 in *The Living Bible*, Paraphrased, reads, "So become more and more in every way like Christ who is the Head of his body, the church." God's purpose is to make you like Christ.

Faith, if it is true faith, is not placed in circumstances or in the directions in which our affairs seem to be moving but in God's character. His character never varies. This is why our faith should not vary and why our gratitude may include all things.

## Glorifies God

God's glory demonstrated in our lives is the greatest good that can come to us. His glory is best demonstrated when our lives reflect His character.

*"We know that all things work together for good to them that love God, to them who are the called according to his purpose. For whom he did foreknow, he also did predestinate to be conformed to the image of his Son, that he might be the firstborn among many brethren. Moreover whom he did predestinate, them he also called: and whom he called, them he also justified: and whom he justified, them he also glorified" (Rom. 8:28-30).*

*"Ye are complete in him, which is the head of all principality and power" (Col. 2:10).*

*"Neither pray I for these alone, but for them also which shall believe on me through their word; that they all may be one; as thou, Father, art in me, and I in thee, that they also may be one in us: that the world may believe that thou hast sent me. And the glory which thou gavest me I have given them; that they may be one, even as we are one: I in them, and thou in me, that they may be made perfect in one; and that the world may know that thou hast sent me, and hast loved them, as thou hast loved me" (John 17:20-23).*

If we knew for an absolute certainty that a series of difficult circumstances would lead to great glory for the Lord, would we be likely to thank God for those difficult circumstances? Yet that outcome—good in all circumstances—is exactly what we are promised!

 Read Romans 8:28-30 in the margin and see how the goal for your life is stated. Record this promise on the chart "Bible Promises," page 221.

Read and summarize the goal in Colossians 2:10, which appears in the margin.

_____

God wants you to attain maturity, reach the measure of the stature of Christ, and become complete in Christ. How do you think your becoming like Christ glorifies God?

_____

_____

_____

In John 17:20-23, in the margin, Jesus said that the world will behold His glory and will know that God sent Christ when it sees Christians who are perfect (mature) and united as one. God receives glory when you let others see Christ in your life.

 On a separate sheet of paper draw or describe the four mental pictures you have for the points today. Bring your drawings to your group session this week.

 Walking in Fellowship with God Today

1. Today try to redefine what is good in your life. Imagine that you are at the judgment right now and God shows you the story of your life, intending to reveal how and why He brought you to this day. What would He be likely to show? Some of the discomforts, tragedies, and disappointments may have revealed a glory you did not recognize at the time.
2. What has brought you to the fifth week of *Disciple's Prayer Life?* What has produced your desire to learn how to pray? Thank God for all of the manifestations of His glory in your life. Exercise your attitude of gratitude again today, using "A Christian's Attitude of Gratitude" in prayer guide 5, "Expressing Gratitude in Prayer," on page 210.
3. As you have your quiet time, complete the Daily Master Communication Guide in the margin on page 67.

# Day 3
# Properly Expressing Gratitude

A Christian's attitude of gratitude should be continuous and permanent.

## In Relationship to Time
*Continuous.* We should overflow with gratitude continuously.

 Read in the margin Paul's description of Christian characteristics in Colossians 2:7. The last phrase says that a Christian should—

_____

Christians are to be like fountains ever pouring forth appreciation for God's goodness. Gratitude should be continuous because God's goodness is continuous and God never changes. God's goodness has no beginning or end. We sometimes think that God demonstrates His goodness only on occasions when we receive extraordinary blessings. We should be grateful for high moments and great favors. Those mountain peaks, however, no more depict God's character than do the valleys. They indicate the process of His working, not His character. The highest gratitude is rejoicing in His character, and His character is eternally the same.

 Read Malachi 3:6 in the margin. What does the Lord say about Himself?

_____

*Permanent.* If gratitude is our response to His goodness, then gratitude, like His goodness, should be continuous. The only way it can be continuous is if it becomes a permanent attitude, not intermittent expressions.

 List things for which you can always be grateful.

_____

_____

If our permanent attitude is fixed on God's permanent goodness, we can and should enter all phases of life with gratitude and confidence in God's goodness. All days, cloudy and sunny, are works of God. Each new phase we enter will bring us nearer the final goal God has in mind for us.

Our prayer, then, begins with our fixed attitude; we "enter into his gates with thanksgiving" (Ps. 100:4). We enter not by saying the right words but by presenting God a heart grateful for Him and for His purposes. Thanksgiving is the proper entrance to prayer, and a spirit of gratefulness is the proper continuation of prayer.

*Today's Learning Goal*
You will demonstrate a commitment to express an attitude of gratitude properly.

*"Rooted and built up in him, and stablished in the faith, as ye have been taught, abounding therein with thanksgiving"* (Col. 2:7).

*"I am the Lord, I change not"* (Mal. 3:6).

## Daily Master Communication Guide

Scripture reference:

_____

*What God said to me:*

_____

_____

_____

_____

_____

_____

_____

*What I said to God:*

_____

_____

_____

_____

_____

_____

_____

What two words describe the time element in Christian gratitude?

1. _____

2. _____

**What are two reasons for this?**

1. _____

2. _____

Review the preceding material if you are unsure of your responses.

### Gratitude for All Things

Christians practice two levels of gratitude and thanksgiving.

*The lower level.* Most believers see God as occasionally intervening in their lives for their good. When He does that, they express thanksgiving. These people are grateful only for God's more spectacular gifts. Few Christians would admit that this is their attitude, but it is what they actually practice. If God wants their attention, He has to attract their interest with a big blessing.

This attitude level has two drawbacks. First and most important, the person has his or her attention on self. The size of the blessing is limited by whatever satisfies self. This person fails to thank God for the greatest blessings—God's character, which is duplicating itself in the Christian, and the expansion of God's kingdom that is realized because of that growth. The definition of *blessing* in terms of self is not as big as the Lord's definition.

Second, but not unimportant, the person who sees a blessing only on the occasion of a spectacular blessing fails to perceive the little blessings. The psalmist wanted to "forget not all his benefits" (Ps. 103:2). We are to be grateful for the little as well as the big if we are to be grateful for all things.

*The higher level.* This level of gratitude realizes that all things indeed work together for good for those who love God. This attitude expresses itself as faith and constantly erupts in outpourings of gratitude to God for small things and great things. This is the attitude the Bible describes as "abounding therein with thanksgiving" (Col. 2:7).

If you were giving a devotional about continuous gratitude, what would you say? On a separate sheet of paper make notes to outline your devotional. List key points, illustrations, and Scriptures you would use. Bring your outline to this week's group session.

Properly expressing gratitude means that you thank God continuously, permanently, and for all things—large and small, "good" and "bad."

1. It is discourteous to ignore someone who is with you, but many people ignore Jesus, who said that He is always with us. Today let these three colors remind you of His presence in your life:
   + Every time you see the color red, silently thank Him for the blood He shed on the cross for you.
   + Whenever you see green, thank Him for life and spiritual growth.
   + Let blue remind you of His purity and your new character in Christ.

   Let these expressions of gratitude become springboards for other thank-yous. Remain grateful all day, using the ideas in prayer guide 5, page 210, during your prayer times.

2. As you have your quiet time, complete the Daily Master Communication Guide in the margin on page 72.

## Day 4
# Ways to Express Gratitude

*Today's Learning Goal*
You will understand three ways to express gratitude and will use them in your fellowship with God.

Gratitude needs to be expressed. If your attitude is genuine, you need to express it. As the attitude of gratitude is expressed outwardly, it becomes stronger.

 Gratitude can be expressed in a number of ways. Read the following Scriptures in the margin and describe one way Old Testament saints expressed gratitude: Genesis 8:20; Joshua 8:30-31; 1 Samuel 7:12.

_____

*"Noah builded an altar unto the Lord; and took of every clean beast, and of every clean fowl, and offered burnt offerings on the altar"* (Gen. 8:20).

### Physical Reminders
The Old Testament saints often built altars (see Gen. 8:20; Josh. 8:30-31) or monuments (see Josh. 4:1-7). Their gratitude found concrete, physical expression. The physical expression also became a tangible reminder of God's goodness. They sometimes gave their monuments names to indicate that they specifically credited the work to God (see 1 Sam. 7:12; *Ebenezer* means *stone of help*).

 If you were engraving your gratitude to God in stone, what words would you use?

_____

_____

*"Joshua built an altar unto the Lord God of Israel in mount Ebal, as Moses the servant of the Lord commanded the children of Israel, as written in the book of the law of Moses, an altar of whole stones, over which no man hath lift up any iron: and they offered thereon burnt offerings unto the Lord, and sacrificed peace offerings"* (Josh. 8:30-31).

*"Samuel took a stone, and set it between Mizpeh and Shen, and called the name of it Eben-ezer, saying, Hitherto hath the Lord helped us"* (1 Sam. 7:12).

Transfer these words to "My Gratitude to God in Stone" in prayer guide 5, page 210. Consider using these words in a plaque, tapestry, cross-stitch, rug, or another physical reminder that you can display in your home.

## Verbal Thanksgivings

The most common expression of gratitude is verbal thanksgiving. This outward expression of thanksgiving results from the inner attitude discussed throughout this week's study. Gratitude itself is bigger than thanksgiving but includes it. If the attitude is proper, it will find expression in many outlets:

- Thanksgiving for past blessings
- Thanksgiving for God's current work in your life
- Thanksgiving for future things that you expect will glorify God, build His kingdom, and edify yourself and others

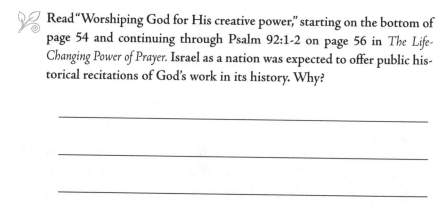 You may not be a poet like David, but try writing an expression of gratitude in two lines that rhyme.

_____

_____

## Prayers, Songs, and Testimonies

We may express gratitude in prayers, songs, and testimonies. Our prayers and songs may be expressed either publicly or privately. The important thing is that God receive the credit for what He has done or is doing. Although a testimony is usually public, we should also privately recount to God our understanding of His work in us.

*The important thing is that God receive the credit for what He has done or is doing.*

Read "Worshiping God for His creative power," starting on the bottom of page 54 and continuing through Psalm 92:1-2 on page 56 in *The Life-Changing Power of Prayer.* Israel as a nation was expected to offer public historical recitations of God's work in its history. Why?

_____

_____

_____

A praise history constantly reminds us of God's activity in our lives. It can draw us into worship. It keeps us from sin. It reminds us of God's blessings when we must walk through a troublesome valley. A praise history can be a valuable spiritual family heirloom.

This may be one of the most challenging yet rewarding assignments you have received in *Disciple's Prayer Life.* You and your family should compose a praise history of God's activity in your family's life together. You may not be able to complete this assignment today, but do your best to complete the assignment before your next group session. Use the suggestions on the following page for your work.

## Preparing a Praise History

1. Secure paper and a pencil. You may prefer to use chart paper or poster board so that all family members can read what is taking shape.

2. Gather your family together, as many members as possible. If you are single, consider involving any relative who lives nearby. If you have no other alternative, you may compose this praise history on your own, phoning absent family members to get ideas.

3. Read aloud examples from praise histories like Exodus 15; Judges 5; Psalms 78; 105; 106; 114; 135; 136; and Ephesians 1:3-14.

4. Jot down statements or refrains you would like to include in your history. For example, "O give thanks unto the Lord; for he is good: for his mercy endureth for ever" (Ps. 106:1).

5. Without evaluating responses, write down all of the significant events and blessings you can think of. Think of good times. Think of troubled times God helped you through. Think of spiritual highlights like a child's salvation.

6. Arrange your list in chronological order. Mark out items you decide not to include.

7. Add some of the biblical verses, phrases, or refrains you listed earlier.

8. When you have finished, take turns reading verses one at a time. After each statement, invite the family to say together, "We thank [or praise] You, O God."

9. When you have completed your praise history, rewrite it and keep it in a safe place.

10. Recite your family's praise history on special occasions like Thanksgiving Day. Add to the history once each year to keep it up-to-date.

11. Send or give copies to family members who no longer live in your home.

### ❧ Walking in Fellowship with God Today ❧

1. Today give God credit for doing in your life the specific things He has done for His purposes and for His glory. Credit and thank Him first for unalterable things—being male or female, the color of your eyes, your height, the pitch of your voice, and so forth.

2. Thank Him for alterable things He has used to conform you to the image of His Son—your salvation, a song that has become meaningful to you, incidents that have turned your mind to Him, sermons that brought a decision, and so forth. During your prayer time read Psalm 66:4. As you pray, refer to the ideas in "Ways to Express Gratitude" in prayer guide 5, page 210.

3. As you have your quiet time, complete the Daily Master Communication Guide in the margin.

---

## Daily Master Communication Guide

SCRIPTURE REFERENCE:

_____

### What God said to me:

_____

_____

_____

_____

_____

_____

_____

### What I said to God:

_____

_____

_____

_____

_____

_____

_____

_____

# Day 5
# Gratitude for Spiritual Blessings

Gratitude should be greater for matters of spiritual importance than for material things. The material world is important only because it mirrors a larger sphere—the spiritual world. We should be grateful for material things, but spiritual blessings weigh more in the minds of spiritual persons.

 The content of Paul's letters indicates the premium he placed on spiritual blessings. Examine parts of Paul's prayers and record the spiritual matters that were the subjects of his prayers and gratitude.

Ephesians 1:3: _____

Colossians 1:4: _____

Colossians 1:10: _____

Colossians 1:11: _____

Colossians 1:12: _____

1 Corinthians 15:56-57: _____

1 Timothy 1:12: _____

*"To all that be in Rome, beloved of God, called to be saints: grace to you and peace from God our Father, and the Lord Jesus Christ. First, I thank my God through Jesus Christ for you all, that your faith is spoken of throughout the whole world"* (Rom. 1:7-8).

*"I thank my God always on your behalf, for the grace of God which is given you by Jesus Christ"* (1 Cor. 1:4).

*"I thank my God upon every remembrance of you, always in every prayer of mine for you all making request with joy, for your fellowship in the gospel from the first day until now" (Phil. 1:3-5).*

*"We give thanks to God always for you all, making mention of you in our prayers" (1 Thess. 1:2).*

Paul was ever grateful for the spiritual blessings God had bestowed on believers. He praised God for blessing us with all spiritual blessings (see Eph. 1:3). He thanked God for giving faith and developing godly love in believers (see Col. 1:4). In Colossians 1:10-12 he stated that believers are given the capacity to walk worthily, bear fruit, and increase in knowledge. They can be strengthened with power to achieve patience, longsuffering, and joy. God has even given us the opportunity to share in the inheritance of the saints by experiencing Christ's salvation. Paul was thankful for victory over sin and death (see 1 Cor. 15:56-57) and for his call into ministry (see 1 Tim. 1:12).

## Thanks for People

Read the verses in the margin and write something else for which Paul expressed gratitude.

_____

Paul's most frequent expression of thanksgiving was for people rather than things. The recipients of these letters were the subjects of Paul's gratitude—the Christians in Rome, Corinth, Philippi, and Thessalonica.

We too should thank the Lord for people, especially those who help us spiritually. We, like Paul, should thank our Lord for a church that has helped us spiritually (see Phil. 1:3-5). Recognition services for faithful church leaders should be times to express gratitude to God for them and for members whose lives and faithfulness have blessed others.

List the names of persons for whom you are grateful.

_____

_____

Now stop and express your gratitude to God for them.

## Thanks for Spiritual Experiences

We should thank God when experiences help us spiritually.

Read Acts 28:15 in the margin. What was Paul's experience for which he was grateful?

_____

Paul was on his way to his Roman imprisonment. Some Christians met him on the way to encourage him. Paul thanked God for the courage they brought.

What personal experience have you had of feeling grateful for being helped by others? What did the other persons do?

_____

_____

## Thanks for Kingdom Advances

Above all, we should thank the Lord for Kingdom advances.

Read 2 Corinthians 9:12-15 in the margin. Why was Paul giving thanks?

_____

_____

Money had been given, the needs of the saints had been supplied, the gospel was being professed, and Paul never forgot to be thankful for God's gift of His Son. As the Kingdom penetrates a world still dark, we can continually thank the Lord as we see His Spirit moving in various places. We can thank God as we see the good news moving into new geographical areas. We should thank Him for souls won, when our missionaries enter a new country, and when we see a new

*"From thence, when the brethren heard of us, they came to meet us as far as Appii forum, and The three taverns: whom when Paul saw, he thanked God, and took courage" (Acts 28:15).*

*"The administration of this service not only supplieth the want of the saints, but is abundant also by many thanksgivings unto God; whiles by the experiment of this ministration they glorify God for your professed subjection unto the gospel of Christ, and for your liberal distribution unto them, and unto all men; and by their prayer for you, which long after you for the exceeding grace of God in you. Thanks be unto God for his unspeakable gift" (2 Cor. 9:12-15).*

## Daily Master Communication Guide

SCRIPTURE REFERENCE:

_____

### What God said to me:

_____

_____

_____

_____

_____

_____

### What I said to God:

_____

_____

_____

_____

_____

_____

church established. As our thanksgiving properly gives God credit, we release His hand in broader measure, and we make ourselves more fit to participate in the very advances we extol.

 What good news have you heard about the spread of the gospel in the world? What spiritual changes have you seen take place? Think hard. List several events or changes for which you are grateful. After writing them, express to God your gratitude for these spiritual victories.

_____

_____

### Public and Private

Gratitude should be public as well as private. Church worship can be a group expression of gratitude. In church prayer meetings, Bible-study groups, and other gatherings, opportunities should be given for expressing gratitude in addition to giving prayer requests. Use your leadership opportunities to train your church friends to express their gratitude in testimony, prayer, or song.

 What opportunities at church have you recently been given to express gratitude for others?

_____

Write this week's memory verse(s) on a separate sheet of paper.

 Walking in Fellowship with God Today

Much of our thanksgiving is for blessings even a non-Christian could name as blessings. A new car (in some cases) might glorify someone's ability to earn money. Your salvation, however, can glorify only God. Glorify God today by thanking Him for the highest and noblest of all His gifts to you. Concentrate on responding to His spiritual blessings with a thankful heart. As you pray, refer to "Gratitude for Spiritual Blessings" in prayer guide 5, page 210.

1. First thank God for as many purely spiritual (unseen) blessings as you can think of—your salvation, a person you have led to Christ, temptations He has enabled you to overcome, a transformation in your personality, new desires, or persons you have influenced to grow spiritually.

2. Thank God for instruments of spiritual blessing in your life—someone who led you to the Lord or has taught you in your Christian growth, a pastor, churches that have blessed you, conferences or courses you may have attended or studied, books you have read, and so forth.

3. Add the more significant thanksgivings to "Praise and Thanksgiving List," page 222.

4. As you have your quiet time, complete the Daily Master Communication Guide in the margin.

# [week 6]
# WORSHIPING GOD IN PRAYER

**Determined to Praise the Lord**

I was going through personal and private grief. Without realizing it, I stopped praising God as I prayed. Although I begged God for relief from the grief, no relief came. I struggled through five praiseless days in this dark mood.

Then on Saturday, the fifth day of the grief and the fifth day without any real worship in my prayer life, suddenly I realized that if I praised God on the mountaintop but refused to praise Him in the valley, I was not praising God at all—I was praising my feelings. I did not feel like praising, but I also knew that much of our commitment to God is a matter of the will, not of feelings. God had not changed! His glory, His majesty, and His eternal purpose were not dimmed or tainted by the events of my life. So I went to my prayer closet, kneeled before the Lord, and concentrated on His unchanging perfections.

I knew that I was still much blessed. My salvation was intact; my family was godly; my job was secure. The dark days had made me concentrate on the unhappiness of the hurt. So I sang the Doxology to the Lord—"praise God from whom all blessings flow!"I began to sense a lightness in my spirit that I had not sensed for days. Then I quoted to the Lord Psalm 103 with its staggering list of benefits. By now the lightness was becoming joy in the Lord's presence, and I marveled at the inner change that praise had worked so quickly.

My experience reminded me of Habakkuk's determination to praise the Lord. Troubled by God's use of the Babylonians to punish Israel, Habakkuk earnestly searched for an explanation. He named six disasters and concluded with a strong resolve:

> Though the fig tree should not blossom,
> And there be no fruit on the vines,
> Though the yield of the olive should fail,
> And the fields produce no food,
> Though the flock should be cut off from the fold,
> And there be no cattle in the stalls,
> Yet I will exult in the Lord,
> I will rejoice in the God of my salvation.
> The Lord God is my strength,
> And He has made my feet like hinds' feet,
> And makes me walk on my high places (Hab. 3:17-19, NASB).

Habakkuk walked the high countries! The path of praise is a high path. Now I understood how Habakkuk could praise in his difficult circumstances. I also learned a new definition of *praise*: Praise is insisting on the truth!

*Key Idea*
God is worthy of your worship. When you worship Him in spirit and truth, He is pleased.

*This Week's Learning Goal*
You will improve your private and public worship by studying biblical models and scriptural teachings on the meaning and ways of worship.

*Verses to Memorize*
"Thou art worthy, O Lord, to receive glory and honour and power: for thou hast created all things, and for thy pleasure they are and were created" (Rev. 4:11).

"God is a Spirit: and they that worship him must worship him in spirit and in truth" (John 4:24).

*Related Prayer Guide*
Prayer guide 6, "Worshiping God in Prayer," page 211

# Day 1
# God Is Worthy

*"I will call on the Lord, who is worthy to be praised"* (2 Sam. 22:4).

*"He is the Rock, his work is perfect, for all his ways are judgment: a God of truth and without iniquity, just, and right is he"* (Deut. 32:4).

*"Great is the Lord, and greatly to be praised; and his greatness is unsearchable"* (Ps. 145:3).

Our English word *worship* comes from an old Anglo-Saxon word, *weorthscipe*, which means *worth-ship*. Worship is evaluating God properly—esteeming Him for all His worth, acknowledging all of His attributes, and crediting His judgments with righteousness.

Worship is placing worth on the person of God Himself. We recognize His worth because He is perfect; there is no blemish in any aspect of His character or work. Read 2 Samuel 22:4 and Deuteronomy 32:4 in the margin.

**God Is Worthy to Be Praised**
Read Psalm 145:3 in the margin. We must attribute worth to the Lord, whose greatness is immeasurable.

 As you examine the following reasons God is worthy of praise, make notes on the chart "Reasons God Is Worthy of Praise" in prayer guide 6 on page 211. Praise Him in your heart or verbally.

*He is infinite.* God is infinite; His qualities are not measurable by any standard we know. We cannot understand infinity, but we can stand in awe of God, who is infinite.

- The psalmist marveled, "He telleth the number of the stars; he calleth them all by their names. Great is our Lord, and of great power: his understanding is infinite" (Ps. 147:4-5).
- Isaiah wondered, "Hast thou not known? hast thou not heard, that the everlasting God, the Lord, the Creator of the ends of the earth, fainteth not, neither is weary? there is no searching of his understanding" (Isa. 40:28).
- This attitude of wonder and awe is maintained throughout the psalms; contemplating how God reverses the ways of men, the psalmist exclaimed, "This is the Lord's doing [this placing of the stone which the builders rejected as the chief cornerstone]; it is marvelous in our eyes" (Ps. 118:23).

*He is transcendent.* We are also to stand in awe of God because He is above and beyond anything else we know; He is other than any of His creatures. Theologians call this quality of otherness transcendence. The psalmist expressed it in awesome words: "Who is like unto the Lord our God, who dwelleth on high?" (Ps. 113:5). He is so vastly beyond anything we can know that Solomon asked, "Will God indeed dwell on the earth? behold, the heaven and heaven of heavens cannot contain thee; how much less this house that I have builded?" (1 Kings 8:27).

*He is unique.* We attribute worth to God because of His uniqueness. Hannah acknowledged, "There is none holy as the Lord: for there is none beside thee: neither is there any rock like our God" (1 Sam. 2:2). Paul told us that "there is no power but of God: the powers that be are ordained of God" (Rom. 13:1). God's uniqueness prompted the command "Thou shalt worship no other god: for the Lord, whose name is Jealous, is a jealous God" (Ex. 34:14). God is the source of all holiness, all strength, and all authority. His worth stands alone; we can value nothing on a par with Him.

*He is wise.* We can attribute worth to God because of His wisdom and knowledge. Paul, who often broke into a doxology as he contemplated God's glory, said, "O the depth of the riches both of the wisdom and knowledge of God! how unsearchable are his judgments, and his ways past finding out!" (Rom. 11:33).

*He is completely perfect.* God's worth is seen in the completeness, the totality, of each of His perfections. The psalmist said, "The judgments of the Lord are true and righteous altogether" (Ps. 19:9) and "The Lord is righteous in all his ways, and holy in all his works" (Ps. 145:17). This totalness of His perfection separates Him from His creatures. We must acknowledge His worth in "worth-ship." He is worthy to be praised!

What five qualities of God show that He alone is worthy to be praised?

_____

_____

Check your work by reviewing the preceding material.

## A Pattern for Worship

The Book of Revelation contains glorious worship of God and His Son, the Lamb of God. Read Revelation 5:8-14 in the margin and answer the following questions to discover a pattern for worship.

In verses 8-10 who was being worshiped? _____

Who did the worshiping? _____

What posture did the four living creatures use in their worship?

_____

What items did they use in worship? _____

In what form did they present their worship? _____

What results of Jesus' death did they praise? _____

In verses 11-14 who besides living creatures and elders joined in worship?

_____

How did they present their worship? _____

What words expressing God's and the Lamb's worth did they use in

praise? _____

"When he had taken the book, the four beasts and four and twenty elders fell down before the Lamb, having every one of them harps, and golden vials full of odours, which are the prayers of saints. And they sung a new song, saying, Thou art worthy to take the book, and to open the seals thereof: for thou wast slain, and hast redeemed us to God by thy blood out of every kindred, and tongue, and people, and nation; and hast made us unto our God kings and priests: and we shall reign on the earth. And I beheld, and I heard the voice of many angels round about the throne and the beasts and the elders: and the number of them was ten thousand times ten thousand, and thousands of thousands; saying with a loud voice, Worthy is the Lamb that was slain to receive power, and riches, and wisdom, and strength, and honour, and glory, and blessing. And every creature which is in heaven, and on the earth, and under the earth, and such as are in the sea, and all that are in them, heard I saying, Blessing, and honour, and glory, and power, be unto him that sitteth upon the throne, and unto the Lamb for ever and ever. And the four beasts said, Amen. And the four and twenty elders fell down and worshipped him that liveth for ever and ever" (Rev. 5:8-14).

## Daily Master Communication Guide

SCRIPTURE REFERENCE:

_____

### What God said to me:

_____

_____

_____

_____

_____

_____

_____

### What I said to God:

_____

_____

_____

_____

_____

_____

_____

_____

The 4 beasts and the 24 elders used harps and golden vials in their worship of the Lamb. The vials contained the prayers of the saints (your prayers and mine) and provided a sweet-smelling incense for worship. They fell down before the Lamb in reverence for His worthiness. As they worshiped Him, they sang a song of praise. They praised Jesus, the Lamb, for redeeming them and for making them kings and priests.

Visualize this picture. The 4 beasts and the 24 elders surrounded God's throne worshiping the Lamb. They were joined by a chorus of angels—100 million plus thousands of thousands. Then all creatures in heaven, on earth, under the earth, and in the sea joined in praising the Lamb. What a worship service that was—and will be!

This mighty choir used words in praise that you too can use. The Lamb is worthy to receive power, wisdom, honor, blessing, riches, strength, and glory. Only an infinite God can be infinitely worthy. The 24 elders and the 4 living creatures fell before His throne and proclaimed, "Thou art worthy, O Lord, to receive glory and honour and power: for thou hast created all things, and for thy pleasure they are and were created" (Rev. 4:11). He is the Creator and the Source who can meet all of our needs. Only one value can we esteem as supreme, infinite, and eternal. We esteem God alone as being gloriously worthy, even beyond our comprehension. You were created for His pleasure. Please God with your worship of Him.

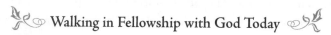 Walking in Fellowship with God Today

Every morning as I begin my quiet time, before I do anything else—before I speak to God, read the Bible, or meditate—I pause for several serious minutes to contemplate whom I am talking to. I can address no one who is more awesome; no greeting is more formidable. Therefore, the first words I utter are words of praise, submission, and adoration.

1. Each day this week as you approach prayer, refer to "He Is Worthy" and to the chart "Reasons God Is Worthy of Praise" in prayer guide 6, "Worshiping God in Prayer," page 211. Spend time contemplating the five qualities above the chart showing that God is worthy to be praised, as well as the notes you recorded on the chart. Pause now to enjoy a time of worship and praise.

   • _God is infinite._ We cannot understand infinity, but try to concentrate on "thinkable" qualities that have no boundary: limitless love, unbounded holiness, never-exhausted mercy and grace.

   • _God is transcendent._ We can't understand His utter otherness—His transcendence—but its essence is fearsome and wonderful.

   • _God is unique._ His uniqueness seems to separate Him from anything He created, but the awesome gulf of His mighty love brings us right to the throne of holiness through the Lord Jesus.

   • _God is wise._ His wisdom means that He can use every detail of our lives to bring glory to Himself.

   • _God is perfect._ Contemplate His perfection in the perfect gifts He has given us—His Son, His Spirit, the Bible, and complete salvation.

2. As you have your quiet time, complete the Daily Master Communication Guide in the margin.

# Day 2
## Worship in Spirit and Truth

### Spiritual Worship

Read Jesus' words in John 4:24, in the margin. Worship must be spiritual, but many Christians are confused by the idea of spiritual worship.

Worship in spirit is worship initiated, empowered, and directed by the Spirit. From your perspective, worshiping in spirit is—
- your appropriate response to the Spirit's initiative;
- your dependence on the power of the Spirit rather than on the strength of the flesh;
- your sensitivity to the Spirit's leadership.

*Today's Learning Goal*
You will understand the meaning of true and false worship and will be able to worship in spirit and truth.

### Worship in Spirit

One way to understand this difficult biblical concept is to place it in sharp relief, to make it stand out. We can place the concept of worshiping in spirit in sharp relief by contrasting it with its opposite. The opposite of the spirit in which we must worship is the flesh. Read in the margin Paul's warning about the flesh.

The usual meaning of *flesh* in the Bible is performing works in our own strength apart from the strength and direction God can give. A *work of the flesh* is an exertion of human effort to satisfy merely human desire. Throughout the New Testament *flesh* is manifested by pride and arrogance. *Flesh* pictures humanity's sinful nature.

*"God is a Spirit: and they that worship him must worship him in spirit and in truth"* ( John 4:24).

*"The flesh lusteth against the Spirit"* (Gal. 5:17).

Read the following Scripture verses and write your own definition of *flesh*: **Romans 8:5-10; Galatians 5:16-25; Galatians 6:7-9; 2 Peter 2:9-12.**

_____

**Read Philippians 3:3 in the margin. What did Paul contrast with worship in spirit?**

_____

*"We are the circumcision, which worship God in the spirit, and rejoice in Christ Jesus, and have no confidence in the flesh"* (Phil. 3:3).

Confidence in the flesh is pride in what a human being can do apart from God. If, for any reason, the act of worship produced pride in anyone, it would be fleshly worship. Paul identified a particular kind of first-century false worship as causing the "worshiper" to be "vainly puffed up by his fleshly mind" (Col. 2:18). Pride, then, is a characteristic of the flesh.

Check the items that characterize worship in the flesh.
- ❑ A human effort to satisfy a human desire
- ❑ A religious action that produces pride
- ❑ A religious experience that makes a person arrogant
- ❑ Confidence in what a person can do apart from God

You should have checked all four items.

1. "Her outfit looks nice today."
2. "That window reminds me of the Trinity at Jesus' baptism."
3. "The preacher is preaching too long today."
4. "I never saw so many great truths in those verses before."
5. "Our choir is surely better than the one at First Church."
6. "I hope her son will accept the Lord publicly today."
7. "That solo helped me feel closer to God."
8. "I think everyone will admire the way I worded that prayer."
9. "If I place my check in the offering plate face up, others will see how faithful I am."

- Your part in a record-breaking attendance day
- Perfect Bible-study attendance for a year
- Your family's prominence in the church
- Your church's size
- Your preacher's eloquence
- Your position in the church
- Your musical or dramatic abilities

*"Among the chief rulers also many believed on him; but because of the Pharisees they did not confess him, lest they should be put out of the synagogue: for they loved the praise of men more than the praise of God"* (John 12:42-43).

 **In the first list in the margin, check the thoughts that seem out of place for worship in spirit.**

You should have checked items 1, 3, 5, 8, and 9.

 **Examine the second list in the margin. Have you ever felt the wrong kind of selfish pride in any areas listed? Check all that apply.**

Legalism has great advantages for the flesh. It is exterior and can be documented. Those who regularly attend church are regarded as "good" Christians. People can feel good about going to church even when their hearts and minds never worship or focus on God.

In contrast, spiritual worship is interior and cannot be documented by human instruments. No person can boast, or would boast, if worship is truly spiritual. If the requirements for worship were dictated by humans, then humans could measure the worship. If they are dictated by God, then only God can measure, and human boasting becomes impossible.

 **John recorded that some rulers preferred to look good to people rather than to God. Read John 12:42-43 in the margin. Who were they? What was the proof that they would rather look good to people?**

_____

_____

The chief rulers were afraid of the Pharisees. They would not confess Christ because they would be barred from worship at the synagogue. Their fleshly worship and their response to Christ will be judged in the last day. Such worship will not measure up to God's expectations (see John 12:44-50).

Fleshly worship is event-centered. It reduces worship to an event such as a church service or even a daily devotional period. Spiritual worship is process-centered. It permeates all of life, although it may be expressed in concentrated periods that are events. A fleshly worshiper, after meeting the requirement of the event, says to himself: *It is finished. Now I can do something else.* A spiritual worshiper seeks to meet the requirement of the Lord, saying: *It is started. The Lord's presence will continue with me.*

 **Think about last Sunday's worship in your church. Decide whether your response to the worship tended toward flesh or toward spirit. The answer might also indicate something about the attitude of the preacher or performer. Focus only on your response. In the margin on page 85, check your responses or write your own responses on the blank lines.**

## Worship in Truth

The worshipers God seeks must worship in spirit and in truth. Read in the margin on the next page Jesus' words to the Samaritan woman in John 4:24.

Worship in truth rejoices in the whole truth of God as He has shown Himself to us. It causes us to seek Him further. It causes us to realize that no matter how much we know of Him now, we have yet to discover and understand much truth about Him.

An opposite of truth is error. Whenever a doctrine is perverted or presented out of a proper balance, its truth is lost. I once knew a preacher who, during a period of immorality in his life, emphasized God's love and mercy to the exclusion of God's holiness. His particular emphasis misled some people into lax moral thinking. Love and mercy, without holiness to balance them, became indulgence and permissiveness. The teaching did not represent God's true love and mercy, which are perfect only when balanced by holiness. That preacher was not leading his people to worship in truth. To worship in error or false belief is an attempt to worship in that which is opposite God's nature.

Another perversion of truth occurs when words that are true in themselves become mere formula—an empty formula of right words recited without applying their meaning. If we worship only in the recitation of formula, we fail to understand that rightness of words is not always the same as rightness of heart (although it is possible for worship in formula to be genuine).

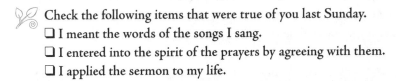 **Check the following items that were true of you last Sunday.**
❑ I meant the words of the songs I sang.
❑ I entered into the spirit of the prayers by agreeing with them.
❑ I applied the sermon to my life.

Certain precise prescriptions characterized the outward forms of Jewish worship. The danger of perversion and of Israel's failure to observe the inward requirements of true worship found expression in the time of Amos. The people's worship had two great wrongs:

1. Their lives were wicked. Their worship did not spring from an inner righteousness. They were observing the technicalities, but they did not worship in spirit.
2. Their worship was insincere. They practiced an outward observance without meaning the words they said. They had the right formulas, but their worship was not in truth.

In the Bible God seldom spoke of hating anything; yet read in the margin what He declared in Amos 5:21-23.

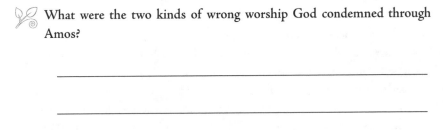 **What were the two kinds of wrong worship God condemned through Amos?**

_____

_____

God condemned worship from a wicked and unrighteous people. He also condemned worship that was insincere, shallow, and meaningless.

I am frightened to think that God, who requires worship in spirit and truth, might say of some of our worship: "I hate, I reject your Sunday-morning services,

*Inappropriate*
*Response (Flesh)*
❑ "She sang very well."
❑ "Our church has excellent
     music."
❑ "He has such a gift of words."
❑ "Our beautiful worship leaves me
     pleased and satisfied."
❑ "He must have had great
     teachers in seminary."
❑ Other: _____
_____
_____
_____

*Appropriate*
*Response (Spirit)*
❑ "I feel that way about God, too."
❑ "Now I know God better."
❑ "God has confronted me."
❑ "I must decide for or against
     God in this matter."
❑ "What a challenge to my living
     for Christ!"
❑ Other: _____
_____
_____
_____

"God is a Spirit: and they that worship him must worship him in spirit and in truth" (John 4:24).

"I hate, I despise your feast days, and I will not smell in your solemn assemblies. Though ye offer me burnt offerings and your meat offerings, I will not accept them: neither will I regard the peace offerings of your fat beasts. Take thou away from me the noise of thy songs; for I will not hear the melody of thy viols" (Amos 5: 21-23).

## Daily Master Communication Guide

SCRIPTURE REFERENCE:

_____

### What God said to me:

_____

_____

_____

_____

_____

_____

### What I said to God:

_____

_____

_____

_____

_____

_____

_____

nor do I delight in your Wednesday-evening services. Even though you offer up to Me a tenth or more of your income, I will not accept it, and I will not even look at your special offerings. Take away from Me the noise of your hymns. I will not even listen to the sound of your pianos and organs."

Worship in spirit and truth is in right response to God and in sincerity of heart, not in the fulfillment of any human prescriptions, whether in time, place, manner, formula, or person. When Jesus said, "I will have mercy, and not sacrifice" (Matt. 12:7), one of the implications was "I desire heart, not form."

### ✤ Walking in Fellowship with God Today ✤

You will need a big imagination for your prayers today, so stretch your mind.

1. Imagine that the angel Gabriel appears to you and says: "You have been chosen for perfect worship. God has commanded that I take you to heaven this morning so that you can never again mistake the nature of worship in spirit and truth. You will never forget the worship you offer God today." Then Gabriel transports you into a realm of perfect glory, light, and beauty. But he explains: "Before you can enter the Lord's presence, you must be utterly clean, so we have a special bath for mortals about to enter His holy presence. You will take a shower with a most unusual cleanser, so don't be surprised by its nature. Just allow the cleanser to do its work on you until you are totally clean."

   The shower proves to be more shocking than you anticipated. You find yourself under a shower of blood! You dare not disobey, so you allow the blood to soak your entire body. To your amazement, everywhere the blood touches turns glisteningly clean, clean in a way you never understood cleanness before. As you emerge, you realize for the first time in your life what "unblemished and spotless" means. Gabriel explains to you that you have been cleansed with the blood of Christ Himself.

   Then Gabriel, gesturing toward a magnificent temple, tells you: "Now you are fit for the presence of the Lord. We will dress you in robes fitting for those who enter the throne room of God." As you wonder at the glory and beauty of robes unlike anything on earth, he explains that you are being dressed in the robes of Christ's righteousness. Fully dressed, you hear the command "Enter His holy of holies!" As you approach the Lord's presence, you sense His yearning for your company. You step into the glory of perfect love with a joy that you wish would last forever.

   This experience is your present possession. When you pray, you come into the presence of formidable holiness, washed in Jesus' blood, dressed in His righteousness. You approach a yearning love and fellowship with a holy God. Your worship must be valid—in spirit—and it must be real—in truth.

   Try to imagine what you would say to Him in these circumstances! As you pray, refer to "He Is Worthy" and to the chart "Reasons God Is Worthy of Praise" in prayer guide 6, page 211. Record your thoughts.

2. As you have your quiet time, complete the Daily Master Communication Guide in the margin.

# Day 3
## Bible Praise Words

One way we can praise is to imitate the praise we find in the Bible. The highest praise in all history is expressed in the Psalms, the hymn book of the Jewish people. The vocabulary of the Psalter ought to be a part of every Christian's prayers. That vocabulary gives useful insights into praise. Some Bible words used in worship that we will study today are *magnify, exalt, ascribe, rejoice, exult, bless,* and *praise.*

### Magnify and Exalt

In Psalm 34:3, in the margin, David urged us to magnify and exalt the Lord with him. We magnify and exalt God when we hold up His greatness and His exalted position so that they will be seen. God's greatness is best seen when we are not obtrusive, when we do not magnify ourselves so that eyes focus on us rather than on Him. God said, "My glory will I not give to another" (Isa. 42:8).

If God knows that your secret motives are to make yourself look good rather than to bring Him glory, He will not accept your praise. Your prayer to magnify or exalt the Lord should be accompanied by a sincere prayer that He will be glorified. Your life of humility allows His glory to shine through.

*"O magnify the Lord with me, and let us exalt his name together"* (Ps. 34:3).

**Write a sentence prayer, using the words** *magnify* **and** *exalt.*

_____

_____

*Ascribe to* **was used when God's qualities and words were attributed to Him. Read Psalm 29:1-2 in the margin. What did the psalmist ascribe to God?**

_____

**In Deuteronomy 32:3, in the margin, what did Moses ascribe to God?**

_____

*"Ascribe to the Lord, O mighty ones, ascribe to the Lord glory and strength.
Ascribe to the Lord the glory due his name;
worship the Lord in the splendor of his holiness"* (Ps. 29:1-2, NIV).

We are to ascribe to the Lord glory, strength, and greatness—to give God credit for what is His, to acknowledge His perfections. We need to recognize Him and His works. David credited God with being Israel's Source when he prayed, "All things come of thee" (1 Chron. 29:14).

*"Because I will publish the name of the Lord: ascribe ye greatness unto our God"* (Deut. 32:3).

### Rejoice and Exult

The Old Testament urges people to rejoice and exult before the Lord. *Exult* means *to rejoice greatly or be jubilant.* A part of the Mosaic law was "Ye shall rejoice before the Lord your God, ye, and your sons, and your daughters, and your menservants, and your maidservants, and the Levite that is within your gates" (Deut. 12:12).

# Daily Master Communication Guide

SCRIPTURE REFERENCE:

_____

## What God said to me:

_____

_____

_____

_____

_____

_____

## What I said to God:

_____

_____

_____

_____

_____

_____

Read each of the following Scriptures, which are printed in the margin on page 89. Why or in what does the psalmist rejoice or exult?

Psalm 19:8: _____

Psalm 20:5: _____

Psalm 9:2: _____

We can rejoice in the Lord's precepts and in His victory. Above all, we can rejoice in God Himself.

## Bless

Can we bless the Lord? The psalmist was wise enough to know that a heartfelt utterance of blessing on the Lord actually accomplished just that—it blessed the Lord. He associated blessing with a review of God's benefits for us (see Ps. 103: 2-5) and with a review of the might and splendor of God's creation (see Ps. 104). The psalmist resolved that Israel would make its utterance of blessing eternal in duration: "we will bless the Lord from this time forth and for evermore" (Ps. 115:18).

## Praise

The most frequently used word in the Bible for the entire activity of praise is _praise_ itself. We enter the Lord's courts not only with thanksgiving but also with praise (see Ps. 100:4). Praise is natural for a believer. _Hallelujah_ or _alleluia_ means "Praise Ye, Jehovah." _Hosanna_ in the New Testament is an exclamation of joy or a shout of welcome to Jesus. When the multitudes were praising Jesus on His triumphal entry into Jerusalem, the Pharisees objected. Jesus' answer was "I tell you that, if these should hold their peace, the stones would immediately cry out" (Luke 19:40).

Define in your own words what each of the following means.

_Magnify_ **and** _exalt:_ _____

_Ascribe:_ _____

_Rejoice_ **and** _exult:_ _____

_Bless:_ _____

_Praise:_ _____

Check your work by referring to the descriptions you read in today's lesson.

1. Read and meditate on Jude 24-25. Record your communication with God.
2. "Bible Praise Words" in prayer guide 6, page 211, lists praise and exclamatory words for use in worship. As you read the terms, utter prayers of praise.
3. Write each of the following Scriptures on a three-by-five-inch card or on a sheet of paper. Pray each of these to the Lord throughout the day.
   * "O magnify the Lord with me, and let us exalt his name together" (Ps. 34:3).
   * "Give unto the Lord the glory due unto his name; worship the Lord in the beauty of holiness" (Ps. 29:2).
   * "Bless the Lord, O my soul: and all that is within me, bless his holy name" (Ps. 103:1).
   * "I will be glad and rejoice in thee: I will sing praise to thy name, O thou most High" (Ps. 9:2).
   * "Praise ye the Lord: for it is good to sing praises unto our God; for it is pleasant; and praise is comely" (Ps. 147:1).
4. As you have your quiet time, complete the Daily Master Communication Guide in the margin on page 88.

*"The statutes of the Lord are right, rejoicing the heart: the commandment of the Lord is pure, enlightening the eyes" (Ps. 19:8).*

*"We will rejoice in thy salvation, and in the name of our God we will set up our banners: the Lord fulfil all thy petitions" (Ps. 20:5).*

*"I will be glad and rejoice in thee: I will sing praise to thy name, O thou most High" (Ps. 9:2).*

# Day 4
# Patterns for Worship

## Praying the Psalms

Another way we can use psalms to praise the Lord is to pray them as though they were our own. The variety in the Psalter lends itself to our various needs, conditions, moods, attitudes, and circumstances. Use these varieties to express your praise in different moods.

Today as you read about the types of psalms, mark them in your Bible with letters that will help you identify them. Marking the psalms will enable you to return to them in your daily devotions and to pray verses as your own.

*Today's Learning Goal*
You will understand ways to use psalms as patterns for worship.

> E—exhortation to worship
> C—contemplation in worship
> R—refuge as a place of worship
> M—majesty as the characteristic of the One worshiped

## Exhortation

Some psalms are exhorting psalms. *To exhort* means *to advise, urge, or entreat another.* Read David's exhortation in Psalm 34:3, in the margin. One characteristic of a heart overflowing to God is the desire to enlist others in our praise. Read Psalm 67:3 in the margin. The last four psalms in the book exhort Israel, natural forces, and musical instruments to praise the Lord.

By placing an *E* in the margin of your Bible beside psalms of exhortation, you will be reminded to join the psalmist in worship. Turn in your Bible to these

*"O magnify the Lord with me, and let us exalt his name together" (Ps. 34:3).*

*"Let the people praise thee, O God; let all the peoples praise thee" (Ps. 67:3).*

## Daily Master Communication Guide

SCRIPTURE REFERENCE:

_____

*What God said to me:*

_____

_____

_____

_____

_____

_____

*What I said to God:*

_____

_____

_____

_____

_____

_____

psalms and mark them with an *E*: Psalm 34:3; 67:3; 147; 148; 149; 150. You will use these psalms for worship later today.

### Contemplation

Other psalms are contemplative psalms in which the psalmist meditates on God's perfections. Psalm 62 portrays David calmly waiting on the Lord as he quietly surveys his salvation by the Lord. Psalm 65 is a meditation in awe on all of God's manifold works. Other psalms useful for quiet meditation and contemplation on God's nature and works are Psalms 1; 42; 84; and 119. Turn to and mark these, as well as Psalms 62 and 65, with a *C*.

### Refuge

A number of refuge psalms are associated with praise. The term *refuge* pictures a place of safety and confidence. Martin Luther was especially fond of Psalm 46; his paraphrase of it is the basis of our hymn "A Mighty Fortress Is Our God."

Psalm 11 can be used for reassurance, and Psalm 16 is especially helpful in inspiring confidence in the meaning of our relationship with God. Many psalms impart a sense of safety, even as we praise the helping strength of the Lord—for example, Psalms 57; 59; 71; 91; 121; 124; and 141. Mark an *R* beside these, as well as Psalms 11 and 16.

### Majesty

The majestic psalms are thrilling, placing us in the presence of a sovereign God, wonderful in power and wonderful to contemplate. Psalms 8; 19; and 24 survey the mighty works of God's hand, and yet they see people in the fellowship of that awesome power. These psalms help you consider our God's might, glory, power, dignity, and imperial rank. Turn to and place an *M* beside the following psalms: 8; 19; 24; 29; 48; 50; 76; 93; 97; and 113.

When you see in your Bible the following letters beside psalms, what will they tell you about the psalms' use in worship? Briefly describe each.

E _____

_____

C _____

_____

R _____

_____

M_____

_____

Using "Psalms to Use in Prayer" in prayer guide 6, page 211, and a separate sheet of paper, complete the following activities. Bring them to your group session this week.

- Read Psalm 147. Write your own psalm that exhorts or calls your *Disciple's Prayer Life* group to join you in praise to God.
- Select a contemplative psalm and read it devotionally. List God's perfections that the psalmist named. Write thoughts that the psalm brings to your mind.
- Read a refuge psalm. List ways God is seen as a refuge, hiding place, or protector. Also list ways you have experienced God as a refuge.
- Select a majestic psalm and read it aloud as your prayer of praise.

## Confident Praise

Christians are prone to praise God when they feel good. If we praise God on the mountaintop but refuse to praise Him in the valley, we are praising not God but our feelings. Often the psalmist begins by reciting his troubles and by desperately pleading for help but moves quickly to praise. Psalm 13 begins by asking, "How long wilt thou forget me, O Lord? for ever?" but moves to confident praise of the Lord through trust: "But I have trusted in thy mercy; my heart shall rejoice in thy salvation. I will sing unto the Lord, because he hath dealt bountifully with me" (vv. 5-6). So praise is partly a matter of the will. We would do well to imitate David's attitude as he began Psalm 9. Note the repeated "I wills" in the verses in the margin.

*"I will praise thee, O Lord, with my whole heart; I will shew forth all thy marvellous works. I will be glad and rejoice in thee: I will sing praise to thy name, O thou most High"* (Ps. 9:1-2).

*≽⌒ Walking in Fellowship with God Today ⌒≼*

1. Pray Psalm 13 and feel the move from depression to faith. Use Psalm 9:1-2 to declare your own will to worship God. As you praise God, refer to "Bible Praise Words" in prayer guide 6, page 211.
2. As you have your quiet time, complete the Daily Master Communication Guide in the margin on page 90.

# Day 5
# Outward Worship

In addition to inner feelings and words spoken in adoration, worship has outward manifestations.

## Body Language

The position of the body and its parts, movements, and gestures show the worshiper's inner attitude. The psalmist's enthusiasm in worship is surprisingly physical for some 20th-century minds.

*Today's Learning Goal*
You will understand ways to use body language, music, and offerings in worship.

*"O clap your hands, all ye people; shout unto God with the voice of triumph" (Ps. 47:1).*

*"Thus will I bless thee while I live: I will lift up my hands in they name" (Ps. 63:4).*

*"Make a joyful noise unto God, all ye lands" (Ps. 66:1).*

*"Praise him with the sound of the trumpet: praise him with the psaltery and harp. Praise him with the timbrel and dance: praise him with stringed instruments and organs. Praise him upon the loud cymbals: praise him upon the high sounding cymbals" (Ps. 150:3-5).*

*"Deliver me from bloodguiltiness, O God, thou God of my salvation: and my tongue shall sing aloud of thy righteousness" (Ps. 51:14).*

*"I will sing of thy power; yea, I will sing aloud of thy mercy in the morning: for thou hast been my defence and refuge in the day of my trouble" (Ps. 59:16).*

*"I will sing of the mercies of the Lord for ever: with my mouth will I make known thy faithfulness to all generations" (Ps. 89:1).*

**Read in the margin the following passages and identify physical ways the psalmist worshiped or invited others to worship.**

Psalm 47:1: _____

Psalm 63:4: _____

Psalm 66:1: _____

Psalm 150:3-5: _____

The psalmist encouraged the use of or declared that he would participate in clapping (47:1), lifting up hands (63:4), shouting (66:1, NASB), and dancing (150:4). He called for using loud instruments to praise the Lord (150:3-5). Our praise may remain silent, but the psalmist certainly gave us examples of worship that is overt, visible, and audible.

## Music

Music expresses worship. The most important overt musical activity is singing. The psalmist wanted us to sing with a harp (see 33:2b) and to sing for joy (see 95:1). Sometimes we are to sing to the Lord (see 13:6; 27:6), and sometimes we are to sing about Him (see 66:2; 89:1). We sing about the entire gamut of His glories.

**What did the psalmist sing about? Discover his subjects in these verses in the margin and write them below: Psalm 51:14; Psalm 59:16; Psalm 89:1.**

_____

_____

Above all, we are to sing praise (see 68:4; 135:3). The psalmist sang praises for God's righteousness, power, mercies, and faithfulness. The psalmist also challenged us to sing a new song (see 96:1; 98:1; 149:1). Reflect on these praises.

**If you were writing a new psalm as the psalmist suggested, what ideas would you include? Write several below.**

_____

_____

**What are some subjects you most enjoy singing about in your worship services at church? Write several below.**

_____

_____

## Offerings

Giving is an activity that praises the Lord. Jesus observed how the multitudes were putting money into the treasury of the temple (see Mark 12:41). His compliment to the widow was not for the amount but for the proportion of her substance she gave. Paul later declared that an offering is "accepted according to that a man hath, and not according to that he hath not" (2 Cor. 8:12). He said that the churches of Macedonia gave in an "abundance of joy" (2 Cor. 8:1-2).

*Giving is an activity that praises the Lord.*

 **When and how have you given an offering to God that was a truly joyous worship experience?**

_____

**When you place an offering in the collection plate, what special feelings of worship do you have?**

_____

**Do you feel that you are giving a present to God? Why or why not?**

_____

**Do you ever give only from habit or a sense of guilt? If so, what could you do to improve your motives for giving?**

_____

As the people of Israel brought their offerings for the building of the temple, the chronicler reported, "The people rejoiced, for that they offered willingly, because with perfect heart they offered willingly to the Lord: and David the king also rejoiced with great joy" (1 Chron. 29:9). Mary of Bethany gave a similar example of offering with a whole heart when she poured out a "very costly" spikenard ointment on Jesus' feet (see John 12:3). Our offering is made with a whole heart when we realize that the offering is simply a token of giving the Lord all of ourselves.

We learn the true meaning of *offering* from David. Read his words in the margin as he blessed the Lord in the temple offering. God is on a high and holy level and does not need anything we can give Him from our level. He does not need our money, our talent, our skills, our intelligence, our education, or anything else we value. God needs nothing to sustain what He is. Our offering is not a way to meet divine need but rather a way to understand and acknowledge that God is the Source of all that is good in us and of all that we have. We can rejoice as we make offerings to God. He has given to us, and we joyfully acknowledge that.

*"All things come of thee, and of thine own have we given thee" (1 Chron. 29:14).*

 **What is one way the offering time in your church's worship services could become a more meaningful worship experience?**

_____

## Daily Master Communication Guide

SCRIPTURE REFERENCE:

_____

*What God said to me:*

_____

_____

_____

_____

_____

_____

*What I said to God:*

_____

_____

_____

_____

_____

_____

**Lifelong Learning**

We have not exhausted worship. Even the psalms do not exhaust worship. It is one of the great major themes of Leviticus, Malachi, and Revelation. Worship is repeatedly seen in the higher moments of the history of the leaders of Israel and the church. Paul's doxologies naturally flow from a life of worship. Worship is a lifetime study, and the greatest prayer warriors, both in the Bible and in Christian history, have made it the major part of their prayer lives. Christians who are serious about their prayer lives will want to commit themselves to exploring the kinds, depths, and glories of worship as long as they live.

Write this week's memory verse(s) on a separate sheet of paper.

### Walking in Fellowship with God Today

1. As you pray and praise privately today, use different physical expressions in your worship. For example, lift your hands to the Lord as you praise Him or clap your hands as you recite a psalm. As you praise Him, refer to the ideas in prayer guide 6 on page 211.
2. Choose a favorite Scripture song or hymn and sing it to the Lord.
3. The next time you make an offering, pray over the money or the check as you prepare it. Dedicate your life to God and let the offering symbolize giving Him all.
4. As you have your quiet time, complete the Daily Master Communication Guide in the margin.

# PRAYING TOGETHER

## United in Prayer

My wife and I established our family altar before we were married. When we entered our mid-50s, Laverne and I rejoiced that we had seen a lifetime of mutual prayer answered. Our son-in-law was as godly as we had prayed for him to be. Our daughter was totally committed to the lordship of Christ. Both were godly, praying Christians. Our grandchildren were already demonstrating the fruit of much prayer. We felt that our family devotions lacked nothing, and we were each growing in the Lord. There was much thanksgiving in our home.

Then Laverne was stricken with cancer. Two things immediately began happening. The first was an instinctive turning to God in deeper dimensions. Grief is often a father to new insights. As God began bringing new understandings of Christ's lordship into our lives, we documented the new understandings—and requirements—in a notebook we titled "For You Are My God," the name of a Scripture song that ministered powerfully to us in the darkest days.

The second thing that happened to us was that we drew closer together. I worked hard to arrange my schedule to be at home with Laverne more, to eat more meals with her, and to take her with me whenever possible. We spent hours in the Bible together, and we prayed together more often. Amazingly, we began to see dramatic answers to prayer.

Laverne developed shingles, a frequent occurrence with the surgery she had. The doctor prepared us for a hard siege. We prayed, and all symptoms were gone in three days!

I had a sabbatical leave approaching during which I was to write a book. We prayed for a computer so that I could have a word processor. I was thinking of the smallest unit on the market, but Laverne was more daring in her requests. Without knowledge of my need, a Christian businessman in Fort Worth bought us one of the top personal computers on the market, with ample software, a modem, and a letter-quality printer!

One night as we were marveling over what seemed to be happening in our prayers together, we were able to articulate a new principle for united prayer: The closer the bond, the more powerful the prayer; the higher the unity, the greater the authority in prayer.

*Key Idea*
United prayer yields increased power and authority in prayer.

*This Week's Learning Goal*
You will learn and begin to practice ways to pray with other Christians in small and large groups.

*Verses to Memorize*
*"If my people, which are called by my name, shall humble themselves, and pray, and seek my face, and turn from their wicked ways; then will I hear from heaven, and will forgive their sin, and will heal their land"* (2 Chron. 7:14).

*"Again I say unto you, that if two of you shall agree on earth as touching any thing that they shall ask, it shall be done for them of my Father which is in heaven. For where two or three are gathered together in my name, there am I in the midst of them"* (Matt. 18:19-20).

*Related Prayer Guide*
Prayer guide 7, "Praying Together," page 212

# Day 1
## Prayer Partners

You will understand the value of praying together with others and will demonstrate your appreciation for united prayer by enlisting a prayer partner.

### Paul and Silas—Bible Prayer Partners

Paul and Silas were prayer partners in the jail at Philippi: "At midnight Paul and Silas prayed, and sang praises unto God: and the prisoners heard them" (Acts 16:25). Luke does not tell us the content of their prayer, but the earthquake and the loosing of their bonds led to the conversion of the Philippian jailer and his household. The first church in Europe had a remarkable beginning, and two prayer partners had a remarkable answer to prayer.

 **Pretend that you are Silas in the Philippian jail with Paul. Read the account of this experience in Acts 16:6-40. List some things you (Silas) and Paul would pray about in such circumstances.**

_____

_____

Paul and Silas praised God in the midst of their troubles. Paul knew from the Macedonian vision (see Acts 16:6-10) that God had a purpose for their being where they were. They may have prayed for Lydia and her family (the first converts in Philippi), for the slave girl God had freed from the demonic spirit, for the men who were responsible for their being in prison, for the men who beat them, for their fellow prisoners, and for the jailer and his family. They probably thanked God that He counted them worthy to suffer for Christ's sake. Their joint prayer in that prison cell must have had a tremendous impact on those who heard them. It certainly did on the jailer and his household!

### Reasons We Need to Pray with Others

 **Read the Scriptures in the margin and write a statement about what is common to all of them.**

_____

Paul asked the churches of his time to pray with him and for him. Someone might ask: "Why must we ask someone to pray for us and with us? Does not God hear the prayers of each one of His children? Would He not hear my prayers for myself?" You should want others to pray with you for at least two reasons:
1. The prayers of others strengthen your praying.
2. Others see factors you may fail to see.

Paul was convinced that other Christians' prayers would strengthen his. Unified prayer is more powerful than individual prayer. Another reason you want to pray with others is that others see factors you may fail to perceive. You may have heard the old saying "Two heads are better than one." Praying with a prayer partner strengthens your faith, broadens your prayer concerns, and adds a special accountability to your prayer habits.

_"… praying always with all prayer and supplication in the Spirit, and watching thereunto with all perseverance and supplication for all saints; and for me, that utterance may be given unto me, that I may open my mouth boldly, to make known the mystery of the gospel" (Eph. 6:18-19)._

_"… withal praying also for us, that God would open unto us a door of utterance, to speak the mystery of Christ, for which I am also in bonds" (Col. 4:3)._

_"Brethren, pray for us, that the word of the Lord may have free course, and be glorified, even as it is with you" (2 Thess. 3:1)._

One of your Scripture-memory verses this week addresses the value of praying together. Read Matthew 18:19-20 on page 95 and summarize the value of praying with others.

_____

_____

Meditate on these verses. Ask God to reveal ways you can pray with others.

## More Bible Prayer Partners

 As you read the following paragraphs, underline or highlight the Bible prayer partners listed.

Hezekiah and Isaiah became prayer partners when Sennacherib threatened Judah. Read 2 Chronicles 32:20-21 in the margin. God answered when the national ruler and the national prophet united in prayer.

God also answered when larger groups prayed together.

 Read Numbers 27:1-11. Who joined together as prayer partners?

_____

You may have answered, "Only Moses prayed." However, the daughters of Zelophehad petitioned Moses for an inheritance. Moses then presented their petition to God. In a sense the daughters and Moses became prayer partners. The answer to their prayer was an expansion of the law of inheritance.

In a war with a coalition of alien tribes, the tribe of Reuben, the tribe of Gad, and the half-tribe of Manasseh "cried to God in the battle, and he was entreated of them; because they put their trust in him" (1 Chron. 5:20). There were only five daughters of Zelophehad who prayed together, but a group of tribes also sought and found an answer to prayer. The size of the group does not matter. God seeks the unity of praying together.

Praying together provides help secured only through mutuality. Even Jesus appealed to His disciples in the garden of Gethsemane, "My soul is exceeding sorrowful, even unto death: tarry ye here, and watch with me" (Matt. 26:38). When He found them sleeping, He told them, "Watch and pray, that ye enter not into temptation" (Matt. 26:41). Paul recognized this help that can come only through mutual prayer. Read in the margin his acknowledgment to the church at Corinth.

God wanted Israel to pray as a nation. He wanted groups of any size to pray together. This conviction affected the apostles' thinking. When they were distracted from their appointed ministry in the early church, they led the church to appoint seven men to take their places in serving tables. Then they announced, "We will give ourselves continually to prayer, and to the ministry of the word" (Acts 6:4). They felt the urgent need to pray together, and evidently the ministry of the Word depended on that joint prayer. Praying together demonstrates that we are God's people.

*"For this cause Hezekiah the king, and the prophet Isaiah the son of Amoz, prayed and cried to heaven. And the Lord sent an angel, which cut off all the mighty men of valour, and the leaders and captains in the camp of the king of Assyria"* (2 Chron. 32:20-21).

*"... ye also helping together by prayer for us, that for the gift bestowed upon us by the means of many persons thanks may be given by many on our behalf"* (2 Cor. 1:11).

## Daily Master Communication Guide

SCRIPTURE REFERENCE:

_____

*What God said to me:*

_____

_____

_____

_____

_____

_____

_____

*What I said to God:*

_____

_____

_____

_____

_____

_____

_____

## Enlist a Prayer Partner

By this time in your *Disciple's Prayer Life* group I hope that you have already become convinced of the value of praying together. Now take another giant step in your prayer walk with God by beginning to pray regularly with a prayer partner. You need to enlist a person to pray with you at least once each week for the next six weeks. You may decide to continue beyond that time.

There are only two restrictions: do not enlist a family member as your prayer partner and do not enlist anyone in your *Disciple's Prayer Life* group. The person does not have to be a member of your church, but you certainly want to enlist a Christian. Consider all of your possibilities, including homebound persons. Your prayer times may be in person or by phone.

On a separate sheet of paper, list persons you would consider as potential prayer partners. Next, pray about and select one person to contact. As you make the contact, explain what you have learned today about praying together. Ask the person for the privileges of sharing and receiving requests for prayer and of praying with that person at least once each week. When he or she says yes, pray together a prayer of commitment to each other. Your first special request will be assigned tomorrow.

Record the name, address, and phone number of your prayer partner.

_____

This week day 5 will be brief so that you will have time to experience praying together. Begin praying and planning now for a special time to pray together with your prayer partner or a small group. Plan to pray together for 30 to 45 minutes.

When you have arranged a time and person(s) to pray with, inform someone in your *Disciple's Prayer Life* group who can pray for you during that time. Write the group member's name below.

_____

With whom will you pray and when?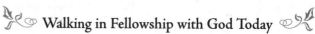

### Walking in Fellowship with God Today

1. Ask God to help you recall things you have learned from others in prayer. These might include faith, discernment, joy, praise, a thankful attitude, a sense of God's presence, and so forth. Thank Him for these things.
2. Pray for God to develop your fellowship with Him in prayer so that it inspires others to learn to pray more effectively. Pray for an opportunity to humbly minister to others through your prayer life.
3. As you have your quiet time, complete the Daily Master Communication Guide in the margin.

# Day 2
## Praying Together at Home, Part 1

Today we will consider the important practice of prayer in the home. If you are single, try to apply today's lesson to your situation. For example, agree to pray regularly with someone close to you, make a commitment to establish a family altar if you marry, determine ways you can use these ideas with roommates, or pray for members of your *Disciple's Prayer Life* group who have families and need to establish family altars.

### Benefits of a Family Altar
The benefits of a family's worshiping and praying together are numerous. The family altar can accomplish things in God's kingdom that nothing else can. The family altar—
❑ gives children a security in the Lord that nothing else can;
❑ provides parents an opportunity to demonstrate and model Christian virtues such as faith, endurance, hope, and concern for the world;
❑ teaches children the meanings of right and wrong;
❑ teaches Bible knowledge if Bible readings are included;
❑ unites the family in seeking God's solutions for its problems;
❑ provides an opportunity for the family to share needs, interests, and concerns for which they can pray;
❑ has power with God and serves the Kingdom by bringing God's will to pass on earth.

The prayer of a united family has unusual power to call forth from God His greater blessings. You may have heard another benefit of a family altar in the saying "The family that prays together stays together." One of the most enriching and rewarding experiences of united prayer occurs in the home. A family that learns to care about one another's concerns and needs, prays together to see God's will accomplished, and demonstrates for one another the change Christ is making in their lives is a family that develops close bonds of love that are difficult to break. In a time when families are breaking up at ungodly rates, Christian families desperately need united family prayer.

 **Reread the benefits listed above and check each benefit that you desire for your family. Pray briefly, asking God to reveal His will for your family altar as you continue today's study.**

### God's Will for Families
God established the first home with Adam and Eve, commanding that they become one (see Gen. 2:24). Jesus commended the home and warned, "What therefore God hath joined together, let not man put asunder" (Matt. 19:6). From the beginning the divine ideal was that the home picture the unity of God and His people or of Christ and His church (see Eph. 5:25-32). God expresses Himself as three Persons, and yet He is one. Likewise, He wants families to be one—to be united. That unity is expressed is through united prayer.

*The prayer of a united family has unusual power to call forth from God His greater blessings.*

## Daily Master Communication Guide

SCRIPTURE REFERENCE:

_____

*What God said to me:*

_____

_____

_____

_____

_____

_____

*What I said to God:*

_____

_____

_____

_____

_____

_____

_____

Read 1 Peter 3:7-9 in the margin on page 101 and briefly summarize what it says about prayer.

_____

_____

The importance of prayer in the home is evident in Peter's injunction. The "your" preceding "prayers" (v. 7) is plural, so the danger of hindered prayers cannot apply to the husband alone. The danger is that their prayers together might be hindered. The obligation to maintain harmony applies to both partners. The verses also imply that prayer in the home is too valuable to neglect. Prayer in the home must not be hindered.

### Biblical Models

Many types of family praying are found in the Bible, including parents praying for their children; husbands and wives praying together; husbands, wives, and children praying together; and families offering thanksgiving at mealtime. Prayer was prominent in many great families of the Bible. These families were pivotal in accomplishing God's plan. The marriages of Abraham and Sarah (see Gen. 12—22), Elkanah and Hannah (see 1 Sam. 1—2:11), Zacharias and Elisabeth (see Luke 1:5-25,57-80), and Joseph and Mary (see Matt. 1:18-25; 2:13-23; Luke 2) accomplished the divine ideal. These godly homes produced godly children.

In every case, one or both parents became famous as Bible pray-ers. Abraham's prayer for a child (see Gen. 15:2-4,6) led to his fathering a great nation. Hannah's famous prayers (see 1 Sam. 1:10-12; 2:1-10) ultimately affected Israel's history. Zacharias prayed for a son (see Luke 1:13), and on the occasion of that son's birth he prayed a great messianic prayer (see Luke 1:68-79). Joseph's visions (see Matt. 1:20; 2:13) indicate that he was a man of prayer, and Mary's Magnificat is one of the greatest praise poems of all time (see Luke 1:46-55). Great prayer was a vital part of these great homes.

List the great Bible pray-er in each of the four families just described. Then read or skim the related Scriptures and write the name of the godly child each home produced.

_____

_____

_____

_____

Praying parents have a tremendous impact on the home. Children in a praying home are blessed. You should have paired Isaac with Abraham, Samuel with Hannah, John the Baptist with Zacharias, and Jesus with Joseph and Mary.

Mentally evaluate your family-altar time. Is it all God wants it to be? With God's desires in mind, dream about what you would like your family to do in praying and worshiping together at home. Write down your dream in detail on a separate sheet of paper, describing what the ideal family-altar time would be for your family.

Contact your prayer partner or one of your *Disciple's Prayer Life* group members and share this dream. Ask this person to pray with you for your family as you seek to do God's will for a family altar. Write the name of your prayer partner and the date and time you prayed together.

Prayer partner: _____

Date: _____ Time: _____

Place this dream sheet in your workbook at "Daily Intercession" on page 223. Pray daily that God will work through you to make the dream a reality. Tomorrow you will reexamine your dream and will develop a plan for starting or improving your family altar.

 Walking in Fellowship with God Today

1. What is God's dream for your family altar? Pray about your commitment to let His will become yours.
2. Find or make an object that reminds you of your family members—a photograph, one of your children's small toys, a hair roller, or even a card with their names listed. Carry this object with you today or place it in a prominent place to remind you several times during the day to pray for your family-altar dreams. Pray for family members. Pray for obstacles to be overcome. Pray for right priorities. Pray for guidance.
3. As you have your quiet time, complete the Daily Master Communication Guide in the margin on page 100.

## Day 3
## Praying Together at Home, Part 2

Turn to the dream sheet you wrote yesterday. What are some things about your family that would have to change in order for that dream to come true?

_____

_____

*"Ye husbands, dwell with them according to knowledge, giving honour unto the wife, as unto the weaker vessel, and as being heirs together of the grace of life; that your prayers be not hindered. Finally, be ye all of one mind, having compassion one of another, love as brethren, be pitiful, be courteous: not rendering evil for evil, or railing for railing: but contrariwise blessing; knowing that ye are thereunto called, that ye should inherit a blessing"* (1 Pet. 3:7-9).

*Today's Learning Goal*
You will understand ways to unite your family in prayer and will demonstrate a dedication to united family prayer.

Read "Prayer in the Home" on pages 127–30 in *The Life-Changing Power of Prayer*. **As you read, underline activities, benefits, and characteristics of a strong family. In the margin beside each item underlined, identify the item by writing *A* for activities, *B* for benefits, or *C* for characteristics. Also circle practical tips for a family-altar time. Bring your book with you to the group session this week so that you can share your findings.**

You may have discovered other tips, but some of them are:
1. The pastor, his wife, and other spiritual leaders in the church should commit their homes to family prayer times to serve as models for others.
2. The husband and the wife can help each other provide spiritual leadership for the family. This is a matter of cooperation, not competition.
3. Elements of the family-altar time can include—
   • reading a Bible passage;
   • sharing opinions and ideas about what you read;
   • talking about your life together;
   • talking about your church;
   • talking about events in the Lord's work that your prayers might touch;
   • talking about family and friends who need prayer;
   • prayer.
4. Do not feel obligated to find solutions to problems discussed.
5. Do not feel that you must appear spiritual or must pray more impressively than another.
6. Pray with great freedom to be yourself.
7. Spend time together in the morning and continue praying for one another throughout the day.
8. If your family altar works best in the evening, sacrifice a TV program for the eternal value of time with God. The best time is probably just before bedtime.

### Planning the Family-Altar Time

*Time of day.* The time for a family altar may be either in the morning or at night. Schedules are usually less cluttered in the morning. If nighttime can be arranged, it provides security for children to end their day together with family and God. But the time of day is less important than regularity.

 **What time of day is best for family worship at your house and why?**

_____

*Procedure.* The procedure in family worship—what is actually done—differs according to family members' ages, knowledge, and abilities. Begin the devotional time by reading a part of the Bible together. If children can read, allow them to participate in the readings. Then the family may want to discuss the Bible passage, or they might discuss the things they want to pray about. All family members who are willing should pray. The order in which they pray is not important, but

---

*The husband and the wife can help each other provide spiritual leadership for the family.*

children gain security if a parent maintains control by directing the order in which the members pray. The prayers need not be long and certainly should not be showy. This simple outline can be a basic guide:

1. Bible reading    2. Discussion    3. Prayers

Imaginative parents can add exciting and interesting variations.

 Compare your dream family-altar plan with the simple outline above. Describe the differences between your plan and this simple guide. Add other ideas you have had.

_____

_____

## Other Helps for Family Worship

Helps for conducting family worship are numerous. Christian book stores have helpful books for leading a family altar. Some families prefer to use a devotional guide for each day. Many excellent guides are available in such periodicals as *Look and Listen, Bible Express, More, Adventure, essential connection, Living with Teenagers, Open Windows,* and *HomeLife.*[1] Look for ways to involve children creatively in discussing the Bible passage.

## Establish Right Priorities

The Bible does not deal with excuses for not having prayer in the home. Prayer in the home is expected. It is the standard, and deviations from it are to be temporary. In our hectic world many families do not allow time for prayer together, except perhaps at meals. This says that other activities have higher priority. Some of today's busiest Christians have regular prayer in their homes. Priorities can be arranged in yours.

The world has not seen what can be done by churches filled with families that pray together. Jesus' High Priestly prayer (see John 17) only hints of the importance He placed on the church's unity. He Himself came from a very godly home, and He expected homes to be unified. The great Kingdom accomplishments of the New Testament church and the achievements of the great families of the Bible came about because they prayed together. Prayer is not optional for the family. The family that prays together stays together, but far more important is what that family calls forth from God through its united prayer. God's eternal purposes are accomplished through praying together.

## Take Responsibility

*Husbands.* Husbands and fathers usually take the initiative in family prayer. Determine before the Lord that you will either initiate a devotional time in your family or improve the one you have.

*Wives.* You can use effective ways to appeal to your husband in humility. In some marriages the wife can simply ask forthrightly for a family altar. In others it is more appropriate to request prayer help in certain areas, to seek direction in

*Daily Master Communication Guide*

SCRIPTURE REFERENCE:

_____

*What God said to me:*

_____

_____

_____

_____

_____

_____

_____

*What I said to God:*

_____

_____

_____

_____

_____

_____

_____

understanding Bible passages or spiritual principles, or to give gentle but appropriate prompting. (Demands, threats, and intimidation are inconsistent with godliness in men or women. Godly encouragement is always in order.) If the husband cannot or will not participate, begin with members of the family who will.

*Single adults.* Join with others in praying that the institution of the home will be preserved. Pray for homes you are acquainted with. Find others to pray with.

 On a separate sheet of paper, list steps you will take to develop a family devotional time. Begin acting on these steps this week. Report to your *Disciple's Prayer Life* group ways others can pray for you and your family.

## Walking in Fellowship with God Today

1. Use the list you just prepared as a prayer list. Pray specifically for each person and detail involved. Review "Tips for a Family-Altar Time" in prayer guide 7, "Praying Together," on page 212. Listen to what God says to you about His plan for your family altar. Pray for His will in this area.
2. As you have your quiet time, complete the Daily Master Communication Guide in the margin on page 103.

---

[1] To obtain additional information or order these periodicals: WRITE LifeWay Church Resources Customer Service, One LifeWay Plaza, Nashville, TN 37234-0113; FAX order to (615) 251-5933; PHONE 1-800-458-2772; EMAIL to CustomerService@lifeway.com; ONLINE at www.lifeway.com; or visit the LifeWay Christian Store serving you..

# Day 4
# Church: A House of Prayer

### The First-Century Christians
The early Christians were united believers who prayed earnestly. The importance of the disciples' unity is repeatedly seen in Jesus' great prayer in John 17.

 Read John 17:11,21-23 in the margin and answer the following questions.

What did Jesus pray for His disciples in each verse?

_____

Jesus wanted the unity of the disciples to be like what?

_____

Why did Jesus want the disciples to be united?

_____

*Today's Learning Goal*
You will understand ways a church can become a house of prayer and will demonstrate your cooperation in developing plans for your church's prayer ministries.

*"Now I am no more in the world, but these are in the world, and I come to thee. Holy Father, keep through thine own name those whom thou hast given me, that they may be one, as we are. That they all may be one; as thou, Father, art in me, and I in thee, that they also may be one in us: that the world may believe that thou hast sent me. And the glory which thou gavest me I have given them; that they may be one, even as we are one: I in them, and thou in me, that they may be made perfect in one; and that the world may know that thou hast sent me, and hast loved them, as thou hast loved me"* (John 17:11,21-23).

Jesus wanted the disciples to be one, to be united with a single purpose and spirit. He wanted them to be united just as He and God the Father are united. When this kind of unity is expressed in the church, the world around knows and believes that Jesus was indeed sent from God. Is it possible that our inadequacies in reaching people for Christ are due in part to our lack of unity? Probably so.

In Matthew 18:19-20 Jesus promised Christians a special presence when they gather together to pray. Read His words in the margin.

Jesus desired that the church be unified and that it pray together. This is exactly what we see in the beginnings of the church. Both the unity and the prayer are conspicuous, along with the results of unified prayer. Read the three passages from Acts in the margin.

This habit of praying together continued and spread to the other churches as they were established across the Mediterranean world. After Paul's visit in Ephesus on his third missionary journey, the church as a body accompanied him to the coast: "When we had accomplished those days, we departed and went our way; and they all brought us on our way, with wives and children, till we were out of the city: and we kneeled down on the shore, and prayed" (Acts 21:5).

 On a separate sheet of paper write a paragraph that describes the early Christians' unity, prayer, and accomplishments.

## A House of Prayer

 Consider occasions when your church prays. How would you evaluate the focus on prayer during the following times? Use the scale below to rate each occasion.

| SCALE | OCCASIONS |
|---|---|
| 0—Little or no attention to prayer | _____ Sunday-morning worship |
| 2—Prayer is mostly a habit. | _____ Sunday-evening worship |
| 5—Prayer time is brief but meaningful. | _____ Wednesday-evening service |
| 8—Sometimes prayer is given much attention due to needs. | _____ Business meetings |
| | _____ Bible study |
| 10—Prayer receives almost exclusive priority during this period. | _____ Discipleship training |
| | _____ Choir practice |
| | _____ Missions-organization meetings |
| | _____ Committee meetings |

Some church activities give greater focus to prayer than others. Each time period has its function in the life of the church. However, prayer should not be ignored in any.

 Read in the margin Jesus' words in Luke 19:46 about a place of worship. Does that description fit your church? ❑ Yes ❑ No   Why or why not?

*"Again I say unto you, That if two of you shall agree on earth as touching any thing that they shall ask, it shall be done for them of my Father which is in heaven. For where two or three are gathered together in my name, there am I in the midst of them"* (Matt. 18:19-20).

*"These all continued with one accord in prayer and supplication, with the women, and Mary the mother of Jesus, and with his brethren"* (Acts 1:14).

*"They continued stedfastly in the apostles' doctrine and fellowship, and in breaking of bread, and in prayers"* (Acts 2:42).

*"They, continuing daily with one accord in the temple, and breaking bread from house to house, did eat their meat with gladness and singleness of heart, praising God, and having favour with all the people. And the Lord added to the church daily such as should be saved"* (Acts 2:46-47).

*"My house is the house of prayer"* (Luke 19:46).

## Daily Master Communication Guide

Scripture reference:

_____

### What God said to me:

_____

_____

_____

_____

_____

_____

_____

### What I said to God:

_____

_____

_____

_____

_____

_____

_____

## Your Church Can Be a House of Prayer

Prayer is offered in almost all church meetings, at least to open and close them. If you are a leader in a church organization, such as a Bible-study teacher, program chairman, choir director, department director, organization president, or pastor, you can lead your church members step-by-step to learn and practice more and better praying.

Many choir directors open their rehearsals with prayer for music missionaries. Department directors might concentrate prayers on aspects of Bible learning—prayers for openness, wisdom, divine direction of teachers, and so forth.

Whether or not you are a leader, you can influence prayer in the groups to which you belong through—

- informal conversations with members and leaders about prayer in the meetings;
- suggestions in committee or business meetings;
- your personal patterns of praying in the group or organization;
- direct teaching or explanation when you lead a prayer time.

 **What opportunities do you currently have to influence your church's prayer life?**

_____

Use these opportunities to increase the quality and quantity of prayer in your church.

## Prayer Ministries

Week 13 provides much more detail about a church's prayer ministries. For now, begin thinking about specific prayer ministries in your church.

Churches emphasize and give priority to prayer in many ways. In addition to the usual church organizations, the following are prayer plans some churches use.

- A bulletin board for posting prayer requests with a section for answers to prayer
- A prayer group that meets before Bible study on Sunday morning to pray for spiritual results of teaching and worship
- A group that prays during the worship service for the pastor, each part of the worship service, visitors, lost persons in the congregation, and so forth
- A morning prayer breakfast with more attention to praying than to eating
- A prayer chain with each member phoning the prayer request to the next name on the list. Requests should be briefly worded and dictated to the next person on the prayer chain. Answers to prayer are passed on the same way.
- A prayer room staffed by volunteers who pray weekly during an assigned hour for requests phoned or sent to the church's prayer ministry. Some churches have prayer for 24, 12, 6, or fewer hours a day, according to the size of the church and the availability of volunteers. Personal, church, and worldwide prayer requests are recorded and systematically prayed for. Answers to prayer are also reported.
- Home prayer meetings for revivals and conferences

- One-day, around-the-clock prayer time for special events or times of decision. One or more people pray during each time slot for a 24-hour period.

There are many other ways to focus on and emphasize prayer. How do you sense God leading you to get involved in your church's prayer ministry?

 Read Luke 19:46 in the margin on page 105 and pray about your involvement in a ministry of prayer. Record your thoughts and feelings. Plan to share these thoughts with your *Disciple's Prayer Life* group this week.

_____

_____

 Walking in Fellowship with God Today

1. Many of us are not in positions of leadership, but we are urged to pray for leaders. Pray pointedly that leaders in your church will be divinely guided in uniting church members in prayer. Pray that organizational leaders will be prayer leaders. Pray that members will catch the spirit of prayerful leaders and will join prayer efforts. Pray for a revival of prayer in your church. Pray that your church will truly be called a house of prayer by all who know about it.
2. As you have your quiet time, complete the Daily Master Communication Guide in the margin on page 106.

# Day 5
# Subjects for Church Prayer

## United Prayer
As mentioned in day 1, today's assignment will be brief so that you can spend time praying together with your prayer partner or a small group. Pray for 30 to 45 minutes.

 With whom have you arranged to pray? When and where will you pray?

_____

Following your prayer time, take a few minutes to write reflections on a separate sheet of paper. Bring this sheet with you to your group session.

## Subjects to Pray For
Some people have difficulty thinking of subjects to pray about when they pray with others. It is appropriate to consider subjects the New Testament church prayed about.

## Daily Master Communication Guide

SCRIPTURE REFERENCE:

_____

_____

### What God said to me:

_____

_____

_____

_____

_____

_____

_____

### What I said to God:

_____

_____

_____

_____

_____

_____

_____

_____

_____

Read the Scriptures on the right and match them with the subjects prayed for or commanded to be prayed for on the left.

| | | |
|---|---|---|
| ____ | 1. Right conduct | a. Matthew 9:38 |
| ____ | 2. All Christians | b. John 15:16 |
| ____ | 3. Christian fruit | c. Acts 4:24-31 |
| ____ | 4. Healing | d. Acts 8:15 |
| ____ | 5. Missionaries | e. Acts 12:5 |
| ____ | 6. Filling of the Holy Spirit | f. Acts 13:2-5 |
| ____ | 7. Church leaders | g. Acts 14:23 |
| ____ | 8. Wisdom | h. 2 Corinthians 5:20 |
| ____ | 9. Calling of Christian workers | i. 2 Corinthians 13:7 |
| ____ | 10. Reconciliation | j. Ephesians 6:18 |
| ____ | 11. Boldness in witnessing | k. Philippians 1:9 |
| ____ | 12. Love, knowledge, judgment | l. 1 Thessalonians 5:23 |
| ____ | 13. Preservation | m. 1 Timothy 2:1-2 |
| ____ | 14. Deliverance | n. James 1:5 |
| ____ | 15. Persons in authority | o. James 5:14-16 |

Check your work by comparing your list with "Subjects to Pray For" in prayer guide 7 on page 212.

Select one of the previous Scriptures and meditate on the request. Record your reflections below.

_____

_____

Read "Prayer in the Church Today" in _The Life-Changing Power of Prayer,_ pages 125–26. As you read, list other subjects for church prayer.

_____

_____

Write this week's memory verse(s) on a separate sheet of paper.

### Walking in Fellowship with God Today

1. Read "Praying for Missionaries and Believers in Communist Countries" in prayer guide 7 on page 212. Pray for the subjects listed during your prayer times today.
2. As you have your quiet time, complete the Daily Master Communication Guide in the margin.

# AGREEING WITH GOD

## The Bride of Christ

We had been disturbed about a lump in my wife's breast. Good news! The radiologist who read her X-rays sent a message to our family doctor that the mammogram was clear.

Six months later, Laverne (my wife) went back to the doctor and reported to him, "This mass in my breast is growing." One look convinced him that she was right, and he sent her to a surgeon for a biopsy. This time the test was clear: Laverne had cancer. The doctor who read the earlier X-rays had somehow failed to detect the growth. At surgery, tests on the lymph nodes indicated that by now the malignancy had spread into her lymph system, and the cancer specialist started her on chemotherapy. He told us that the chances were 50-50 that the cancer could be destroyed without recurrence.

Laverne and our daughter handled the shock beautifully. I did outwardly, but inwardly I was reeling. When we were together, I somehow managed a smile; alone I would weep. The climax came when I could go no farther. I locked my office door, fell on my face, and shattered into a thousand pieces. I knew that the Lord had purposes beyond my knowing, and I wanted desperately to participate in His work. I cried out for the Lord to give meaning to this hurt.

Later, a remark by a former pastor opened a new world for me. He said: "Jesus understands how you feel. After all, He loves His bride, too." The church is the bride of Christ! My prayer took a new direction. Suddenly it was all quite clear. I teach a seminar on *The Mind of Christ*, but there was a dimension of the mind of Christ I did not yet understand. Cancer in my wife's body was a severe pain, a grief to me. Sin in the church is far more painful to her glorious Husband than I had realized. If I am to know the meaning, the what, and the how of His mind and His thinking, I cannot ignore the painful aspects of His being Husband to the church.

I fell on my face in agreement with His mighty love, grief, and long-suffering in His dealing with cancers in the body of Christ. For the first time I saw them in the horror of their ugliness. I had learned what it meant to agree with God about my personal sin. Now I had to agree with Him about something far more grand and formidable—the glory of the church and the horror of sin in God's own people. I did not ask to have sin in Christ's bride revealed to me. However, I prayed more fervently when I saw arrogance, anger, or any secret sin that is an affront to corporate life. This made my own sin more loathsome to me and gave me a new eagerness to remain in constant, unbroken agreement in my prayers with the Lord.

As of this writing, my wife's cancer is in remission. I am inexpressibly grateful that she is in a condition to agree with me, to be a real helpmeet. I am also more eager to abide in agreement with God than I have ever been. One of the strongest prayers of my heart now is that the bride of Christ will complement His glory and purity, without blemish and without spot.

---

### Key Idea
Agreement with God is the essence of the Christian life and of prayer itself.

### This Week's Learning Goal
You will understand the biblical meaning of confession, its importance, and the kinds of confessions Christians need to make.

### Verses to Memorize
"If we confess our sins, he is faithful and just to forgive us our sins, and to cleanse us from all unrighteousness" (1 John 1:9).

"At the name of Jesus every knee should bow, of things in heaven, and things in earth, and things under the earth; and that every tongue should confess that Jesus Christ is Lord, to the glory of God the Father" (Phil. 2:10-11).

### Related Prayer Guide
Prayer guide 8, "Agreeing with God," page 213

---

# Day 1
# The Meaning of Confession

*Today's Learning Goal*
You will understand the difference between the broad meaning of confession and the confession of sin.

 **Schedule a time to pray with your prayer partner this week. Write the day and time here.**

_____

Let's quickly review some of the qualities of God.
- God is omniscient—all-knowing. He created you, so He always knows what is best for you.
- God is righteous.
- God is just.
- God is wise.
- God is faithful.
- God is loving.

These are God's traits not just some of the time but all of the time. He possesses these qualities completely; He is perfectly knowledgeable, righteous, just, wise, faithful, and loving. Would it make sense to disagree with Him? The answer is obvious! Disagreeing with God makes no sense. Yet some people live their lives in disagreement with God, and they must suffer the consequences of living apart from God's will.

**The Importance of Agreeing with God**
We can disagree with God. This usually means that we think our opinions or our ways are better than His.

 **Read in the margin Peter's experience in Matthew 16:21-23. Was his thinking in accord with God's plan?  ❑ Yes  ❑ No**

Jesus had predicted that He would die by Roman crucifixion. Peter thought that his intentions were right when he disagreed with Jesus by attempting to forbid Him the death of the cross. As strange as that dreadful word seemed at the time, Peter's (seemingly well-intentioned) opinion was wrong. Jesus' opinion was right. Peter disagreed even while he was calling Jesus Lord.

Jesus is our model. He lived a life in perfect agreement with His Father. He had to be in His Father's house (see Luke 2:49). In His temptations Jesus disagreed with Satan, and He agreed with the Father by quoting God's Word. The High Priestly prayer of John 17 is awesome in its picture of the perfect unity of the Father and the Son. That agreement was so perfect that He could say, "I and my Father are one" (John 10:30).

Others have lived in agreement with God. "Enoch walked with God"; he was "in step," in agreement (see Gen. 5:22). Noah was in agreement with God. He was pure in an impure age (see Gen. 6:8-9,11-12). Abraham so agreed with God that he came to be called the "Friend of God" (see Jas. 2:23). Agreement with God is sensible. It is the only way you can have intimate fellowship with Him.

*"From that time forth began Jesus to shew unto his disciples, how that he must go unto Jerusalem, and suffer many things of the elders and chief priests and scribes, and be killed, and be raised again the third day. Then Peter took him, and began to rebuke him, saying, Be it far from thee, Lord: this shall not be unto thee. But he turned, and said unto Peter, Get thee behind me, Satan: thou art an offence unto me: for thou savourest not the things that be of God, but those that be of men" (Matt. 16:21-23).*

Read Amos 3:3 in the margin. What does it say about agreement with God?

_____

*"Can two walk together, except they be agreed?" (Amos 3:3).*

Israel had sinned against God. Because of its iniquities, God had to punish it. Amos basically said, "Your iniquity has broken your fellowship with God." Agreeing with God means praying according to His desires, putting into practice His actions, living according to His nature, and thinking His kind of thoughts. Sin—choosing your own way instead of God's way—breaks fellowship with God.

If you do not agree with God, you cannot walk with God. Since all have sinned (see Rom. 3:23), confession, repentance, and forgiveness are important in restoring fellowship with God. During the next three days we will study these concepts.

*If you do not agree with God, you cannot walk with God.*

## Confession

The subject of confession is much broader than what we usually include under confessing or acknowledging someone's sins. The word in the Greek New Testament for *confess* means *to speak the same thing* God speaks. We are to agree with Him. This is the essence of the Christian life and of prayer itself—praying in agreement with God and living in agreement with God.

 Write your own definition of *confession*. Confession is _____

_____

This week you will learn to—
+ confess sin;
+ confess needs;
+ confess Jesus as Lord and Savior;
+ confess truth.

## David's Confession of Sin

King David committed adultery with Bathsheba and then had her husband killed trying to hide his sin. When Nathan confronted David with his sin, David was broken before the Lord. If you are not familiar with the account, read 2 Samuel 11—12. This situation in David's life led to his writing Psalm 51.

 Study David's prayer in Psalm 51 and answer the following questions.

What four different words did the king use in speaking about his wrongdoing?

_____

What words (verbs) or phrases did David use to describe what he wanted God's forgiveness to do for him? Answer on the following page.

## Daily Master Communication Guide

SCRIPTURE REFERENCE:

_____

### What God said to me:

_____

_____

_____

_____

_____

_____

### What I said to God:

_____

_____

_____

_____

_____

Verse 1: _____

Verse 2: _____

Verse 7: _____

Verse 14: _____

Verse 15: _____

What change did David ask God to bring about in his life as a result of his repentance and confession?

Verse 6: _____

Verse 7: _____

Verse 8: _____

Verse 10: _____

Verse 12: _____

Compare your answers to "A Model Confession of Sin" in prayer guide 8, "Agreeing with God," on page 213.

David learned to agree with God about his sin. There was no place for arguing with God or trying to justify his actions. He saw the ugliness of his sin the way God saw it. He saw sin's terrible impact on his life the way God saw it. He recognized the need for forgiveness and change the same way God did. David learned to agree with God. No wonder he is known as a man after God's own heart!

What verse(s) in Psalm 51 would you use in your prayers when you are convicted of sin?

_____

Read the first five paragraphs under "Prayer of Repentance" in _The Life-Changing Power of Prayer_, **page 65–66. Write a summary of what God expects when you confess your sins to Him.**

_____

_____

Your response may have included several ideas. It should have dealt with your need to agree with God about the nature of your actions and to align yourself with His attitude toward them.

1. Confession should always be immediate. Unconfessed sin compounds itself (see Jas. 3:16) and breaks fellowship with God. Quietly, in God's presence ask Him to show you any sin or sins in your life that you have not confessed or about which you have not come into agreement with Him. Referring to "A Model Confession of Sin" in prayer guide 8, page 213, use some of David's words to confess your sins.

2. Reread Psalm 51 and record your thoughts.

3. Pray for confession and restoration to be experienced by any Christians you know who need to confess their iniquities to God.

4. As you have your quiet time, complete the Daily Master Communication Guide in the margin on page 112.

# Day 2
# Steps in Confessing Sin, Part 1

| STEPS IN CONFESSING SIN |
| --- |
| 1. Acknowledge that the sin was committed. |
| 2. Repent or turn from the sin. |
| 3. Accept God's forgiveness. |

*Today's Learning Goal*
You will understand the need to deal with the guilt of sin by acknowledging it and repenting.

## Acknowledge the Sin

A very crucial area of agreeing with God concerns your guilt when you sin. In this case confession is a realignment of your agreement. The first step in coming into agreement with God about your sin is to recognize that you have sinned. You must acknowledge your sin. God commanded Israel, "Only acknowledge thine iniquity, that thou hast transgressed against the Lord thy God" (Jer. 3:13). David did just that when he prayed, "I acknowledged my sin unto thee" (Ps. 32:5). The primary meaning of the word *acknowledged* in Psalm 32:5 is *to know* or *to perceive*. You need to know sin when you see it or do it. The same word used in Psalm 32:5 for *acknowledged* is translated in the *New American Standard Bible* in Psalm 51:3 as *know*:

> I know my transgressions,
> And my sin is ever before me.

Both in Old Testament and New Testament times people were told to acknowledge or confess their sins. Consider three Bible experiences of confession: the Israelites, the followers of John the Baptist, and the prodigal son.

🌱 In the laws of Moses as recorded in Leviticus, provision was made for handling guilt. Read Leviticus 5:4-6 in the margin and arrange in the right order the three events that related to an Israelite's sin and confession. Write *1, 2,* and *3* on the following page to indicate the right order.

*"If a soul swear, pronouncing with his lips to do evil, or to do good, whatsoever it be that a man shall pronounce with an oath, and it be hid from him; when he knoweth of it, then he shall be guilty in one of these. And it shall be, when he shall be guilty in one of these things, that he shall confess that he hath sinned in that thing: and he shall bring his trespass offering unto the Lord for his sin which he hath sinned, a female from the flock, a lamb or a kid of the goats, for a sin offering; and the priest shall make an atonement for him concerning his sin" (Lev. 5:4-6).*

_____ Brought a trespass or guilt offering.
_____ Did or said something wrong.
_____ Confessed exactly what he had done wrong.

**Read Matthew 3:1-2,5-6 in the margin.** **What did the people do before they were baptized?**

_____

**Read the parable in Luke 15:11-21. Record the prodigal son's words of confession.**

_____

_____

*"In those days came John the Baptist, preaching in the wilderness of Judaea, and saying, Repent ye: for the kingdom of heaven is at hand. Then went out to him Jerusalem, and all Judaea, and all the region round about Jordan, and were baptized of him in Jordan, confessing their sins" (Matt. 3:1-2,5-6).*

*"When I kept silence, my bones waxed old through my roaring all the day long" (Ps. 32:3).*

*"At the evening sacrifice I arose up from my heaviness; and having rent my garment and my mantle, I fell upon my knees, and spread out my hands unto the Lord my God, and said, O my God, I am ashamed and blush to lift up my face to thee, my God: for our iniquities are increased over our head, and our trespass is grown up unto the heavens" (Ezra 9:5-6).*

The first words of the returning prodigal to his father were "Father, I have sinned against heaven, and before thee, and am no more worthy to be called thy son" (Luke 15:18-19). John the Baptist's followers confessed their sins and were called to repentance. When an Israelite sinned, he was to confess his sin and then bring a trespass offering to the Lord.

**The Bible also teaches the effectiveness of confessing sin. One of this week's Scripture-memory verses, 1 John 1:9, is a precious promise about the confession of sin. Read that verse in the margin on page 109. What are the results of confessing sin?**

_____

**Spend a few moments meditating on 1 John 1:9. Talk to God about your relationship with Him and this promise. Record your thoughts.**

_____

_____

Remember to complete your written assignments as you work through *Disciple's Prayer Life*. Do not shortchange your learning experience.

The Holy Spirit speaks to a believer's new nature when he or she sins. We are not to grieve the Holy Spirit (see Eph. 4:30). The offense to His holy nature is more serious than the contradiction of our new nature. Doing what we know to be wrong is dreadfully serious to God. We need to acknowledge as quickly as possible the contrary nature of our offense and to agree with God about the truth of His nature and His ways. In acknowledging your sin, you could say: "Lord, I acknowledge that what I have done is not Your nature and is not a part of my new nature. I confess my sin to You. I agree with You about the nature of this action. In Jesus' name I disapprove of my actions and turn back to follow Your ways."

If a person knows God, failure to confess brings discomfort. Read Psalm 32:3 on page 114. Confession is returning to what our true nature agrees with.

 **What is the first step in confessing sin?**

_____

### Repentance

The second step in confession is repentance, or feeling sorry for the sin and turning from sin. Agreeing with God means that we are sorry about our sin. We reject it. Repentance is more than feeling sorry. We turn from our sin in our preference for God's ways. The Bible calls this turning from sin repentance. Read in the margin on page 114 about Ezra's feeling of grief (Ezra 9:5-6).

Repentance at the time of your salvation was your first step in coming to agree with God. He was, is, and always will be right. You were wrong in your old ways. That was the most powerful turn you will ever make.

Repentance includes more than sorrow and tears. True repentance includes turning from sin and doing the things that please God. Genuine repentance requires radical changes in the things you do.

 **Explain the first two steps to deal with the guilt of sin.**

   1. Acknowledge the sin. _____

   _____

   2. Repent. _____

   _____

 **Walking in Fellowship with God Today**

There is a difference between the accusing voice of Satan (see Rev. 12:10) and the convicting voice of the Holy Spirit. The better you know the Lord, the more easily you can distinguish between Satan's angry accusations and the Holy Spirit's grief when you sin (see Eph. 4:30). Sensitive, mature Christians so agree with God—so personally identify with Christ—that they quickly sense the Holy Spirit's grief.

1. Ask God today for a more intimate knowledge of Him. Ask Him to sensitize you to His presence so that you live in minute-by-minute agreement with Him. If you accept His reaction to your thoughts and actions and tune yourself to His mind, you will experience joy in communion with Him and grief when anything breaks that communion. Confess your sins to Him, referring to "Steps in Confessing Sin" in prayer guide 8, page 213. Live in agreement with God.

2. As you have your quiet time, complete the Daily Master Communication Guide in the margin.

---

*Daily Master Communication Guide*

Scripture reference:

_____

*What God said to me:*

_____

_____

_____

_____

_____

_____

_____

*What I said to God:*

_____

_____

_____

_____

_____

_____

_____

# Day 3
## Steps in Confessing Sin, Part 2

*Today's Learning Goal*
You will understand four reasons you can know that God forgives you when you confess your sins.

 Review by listing the first two steps in confessing sin.

1. _____

2. _____

3. Accept God's forgiveness.

> **REASONS TO BELIEVE THAT SIN IS FORGIVEN**
> 1. Scripture promises forgiveness.
> 2. Scripture pictures sin as being removed.
> 3. Christ's blood cleanses the conscience.
> 4. Forgiven people can forgive others.

### Scripture Promises Forgiveness

First, you can believe that confessed sins are forgiven because Scripture gives you this promise. Read 1 John 1:9 in the margin.

*"If we confess our sins, he is faithful and just to forgive us our sins, and to cleanse us from all unrighteousness" (1 John 1:9).*

 What does Proverbs 28:13, in the margin, promise if you confess your sins?

_____

*"He that covereth his sins shall not prosper: but whoso confesseth and forsaketh them shall have mercy" (Prov. 28:13).*

Trying to hide your sins will only frustrate everything you try to do. God gives mercy to those who confess their sins.

### Scripture Pictures Forgiven Sin as Being Removed

The second reason for believing in forgiveness is that Scripture pictures confessed sins as being removed.

*"Who is a God like unto thee, that pardoneth iniquity, and passeth by the transgression of the remnant of his heritage? he retaineth not his anger for ever, because he delighteth in mercy. He will turn again, he will have compassion upon us; he will subdue our iniquities; and thou wilt cast all their sins into the depths of the sea" (Mic. 7:18-19).*

*"Behold, for peace I had great bitterness: but thou hast in love to my soul delivered it from the pit of corruption: for thou hast cast all my sins behind thy back" (Isa. 38:17).*

*"As far as the east is from the west, so far hath he removed our transgressions from us" (Ps. 103:12).*

Read the following Scriptures in the margin and draw simple pictures of what happens to forgiven sins.

| Micah 7:18-19 | Isaiah 38:17 | Psalm 103:12 |
| --- | --- | --- |
|  |  |  |

Amazingly, some Old Testament saints, without knowing the effectiveness of Jesus' cross, could accept God's forgiveness more easily than some Christians. Micah used a picturesque phrase to portray in understandable terms what God's forgiveness means: "Thou wilt cast all their sins into the depths of the sea." Hezekiah described the thoroughness of forgiveness by praying, "Thou hast cast all my sins behind thy back." The psalmist described forgiven sin as being from us "as far as the east is from the west." Your pictures will probably mean more to you than ours. However, as a future reminder of this point, three pictures of forgiven sin are included in prayer guide 8, page 213.

### Christ's Blood Cleanses the Conscience

A third reason for assurance of forgiveness is that Jesus' death provided the blood that cleanses even the consciences of repentant sinners. If Micah and Hezekiah, in their time, understood as much as they did of God's ways, how much more should we, who understand the victory of Christ's death and resurrection, rejoice in the unquestionable totality of God's forgiveness! Read Hebrews 9:13-14 in the margin.

If people like David and Isaiah, in Old Testament times, could believe that God had forgiven their sins, what stronger reason could you have for assurance or forgiveness? There is none.

### Forgiven People Can Forgive Others

A fourth evidence that confessed sins are forgiven is in the life and actions of the person who has been forgiven. One of the greatest assurances you have of forgiveness is your willingness to forgive others. If you can forgive offenses, you can be certain that God, who describes Himself as merciful, will forgive you. Jesus told us to pray, "Forgive us our debts, as we forgive our debtors" (Matt. 6:12). We who have been forgiven much can find it in our nature to become like the merciful God who forgave us.

Jesus issued a great promise and a strong caution in Matthew 6:14-15. Read those verses in the margin. Agreeing with God must include duplicating His character in every way.

The heavenly court works differently than an earthly court. If we confess a crime before an earthly court, we are sentenced. But confessing sin in God's court means that the past is canceled, because confessing is agreeing with God. It is saying: "I am really like You, Lord, because of my new nature. I prefer Your ways." That aligns you with God's hatred of sin and removes you from the camp of the guilty.

List four reasons you can believe that confessed sins are forgiven.

1. _____

2. _____

3. _____

4. _____

*"If the blood of bulls and of goats, and the ashes of an heifer sprinkling the unclean, sanctifieth to the purifying of the flesh: how much more shall the blood of Christ, who through the eternal Spirit offered himself without spot to God, purge your conscience from dead works to serve the living God?" (Heb. 9:13-14).*

*"If ye forgive men their trespasses, your heavenly Father will also forgive you: but if ye forgive not men their trespasses, neither will your Father forgive your trespasses" (Matt. 6:14-15).*

*"They shall teach no more every man his neighbour, and every man his brother, saying, Know the Lord: for they shall all know me, from the least of them unto the greatest of them, saith the Lord: for I will forgive their iniquity, and I will remember their sin no more" (Jer. 31:34).*

*"I, even I, am he that blotteth out thy transgressions for mine own sake, and will not remember thy sins" (Isa. 43:25).*

## Daily Master
## Communication Guide

SCRIPTURE REFERENCE:

_____

_____

*What God said to me:*

_____

_____

_____

_____

_____

_____

_____

*What I said to God:*

_____

_____

_____

_____

_____

_____

_____

If a person felt that his or her sin was unforgivable, how would you use these reasons to explain that confessed sins are forgiven? Write your answer on a separate sheet of paper.

### Forgetting

If you are totally forgiven, you should forget past sins. God Himself said that in the coming of the new covenant He would not remember iniquity. Read Jeremiah 31:34 and Isaiah 43:25 in the margin on the previous page. If God refuses to remember, so should you. If you do not forget your sins, you have not really accepted God's forgiveness. This is not to say that the consequences of sin do not continue; they certainly do, sometimes tragically. But the mental acceptance of forgiveness means that you move onward in your relationship with God, not backward. You do not forget the consequences; you forget guilt of the sin. The consequences can be a reminder of God's grace in the future. Not to accept the reality of forgiveness is to make God a liar, to disagree with what He says that He will do. Agreeing with God means that you put your sins behind your back, as God does.

### ❧ Walking in Fellowship with God Today ❧

Yesterday you took an important step in asking for more sensitivity to God. Growth in Christ is upward and forward, never downward and backward. Failure to accept forgiveness is really a determined retrogression. The basis for forgiveness is the cleansing effected by Christ's blood.

1. Ask yourself: *If God forgives, how forgiven is my sin? If God does anything, how thoroughly is it done?* Quote Hebrews 9:13-14 to the Lord, using "my conscience" in verse 14 instead of "your conscience." Reflect on the pictures you drew of forgiven sin or on the ones in "Biblical Pictures of Sin's Forgiveness" in prayer guide 8, page 213.
2. Reflect on God's forgiveness of your sin. Remind yourself of the four reasons you can believe that sin is forgiven by referring to "Reasons to Believe That Sin Is Forgiven" in prayer guide 8, page 213.
3. As you have your quiet time, complete the Daily Master Communication Guide in the margin.

## Day 4
## Other Confessions, Part 1

### Confessing Needs

Confessing your needs and the needs of others is another way to agree with God in prayer. God cares about the needs in the world and responds when His followers agree about those needs. Once you agree with God on the needs in your life or in another person's life, you also need to agree that God has the desire and the ability to meet the needs.

Read Psalm 146:7-9 in the margin and list types of people for whom God is concerned.

_____

_____

Today's Learning Goal
You will understand the value of confessing your needs to God and the value and necessity of confessing to others.

God cares about the needs of the oppressed, the hungry, prisoners, the blind, those who are bowed down, the righteous, strangers, orphans, and widows. Certainly He cares about all people, but He seems to have a special concern for these.

Pray about your concern for these types of people. Record your prayer.

_____

_____

"… which executeth judgment for the oppressed: which giveth food to the hungry. The Lord looseth the prisoners: the Lord openeth the eyes of the blind: the Lord raiseth them that are bowed down: the Lord loveth the righteous: the Lord preserveth the strangers; he relieveth the fatherless and widow: but the way of the wicked he turneth upside down" (Ps. 146:7-9).

The many petitions to Christ for healing were confessions of need. Note the vocabulary in these Scriptures: "The dogs eat of the crumbs which fall from their masters' table" (Matt. 15:27). "My little daughter lieth at the point of death; I pray thee, come and lay thy hands on her" (Mark 5:23). "Thou Son of David, have mercy on us" (Matt. 9:27). Jesus agreed with the Father in the way He met needs. Read in the margin His words in Luke 4:18.

Still, we must remember that our greatest needs are spiritual. We obviously need salvation, spiritual growth, the Holy Spirit's blessing and work in our lives, and fellowship with other Christians. For Paul, preaching was a need (see 1 Cor. 9:16). In short, we need God unceasingly in every aspect of our lives.

"The Spirit of the Lord is upon me, because he hath anointed me to preach the gospel to the poor; he hath sent me to heal the brokenhearted, to preach deliverance to the captives, and recovering of sight to the blind, to set at liberty them that are bruised" (Luke 4:18).

What are at least three spiritual needs of your own that you would like to confess to God in prayer?

_____

_____

What are three spiritual needs of other people that you should confess to the Lord in prayer?

_____

_____

Stop and spend time confessing these needs to the Lord.

## Confessing to Others

Read James's words in the margin. Confessing to others may involve two kinds of confession. In one we need the prayer-help of others; this is the subject of the

"Confess your faults one to another, and pray one for another, that ye may be healed" (Jas. 5:16).

James passage. In the other we need forgiveness and restitution from a group.

*Prayer-help of others.* Because the promise in James is that healing will grow from the confession, the confession itself should be something that is capable of being healed by mutual prayer. Mutual help through prayer is especially available in the areas of sin-weaknesses, such as a besetting habit. Mutual prayer, as we saw in week 7, is stronger than solo prayer.

Discretion is needed in mutual confession. The clue to how widely sin should be confessed lies in the expectation of healing in James 5:16. Sometimes we may want to lay burdens on others for the sake of personal purification. However, personal healing, in this case, may bring hurt to others rather than healing. True healing from God is total, involving self and others. If the confession can bring healing from the Lord without damaging others—either the individual making the confession or those hearing the confession—it is legitimate.

 Which best summarizes the first type of confession to others?
❑ When I need someone to pray with me about a fault or a sin-weakness, I should confess the fault to a trustworthy person who can pray with and for me. I should confess to someone only when the confession will not hurt or damage another person.
❑ When I need someone to pray with me about a fault or a sin-weakness, I should confess the fault before my church congregation. I need to be healed even if my confession could hurt or damage another person's feelings or reputation.

The first statement best summarizes this type of confession. Mutual prayer can be very beneficial. You should not seek your own cleansing, however, at the expense of another's feelings or reputation.

*Forgiveness and restitution from a group.* Sometimes even a private sin can hurt others, your family, your friends, your employer, or your church. When Achan sinned privately, God's anger burned against Israel. Thirty-six men lost their lives, and the "hearts of the people melted" (Josh. 7:5). The sin had hurt the nation and had to be confessed publicly (see Josh. 7:18-26).

First John 1:5-9, in the margin, implies that fellowship can be marred by a failure to confess sin. When sin damages a group (such as Achan's sin), confession should be made to the group, even if it is a private sin. Such confession should be limited to the group. In making public confession, follow this principle: Public confession should be limited to the circle of the offense. It should never endanger anyone else's privacy or reputation.

 Select the appropriate responses in the following situations by circling the letters beside your answers.
1. John lost his temper at a church business meeting and said things that hurt other persons' feelings. He should confess his sin to—
a. God only;
b. only the persons whose feelings were hurt;
c. the church;
d. God and the church.

*Mutual help through prayer is especially available in the areas of sin-weaknesses.*

*"This then is the message which we have heard of him, and declare unto you, that God is light, and in him is no darkness at all. If we say that we have fellowship with him, and walk in darkness, we lie, and do not the truth: but if we walk in the light, as he is in the light, we have fellowship one with another, and the blood of Jesus Christ his Son cleanseth us from all sin. If we say that we have no sin, we deceive ourselves, and the truth is not in us. If we confess our sins, he is faithful and just to forgive us our sins, and to cleanse us from all unrighteousness" (1 John 1:5-9).*

2. Sid strayed from the Lord and became involved in an affair with another man's wife. Sid's wife and the woman's husband found out. Sid's guilt became so great that he ended the affair and repented of his sin before the Lord. Now he needs to confess his sin to—

   a. his wife;

   b. the woman's husband;

   c. the woman;

   d. the church;

   e. the parties in a, b, and c.

3. Mary is a key leader in her church and is well respected in the community for her church involvement. She became involved in an embezzlement scheme at work and got caught. The news media reported the whole story. Mary's action brought public reproach on her church. She repented of her sin before the Lord. Now she needs to confess her sin to—

   a. no one else; God is enough;

   b. her church;

   c. the entire community.

Sin is an ugly thing. Once sin is revealed, there are no nice ways to handle it. Confession of sin should be limited to the circle of offense. It should also include those offended by the sin. In the first situation John sinned against God and the church. Since his sin was public, he needs to seek forgiveness from both God and the church. The answer is *d*.

In Sid's case the sin was more private. He was correct in seeking God's forgiveness, but he also needs to seek forgiveness from the other three persons hurt by the sin. To share this confession with the church would be harmful to all involved. You should have chosen *e*.

Mary's offense is so widely known that only confession to the entire community is sufficient. Her church was hurt due to the publicity. She needs to seek not only God's forgiveness but also the forgiveness of her church and community. The correct answer is *c*.

### Walking in Fellowship with God Today

1. Name to God His attributes that you wish to share with Him (perhaps Gal. 5:22-23 or Jas. 3:17).
2. Ask God to let Jesus express Himself in you, as His new creation, to at least one special person today. Do not ask that Jesus control you; ask that He live through you. At the end of the day, ask yourself: *Did I demonstrate a new creation in Christ today? Who would have seen Christ in me today?*
3. As you have your quiet time, complete the Daily Master Communication Guide in the margin.

*Daily Master Communication Guide*

SCRIPTURE REFERENCE:

_____

*What God said to me:*

_____

_____

_____

_____

_____

_____

_____

*What I said to God:*

_____

_____

_____

_____

_____

_____

_____

# Other Confessions, Part 2

*Today's Learning Goal*
You will understand how the initial confession of Christ relates to the continuing confessions that accompany the new life in Christ.

We enter the new life by confessing Jesus as Savior. We must also confess Jesus as Lord of our lives. We continue the new life by agreeing with God about what the new life should include.

## Confessing Jesus as Savior

The Bible uses the word *confess* to refer to our agreement with God on matters other than our sin. We are to confess Christ; that is, we agree with God the Father about His Son. As you can see in Matthew 10:32-33, in the margin, the opposite of confessing Jesus as Savior is denying Him.

## Confessing Jesus as Lord

We who have confessed Jesus as Savior should be certain that we have also confessed Him as Lord. A lovely first-century hymn said that "every tongue should confess that Jesus Christ is Lord" (Phil. 2:11).

*"Whosoever therefore shall confess me before men, him will I confess also before my Father which is in heaven. But whosoever shall deny me before men, him will I also deny before my Father which is in heaven"
(Matt. 10:32-33).*

 **In confessing Jesus, you could hardly improve on the confessions of men who knew Him. What did the following persons confess about Jesus?**

Peter (see Matt. 16:16 in the margin): _____

Nathanael (see John 1:49 in the margin): _____

Thomas (see John 20:28 in the margin): _____

**Pray these confessions to Christ now.**

*"Thou art the Christ, the Son of the living God" (Matt. 16:16).*

*"Rabbi, thou art the Son of God; thou art the King of Israel"
(John 1:49).*

*"My Lord and my God"
(John 20:28).*

You should continue throughout your life confessing Christ as your Lord, as the Holy One, as your King, and as your God. The world needs that confession, and it helps you establish and remember your identity with Him. Confession is an important demonstration of your continual agreement with God. John gave us reassurance in 1 John 4:15, in the margin.

Sometimes Christians continue in the old ways they practiced before conversion. The whole tenor of the New Testament indicates that a preference for the old ways is abnormal. The old ways are out of agreement with the true self, the newly created person whom God "also did predestinate to be conformed to the image of his Son" (Rom. 8:29). You have learned about confessing sin. Now let's discover the place of confession in the lives of those who are new creatures in Christ.

*"Whosoever shall confess that Jesus is the Son of God, God dwelleth in him, and he in God" (1 John 4:15).*

## Confessing Your New Nature

Adam was created in God's image. When Adam fell, the God-image was spoiled by sin. Jesus came into the world to function as a second Adam, a new kind of man (the kind Adam was intended to be). Through His sacrifice, we who accept Him can become a new kind of person. Read 2 Corinthians 5:17 in the margin.

*"If any man be in Christ, he is a new creature; old things are passed away; behold, all things are become new"
(2 Cor. 5:17).*

**What else do the Scriptures say about the newness of the believer's life? Read the following verses in the margin and write what is new.**

Ephesians 4:24: _____

Romans 6:4: _____

Romans 7:6: _____

"… that ye put on the new man, which after God is created in righteousness and true holiness" (Eph. 4:24).

One of the Christian's main pursuits in life should be discovering the meaning of the new life in Christ. We are to "put on the new man" (Eph. 4:24)—what God has made of us. We are to "walk in newness of life" (Rom. 6:4); we "serve in newness of spirit" (Rom. 7:6). In Christ we really are clean and new. The new creature is like Christ, who lived in perfect agreement with God. God is bending all of His efforts to bring us to "bear the image of the heavenly" (1 Cor. 15:49).

"We are buried with him by baptism into death: that like as Christ was raised up from the dead by the glory of the Father, even so we also should walk in newness of life" (Rom. 6:4).

"Now we are delivered from the law, that being dead wherein we were held; that we should serve in newness of spirit, and not in the oldness of the letter" (Rom. 7:6).

 **In the margin check the qualities God gives us in our new nature.**

Perfect likeness to Christ would result in perfect agreement with God. Each quality listed in the margin ought to be part of your new nature. In confessing your new nature, you agree with what you are like.

Anytime you return to the ways of the old nature, you should feel guilt. That guilt is natural, for the new creature was not made to do those things. When you do them, you are acting against God and also against yourself—that truest part of yourself that will last forever.

When you sin, you deliberately return to the old creature, the unredeemed and uncleansed person. Oldness amid so much newness is a jarring abnormality. The old nature is out of agreement with the great work God has done in creating the new nature in Christ. Your job is to seek to be in agreement with God in every way. Confession of sin is an important remedy, but confession of your new nature can also be of great value.

In confession you always speak with God (our English word *confess* comes from a Latin root that means *to speak with*). You agree with God, saying: "Yes, Father, I am a new creature. I have a new nature that bears the image of Your Son, Jesus Christ. Please continue to manifest this new nature in my life."

The new creature in Christ will live joyfully with God in eternity, and by agreeing with God, we can live joyfully with Him on earth.

☐ An eternal destiny
☐ Love for God's people
☐ A preference for the holy
☐ Commitment to the truth
☐ Joy in serving Him
☐ Peace
☐ Courage
☐ Patience
☐ Faith
☐ Hope
☐ Gentleness
☐ Discipline given by the Holy Spirit

**Read again 2 Corinthians 5:17 in the margin on page 122. Spend time with God examining the nature you express in your life. Do you need to confess some old things? What new things can you rejoice in?**

## Agreeing with God's Ways

When Christ is Lord of your life, He is the Master, and you are the obedient servant. Obedience to God's will is the best confession of agreement with God. A final aspect of agreement is the implication that agreement implies obedience. Although Jesus' disciples at times demonstrated the defects of awkwardness and

"I in them, and thou in me, that they may be made perfect in one; and that the world may know that thou hast sent me, and hast loved them, as thou hast loved me" (John 17:23).

## Daily Master Communication Guide

<small>SCRIPTURE REFERENCE:</small>

_____

_____

*What God said to me:*

_____

_____

_____

_____

_____

_____

_____

*What I said to God:*

_____

_____

_____

_____

_____

_____

_____

misunderstanding, their record of obedience is worth imitating. They did not hesitate at His commands. When He beckoned, "Follow me" (Matt. 4:19), they immediately left their nets. When He said, "If any man will come after me, let him deny himself, and take up his cross, and follow me" (Matt. 16:24), they left family and the familiar lives they knew in order to be His disciples.

If we are in agreement with God, a call from Him means that we do not need to make a decision. He has spoken; our desire is to be in agreement with Him, to obey Him. All of life is to constantly reaffirm the rightness of God and His ways.

 Read the following passages and list other things you can confess to God.

Psalm 8; 19:1-6; 104: _____

Matthew 19:5-6: _____

Matthew 28:19-20: _____

Ephesians 5:27: _____

We can confess to Him the beauty of His creation (Ps. 8; 19:1-6; 104). We can confess the rightness of His plan for marriage (Matt. 19:5-6), the rightness of His commandments (Matt. 28:19-20), and the glory of His church (Eph. 5:27).

Your life is to be a confession, an agreement, that God is true, just, and right. You are to be one with the Godhead, just as Jesus is one with His Father (see John 17:23 in the margin on the previous page).

 Using a separate sheet of paper, list truths about God and His ways that you can confess or agree with Him about. Refer to "Subjects for Confession" in prayer guide 8, page 213. Spend time in prayer agreeing with God about these things. Bring this list to this week's group session.

Write this week's memory verse(s) on a separate sheet of paper.

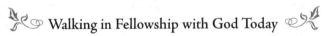 Walking in Fellowship with God Today

1. In your mind, picture Jesus stepping into this day to face it with you. If He were to walk through your duties, work, and steps today, what would He do? Picture yourself throughout the day following in His steps, hearing His voice, instantly obeying every step and turn He would take. Commit yourself to follow Him. Do not try to lead Him or tell Him how or where to go. Simply follow in His steps today. At the end of the day, pause to reflect on what difference this thinking has made in the way you lived the day.

2. Review and pray the confessions in "Confessing Christ" in prayer guide 8, page 213.

3. As you have your quiet time, complete the Daily Master Communication Guide in the margin.

# APPLYING THE PRINCIPLES OF ASKING

## Praying in Faith

Delores had an urgent prayer request during our weekly Wednesday-morning prayer meeting at seminary. Having befriended a high-school girl named Becky, Delores was trying to explain salvation to her but had not made much progress. Early that morning Becky's mother had called Delores with the terrifying news that Becky had run away. At that time drug rings in our city had formed small bands that sheltered runaways so that their parents could not find them. We feared for Becky's safety, but we feared more for her spirit, lost without God.

The group started praying fervently. As we prayed, we felt led to ask the Holy Spirit to prompt Becky to return home on her own. We asked that Delores would have a new opportunity to witness to Becky and that God would give Delores great spiritual power in that witness. Faith grew strong as we asked; each person's faith encouraged others. Somehow we saw Becky's return and conversion as completed facts.

That afternoon Becky called her mother, asked her mother to pick her up, and gave the location where she could find her. Delores went straight to Becky's home and lovingly shared with Becky the meaning of true friendship, introducing her to the greatest of all friends, the Lord Jesus. She explained that He is willing to forgive His friends of everything in their past if they repent.

Becky asked Jesus to save her and to be her Friend. My wife and I went to visit her and to share with her how many friends she could have in our church. The next Sunday morning Becky was warmly welcomed by our church's youth group. She made a public profession of faith in the worship service, was later baptized, and became a strong witness for the Lord. Our Wednesday-morning prayer group grew in our understanding of praying in faith.

### Key Idea
When you make a request of God, you must ask within God's will, with the right attitudes, and according to His principles and procedures.

### This Week's Learning Goal
You will understand and be able to follow biblical principles when making requests of God in prayer.

### Verses to Memorize
*"Call unto me, and I will answer thee, and shew thee great and mighty things which thou knowest not"* (Jer. 33:3).

*"If ye shall ask any thing in my name, I will do it"* (John 14:14).

### Related Prayer Guide
Prayer guide 9, "Principles of Asking," page 214

# Day 1
## God's Invitation and Your Orientation

*Today's Learning Goal*
You will know that God invites asking and will understand ways Paul practiced principles of asking in his prayers.

 Schedule a time to pray with your prayer partner this week. Write the day and time here.

_____

As you begin today's study, turn to prayer guide 1 on page 205 and review "Reasons God Answers Prayer." How frequently are you giving God reasons to answer your prayers?

❑ Always. I constantly ask myself the question, *Why should God answer this request?*
❑ Most of the time
❑ Some of the time
❑ Seldom. I still need to learn to pray from God's perspective instead of my own.

During the first week's study you learned four bases for asking. Basing your prayer on one of them gives God a reason to answer your request. I hope you are developing a pattern in your prayer life that constantly seeks God's perspective in prayer.

This week you will study eight principles that should guide what you ask and the way you ask. These principles, pictured below, form a framework for evaluating the characteristics of your intercession.

## PRINCIPLES OF ASKING

*"Ask, and it shall be given you; seek, and ye shall find; knock, and it shall be opened unto you" (Matt. 7:7).*

*"If ye shall ask any thing in my name, I will do it" (John 14:14).*

*"If ye abide in me, and my words abide in you, ye shall ask what ye will, and it shall be done unto you" (John 15:7).*

*"Hitherto have ye asked nothing in my name: ask, and ye shall receive, that your joy may be full" (John 16:24).*

### God Invites Asking

A major reason for offering prayers that ask things of God is that Jesus told His followers to ask. He repeatedly instructed us to bring our requests to God.

 **In the following Scriptures, printed in the margin, what did Jesus promise to those who ask?**

Matthew 7:7: _____

John 14:14: _____

John 15:7: _____

John 16:24: _____

**Turn to the chart "Bible Promises" on page 221. If you have not already included these particular promises there, do so now. Which promise is most meaningful to you today?**

_____

**Stop and pray now.**

God invites you to ask, and He expects to be asked. But He invites asking only within the framework of His will, His principles, and His procedure.

## A New Orientation

Contrary to popular opinion, Jesus' injunctions to ask are not blank checks. They have a purpose—our participation in the Kingdom. The injunctions in Matthew 7:7 are in the context of the Sermon on the Mount, with all it requires in life. The commands to ask in John are in the context of Jesus' last major discourse, or speech. They deal primarily with displaying His glory after the Holy Spirit is given. Ultimately, every prayer warrior needs to master these two great discourses.

Commit to orient yourself to the outlook in Matthew 5—7 and to the purposes of Christ as Head of the church in John 14—17. This is a lifetime task. You are far enough into *Disciple's Prayer Life* now that you should ask in God's way more and more effectively as you pray.

Write the headings *Matthew 5—7* and *John 14—17* at the tops of two sheets of paper. As you scan these passages, begin listing concepts that should affect the way you pray. Commit yourself to live and pray according to the outlooks you find in these commands and promises. Keep these two lists and continue to add to them. Regularly refer to them to evaluate your living and your praying. Bring your work to the group session.

### Walking in Fellowship with God Today

1. Spend time meditating on and praying about these concepts from Matthew and John in relation to your specific requests today. Review the Scriptures in "God Invites Asking" in prayer guide 9, "Principles of Asking," on page 214. Focus on one verse, concept, command, or promise. Saturate your thinking today with what God might want to say to you through that passage.
2. As you have your quiet time, complete the Daily Master Communication Guide in the margin.

## Daily Master Communication Guide

SCRIPTURE REFERENCE:

_____

*What God said to me:*

_____
_____
_____
_____
_____
_____
_____

*What I said to God:*

_____
_____
_____
_____
_____
_____
_____

Day 2
# Asking in the Spirit and with the Mind

**Today's Learning Goal**
You will understand what it means to ask in the Spirit and with the mind.

*"I shall pray with the spirit and I shall pray with the mind also"* (1 Cor. 14:15, NASB).

Jesus told His followers to ask in prayer but within the framework of His principles. Read in the margin Paul's testimony in 1 Corinthians 14:15. Prayer is imperfect and out of balance if we neglect either the spirit or the mind.

Asking in the Spirit of God is important because power is unleashed only from God's Spirit. The Lord Himself cautioned, "Not by might, nor by power, but by my Spirit" (Zech. 4:6). If something is a divine work, it is done not by human means or strength but through the power of God's Spirit. God's method does what human means cannot. Paul wrote that spiritual strength comes by putting on the whole armour of God and "praying always with all prayer and supplication in the Spirit" (Eph. 6:18).

The first step in praying in the Spirit is to be filled with the Spirit (see Eph. 5:18).

 Read about being filled with the Spirit on pages 49–50 in *The Life-Changing Power of Prayer*. **Then summarize in your own words what being filled with the Spirit means.**

_____

_____

Being filled implies totality. We can hold nothing outside the Spirit's reach. We can withhold nothing from His purifying. If we obey the command to be filled, the Spirit will touch, influence, and control everything in our lives. We are to submit everything to Him.

To ask in the Spirit means that every petition proceeds from the mind of the Spirit, not from selfish motives or self-serving ends. You must avoid two dangers if the Holy Spirit is to enable you to pray in the Spirit.

*"Grieve not the holy Spirit of God, whereby ye are sealed unto the day of redemption"* (Eph. 4:30).

*"Quench not the Spirit"* (1 Thess. 5:19).

**Read the following Scriptures in the margin and identify two things a Christian is *not* to do.**

Ephesians 4:30: _____

1 Thessalonians 5:19: _____

---

We must not grieve the Spirit with sin in our lives; His name is Holy. The Holy Spirit is grieved when a person commits sins that bring sorrow to His holy nature and offend Him. The second danger to avoid is quenching the Holy Spirit. The Holy Spirit is quenched when a believer does not respond to the Spirit's prompting. The Spirit can be quenched by our disobedience or by our refusing Him access to any part of ourselves.

These are our commands; conformity to them is a matter of our will. Whenever the Bible gives a direct command (such as "Be filled with the Spirit"), our job is simple obedience. God is willing to fill anyone with His Spirit who asks, provided the person does not counter his or her own request by disobeying the direct command of Ephesians 4:30 or 1 Thessalonians 5:19.

**Identify the dangers involved in the following actions. Write a letter in each blank:** G for *grieve the Spirit* or Q for *quench the Spirit.*

_____ 1. You know that God wants you to write a letter to an unsaved relative, and you keep putting it off.

_____ 2. You fly into a rage and say bitter, sarcastic words.

How do we grieve the Spirit? _____

How do we quench the Spirit? _____

We grieve the Spirit when we sin, offending the Spirit's holy nature. We quench the Spirit when we refuse to obey the Spirit's leadership or prompting. Your answers should be 1. Q and 2. G.

**Pause now and pray about your relationship with the Holy Spirit. Can you discern any ways you are grieving or quenching Him?**

To ask in the Spirit means that we pray in agreement with the Holy Spirit. Our will must correspond to His will, our desires to His desires. We cannot pray for something He does not want. We must earnestly seek to know God's will for every issue we pray for. Praying in the Spirit means more than being filled with the Spirit. It includes letting Him pray through you, listening to His prompting, and following it.

## Ask with the Mind

The mind is important because the spirit without the mind is immature. Read in the margin Paul's words of caution in 1 Corinthians 14:20. A maturing prayer life is growing in every way, spiritually *and* intellectually.

**Read in the margin the advice of the preacher in Ecclesiastes 5:1-2. What do these verses say about praying with the mind?**

_____

_____

*"Brethren, be not children in understanding" (1 Cor. 14:20).*

*"Keep thy foot when thou goest to the house of God, and be more ready to hear, than to give the sacrifice of fools: for they consider not that they do evil. Be not rash with thy mouth, and let not thine heart be hasty to utter any thing before God: for God is in heaven, and thou upon earth: therefore let thy words be few" (Eccl. 5:1-2).*

*"If the trumpet give an uncertain sound, who shall prepare himself to the battle?" (1 Cor. 14:8).*

_____

## Daily Master Communication Guide

SCRIPTURE REFERENCE:

_____

_____

*What God said to me:*

_____

_____

_____

_____

_____

_____

*What I said to God:*

_____

_____

_____

_____

_____

_____

The mind is the instrument by which you are able to form your requests. With the mind you make your requests precise and specific. Read 1 Corinthians 14:8 in the margin on page 129. Generalities in prayer do not work, because they give God neither a direction for answering nor a measure to fill. According to the preacher in Ecclesiastes, your words should be few and well thought out. You should definitely "keep your mind on your praying."

This does not suggest that you read a stiff, formal prayer. It suggests that you come prepared to present to God what you have thoughtfully determined to be important in His dealings with you. Prayer lists help make your prayer well-rounded and help you avoid missing important items you should pray for.

Read "Daily Intercession" on page 223. Using the master on page 224, prepare lists for the two daily categories mentioned. Begin listing concerns on each list. Read "Weekly Intercession" on page 223 and prepare the lists you will need for each day of the week, using the master on page 225. You will learn more about who and what to add to your prayer lists in the coming weeks.

Using prayer lists helps you practice the principle of asking with the mind by helping you pray clear, precise, and specific requests. It also prevents daydreaming or allowing your mind to wander during your prayer time.

Praying with the spirit does not imply a mindless spirit, and praying with the mind does not mean that we pray with a spiritless mind. If you are filled with the Spirit and your mind controls your praying, the Spirit is not hindered. Your sensitivity to the Holy Spirit allows Him to control your mind and spirit.

### Walking in Fellowship with God Today

1. Turn to the daily prayer lists you prepared today. One by one pray for each need you listed. Ask God to guide you through His Holy Spirit as you pray for the requests on the lists. Do you feel any strong impressions about the importance of those needs? Do some concerns burden you more than others? This may seem to be subjective, but you have the Holy Spirit within you. His business is to lead you in your prayer. Pause and emphasize in your prayer what He wants you to emphasize, but use your mind also. He will not lead you to dwell on nonsense. Keep moving until you have a strong desire or impression to dwell on an item. Don't dawdle over it; pray over it. You are learning to pray in the Spirit and with the mind. As you pray, review the principles of asking in the Spirit and with the mind in prayer guide 9 on page 214.

2. As you have your quiet time, complete the Daily Master Communication Guide in the margin.

# Day 3
## Asking in Jesus' Name While Abiding in Christ

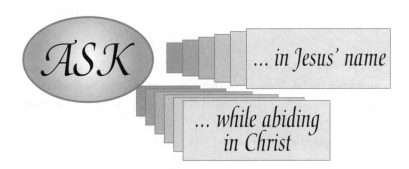

Have you prepared the lists recommended yesterday for use in your daily and weekly intercession? If not, do so before the end of this week.

### Ask in Jesus' Name

Read in the margin Jesus' words in John 14:14. Which of the following do you think best describes what Jesus meant? Check your choice.
❑ "Anything you want."
❑ "If you have my heart and mind, ask what you will."

*"If ye shall ask any thing in my name, I will do it"* (John 14:14).

You should have checked the second choice. Let's study in more detail the principle of asking in Jesus' name.

Read "Why Do Christians Pray in Jesus' Name?" beginning on page 82 in *The Life-Changing Power of Prayer.* As you read, write notes or illustrations below that help you better understand what praying in Jesus' name means.

_____

_____

_____

The context of John 14:14 indicates that this promise is for disciples, learners of Jesus anxious to do His will. The name of Jesus is your legal authorization for prayer. Without Him you would have no claim on God's attention. However, when you offer your prayer in Jesus' name, you base your prayer on Jesus' moral worth, His purity, and His value to the Father. You base your requests on the legal authority of His name. When you approach prayer from the standpoint of Jesus' desires and reputation, your answered prayers bring God glory. Read John 15:7 in the margin.

*"If ye abide in me, and my words abide in you, ye shall ask what ye will, and it shall be done unto you"* (John 15:7).

When you prepare to make a request in Jesus' name, first ask yourself, *What would Jesus want in this situation?* Let His desires become your desires. When you use His name, you claim to represent Him and to act like Him. You have His desires, His qualities, His gratitude, and His outlook.

This fact is one reason you need to allow the Holy Spirit to develop in you the mind of Christ (see Phil. 2:5-11; 1 Cor. 2:10-16). Without the mind of Christ you cannot know His desires, His qualities, His gratitude, and His outlook. Paul used this principle in his prayer for the Christians at Thessalonica. Read 2 Thessalonians 1:11-12 in the margin.

 **Pray this prayer of Paul's for a Christian friend. In place of the pronoun** *you*, **name your friend. Remember that you want Jesus to be glorified in what occurs in your friend's life. Pray this verse again for another person.**

**Write the names of those you prayed for:** _____

### Do Not Carelessly Use Jesus' Name

The use of Jesus' name is not a ritual that produces magical results. It reflects your taking on Jesus' character. The use of a name demands integrity.

In Scripture using a name wrongly is very serious. After Elisha's prayer healed Naaman the Syrian of leprosy, Naaman offered Elisha a payment. Elisha refused, but his servant, Gehazi, secretly followed Naaman and used Elisha's name to secure two talents of silver and two changes of clothing from Naaman. Gehazi used Elisha's name outside Elisha's character, and Gehazi's deception brought leprosy on him. (See 2 Kings 5:20-27.)

After seeing Paul perform miracles in Jesus' name, seven sons of a Jewish priest named Sceva attempted to use Jesus' name outside His character. The evil spirit they were attempting to cast out said, "Jesus I know, and Paul I know; but who are ye?" The demoniac they were trying to exorcise leaped on them and overpowered them. (See Acts 19:13-16.)

The use of Jesus' name is especially serious. When you use it, you represent Jesus, His kingdom, and His character. The name stands for the person, and the use of a name involves all the person stands for. Do not carelessly use Jesus' name.

 **How would you summarize the principle of asking in Jesus' name?**

_____

_____

Turn to prayer guide 9 on page 214 to check your work.

### Ask While Abiding in Christ

Reread Jesus' words in John 15:7 in the margin on page 131. *Abide* means *to remain, to continue in, to persist, to accept without objection.* If Christ's message abides or remains in us over a period of time, the way we think and the way we pray are affected. These prove that we really are learners of Him. He said, "If you abide in My word, then you are truly disciples of Mine" (John 8:31, NASB). Abiding in Christ is expressed in many ways. Prayer, however, is both a means of abiding in Christ and a result of abiding in Christ.

*Prayer is both a means of abiding in Christ and a result of abiding in Christ.*

Abiding in Christ has important implications in your life. Your time with the Lord is regular and continuous. You constantly walk in fellowship with God. By definition, abiding cannot be intermittent. When you abide in Christ, you pray without ceasing (see 1 Thess. 5:17). One thing you do without ceasing is breathing. Prayer is as needful and indispensable to your spiritual life as breathing is to your physical life. Again, Bible pray-ers give us our best examples to follow.

 **Read the following Scriptures in the margin and answer the questions.**

**Read Daniel 6:10. What was Daniel's habit even when it endangered his life?**

_____

**Read Acts 2:42. What was the prayer habit in the newly born church in Jerusalem?**

_____

**Read Acts 6:4. What did the apostles want regarding prayer?**

_____

**Read Romans 1:9; Colossians 1:9; and 1 Thessalonians 1:2-3. What did Paul say to the churches about his frequency in prayer?**

_____

Daniel prayed three times each day, even at the risk of his life. The church in Jerusalem continued steadfastly in prayer. The apostles wanted the seven servants of the church to be appointed so that they could devote themselves to prayer and the ministry of the Word. Paul prayed for the churches without ceasing, always. These Bible pray-ers give us examples of abiding in prayer.

Abiding in the Word of Christ means that you keep His commandments. You take His Word seriously. You keep your commitment to pray.

 Jesus said: "Abide in me, and I in you. As the branch cannot bear fruit of itself, except it abide in the vine; no more can ye, except ye abide in me. I am the vine, ye are the branches: He that abideth in me, and I in him, the same bringeth forth much fruit: for without me ye can do nothing" (John 15:4-5). What marvelous promise did Jesus make about the results of a life that abides in Christ?

_____

_____

"When Daniel knew that the writing was signed, he went into his house; and his windows being open in his chamber toward Jerusalem, he kneeled upon his knees three times a day, and prayed, and gave thanks before his God, as he did aforetime" (Dan. 6:10).

"They continued stedfastly in the apostles' doctrine and fellowship, and in breaking of bread, and in prayers" (Acts 2:42).

"We will give ourselves continually to prayer, and to the ministry of the word" (Acts 6:4).

"God is my witness, whom I serve with my spirit in the gospel of his Son, that without ceasing I make mention of you always in my prayers" (Rom. 1:9).

"For this cause we also, since the day we heard it, do not cease to pray for you, and to desire that ye might be filled with the knowledge of his will in all wisdom and spiritual understanding" (Col. 1:9).

"We give thanks to God always for you all, making mention of you in our prayers; remembering without ceasing your work of faith, and labour of love, and patience of hope in our Lord Jesus Christ, in the sight of God and our Father" (1 Thess. 1:2-3).

## Daily Master Communication Guide

Scripture reference:

_____

### What God said to me:

_____

_____

_____

_____

_____

_____

_____

### What I said to God:

_____

_____

_____

_____

_____

_____

Write this promise on the chart "Bible Promises" on page 221. In prayer reflect on the quality of your abiding in Christ. Write the results of your conversation with the Lord.

_____

_____

How would you summarize the principle of asking while abiding in Christ?

_____

_____

Turn to prayer guide 9 on page 214 to check your work.

### Walking in Fellowship with God Today

1. Begin your prayer today by contemplating the wonder of the person of Jesus. Tell Him briefly, according to your present knowledge, what each of the following means to you as you reflect on His name.
   - He is divine. You might tell Him that His name is perfect because it represents who He is or that His name is a name of glory because He is eternally God.
   - He became human. You might express appreciation that His name was never tarnished by sin or that we are lifted into new glory by His name.
   - He performed miracles. You might tell Him that His name is worthy of awe because of the wonders it has worked or that His miracles set His name apart because they are perfect.
   - He told parables. You might tell Him that His name is worthy of great respect as a teacher or that His name ennobles ordinary occupations like farming, sowing, tending sheep, renting farmland, and so forth.
   - He died. You might thank Him that His death gave you His name—Christian—or express wonder at the awesome humiliation He allowed His name and reputation to assume in His trial.
   - He arose. You might glorify His name because of the power it represents for you or praise the might of His name in the conclusion of a perfect work.

2. As you grow in prayer, glorify His name in many areas: His sinlessness, His teaching, His servanthood, His love, and so forth. Today bow your knees in honor of His name. Tell God the Father that you pray not in your worth but in the legal worth of Jesus' name. As you pray, review the principles of asking in Jesus' name and abiding in Christ in prayer guide 9, page 214.

3. As you have your quiet time, complete the Daily Master Communication Guide in the margin.

# Day 4
## Asking in Faith and Humility

### Ask in Faith

Faith and humility are additional attitudes that guide your asking. The most important attitude you bring to prayer is the attitude of faith. Faith is the very basis of your relationship with God, as stated in Hebrews 11:6, in the margin.

*"Without faith it is impossible to please him: for he that cometh to God must believe that he is, and that he is a rewarder of them that diligently seek him" (Heb. 11:6).*

> PRAYING IN FAITH INVOLVES—
> • asking without doubt in your heart;
> • believing that the things you ask will come to pass;
> • reflecting God's character of constancy;
> • recognizing God's authority and power to answer;
> • having confidence in God's care and purposes for your life;
> • claiming a Bible promise and holding God to His Word.

As you read about the following aspects of praying in faith—
? place a question mark beside any you do not understand;
✳ draw a star beside the one that will best help you cultivate an attitude of praying in faith;
○ draw a circle beside the one you have the greatest difficulty doing;
→ draw an arrow beside the one you want to work on in a special way.

*Without doubt and believing.* When Jesus wanted to stimulate faith, He made a seemingly extravagant promise. In the days just prior to His crucifixion, Jesus saw the need for His disciples to have greater faith. The disciples were facing a crucial period, and Jesus took extraordinary action. He cursed a fig tree that had failed to bear fruit. The tree quickly withered. When the disciples were amazed, Jesus told them: "Have faith in God. For verily I say unto you, that whosoever shall say unto this mountain, Be thou removed, and be thou cast into the sea; and shall not doubt in his heart, but shall believe that those things which he saith shall come to pass; he shall have whatsoever he saith" (Mark 11:22-23). Two aspects of asking in faith are presented in this promise: ask without doubting and believe that what you ask will come to pass.

*Characterized by constancy, not wavering.* One of God's purposes for your prayer life is for His character to be duplicated in you. You are to use His name within the bounds of His character. Your faith mirrors His constancy or steadfastness. Wavering is the opposite of God's character. James told that us we could ask God for wisdom; then He said: "But let him ask in faith, nothing wavering. For he that

*Your faith mirrors His constancy or steadfastness.*

wavereth is like a wave of the sea driven with the wind and tossed. For let not that man think that he shall receive any thing of the Lord" (Jas. 1:6-7). Faith is characterized by constancy.

*Recognizing God's authority and power to answer.* A Roman centurion asked Jesus to heal his servant. Jesus offered to go to the man and heal him. The centurion protested, "Lord, I am not worthy that thou shouldest come under my roof: but speak the word only, and my servant shall be healed." In a rare flash of insight the centurion recognized an authority in Jesus that most Jews of that day could not perceive. We have few examples in Scripture of compliments Jesus gave, but this is one of them. He told the group around Him, "Verily I say unto you, I have not found so great faith, no, not in Israel." Jesus told the centurion, "Go thy way; and as thou hast believed, so be it done unto thee" (Matt. 8:5-13). On another occasion Jesus healed two blind men. He asked them, "Believe ye that I am able to do this?" Their affirmative answer caused Him to say, "According to your faith be it unto you" (Matt. 9:28-29).

*Confidence in God's care and purposes.* The gospel itself is an incentive to faith. The gospel inspires us to profound confidence in God's care and purposes for us. Paul said that the gospel is a basis for faith: "Faith cometh by hearing, and hearing by the word of God" (Rom. 10:17). That "word of God" is the good news of Jesus and His work for us. Surely if we believe the message of Jesus, as grand and noble as it is, we can believe God in His other words!

*Holding God to His Word.* God has given us many precious promises. He is able and willing to keep them when His conditions are met. Faith is believing that God will be faithful to keep His promises. This is why basing your requests on God's promises (see week 4, day 2) can strengthen your faith. Mark, memorize, and repeat prayer promises. Base your prayers on the promises of a faithful God.

 **Read Mark 9:14-27. What was the father's prayer in verse 24?**

_____

**Consider your asking in faith. If you need to, pray the prayer of this father. Write what you say to God.**

_____

_____

## Ask in Humility

In the Bible humility is an extremely important attitude. Read in the margin the Lord's words to Solomon.

An exact fulfillment of this promise is seen in Josiah's restoration of temple worship and his return to the Lord 27 chapters later. God assured him, "Because thine heart was tender, and thou didst humble thyself before God, when thou heardest his words against this place, and against the inhabitants thereof, and humbledst thyself before me … I have even heard thee also" (2 Chron. 34:27).

*The gospel inspires us to profound confidence in God's care and purposes for us.*

*"If I shut up heaven that there be no rain, or if I command the locusts to devour the land, or if I send pestilence among my people; if my people, which are called by my name, shall humble themselves, and pray, and seek my face, and turn from their wicked ways; then will I hear from heaven, and will forgive their sin, and will heal their land"*
*(2 Chron. 7:13-14).*

🌿 Read Luke 18:10-14. Describe the contrast between the men's attitudes.

_____

_____

Jesus commended the humility of the tax gatherer who was unwilling to lift his eyes heavenward and prayed, "God be merciful to me a sinner." At the same time, Jesus condemned the pride of the Pharisee who thanked God that he was "not as other men are." In his contempt the Pharisee specifically pointed out his superiority to the tax gatherer. He was confessing that he needed no one; he was sufficient for his own righteousness.

🌿 In the box below draw a picture that illustrates humility.

┌─────────────────────────────────────────────┐
│                                               │
│                                               │
│                                               │
│                                               │
│                                               │
│                                               │
│                                               │
└─────────────────────────────────────────────┘

Humility needs others. Praying in humility recognizes our need of God. Humility submits to God. Pride, arrogance, and independence prevent an attitude of humility. An outward mark of humility is kneeling. Humility does not require kneeling, but kneeling indicates humility. Kneeling seems instinctive to the psalmist: "O come, let us worship and bow down: let us kneel before the Lord our maker" (Ps. 95:6). Some of the great Bible pray-ers, Daniel (see Dan. 6:10), Peter (see Acts 9:40), and Paul (see Eph. 3:14), often knelt to pray.

🌿 Walking in Fellowship with God Today 🌿

1. A lack of faith is a lack of trust. We sometimes do not trust because we do not recognize God's own proofs of His trustworthiness. Tell God today that you are anxious for Him to build trust in you. Ask Him to lead you to understand His trustworthiness. In prayer name everything you can think of that He has done for you. Count your many blessings. With each item tell Him, "You are trustworthy; You keep Your word." As you pray, review the principle of asking in faith in prayer guide 9, page 214.

2. The secret to humility is understanding who God is. Pride always indicates that you have failed to perceive His greatness. Ask God to keep you so mindful of His glory, holiness, and greatness that you are perfectly humble before Him. As you pray, review the principle of asking in humility in prayer guide 9, page 214.

3. As you have your quiet time, complete the Daily Master Communication Guide in the margin.

_Daily Master Communication Guide_

SCRIPTURE REFERENCE:

_____

_What God said to me:_

_____
_____
_____
_____
_____
_____
_____

_What I said to God:_

_____
_____
_____
_____
_____
_____
_____

# Asking in Sincerity and with Perseverance

## Ask in Sincerity

Another attitude indispensable to God-pleasing prayer is sincerity. Sincere prayer in the Bible is genuine and heartfelt. The deep emotional belief in the importance of the prayer leads to earnest and fervent praying. After telling us that "the effectual fervent prayer of a righteous man availeth much," James gave Elijah as an example of a man who "prayed earnestly that it might not rain: and it rained not on the earth by the space of three years and six months" (Jas. 5:16-17).

 **Read 2 Kings 20:1-5; Colossians 4:12-13; and Luke 22:44 in the margin and describe the characteristic of the prayers.**

_____

Earnestness throughout the Bible is associated with power in prayer. Hezekiah wept bitterly. Paul told the Colossians that Epaphras was "always labouring fervently for you in prayers." As our supreme example, Jesus prayed so sincerely, or fervently, that "his sweat was as it were great drops of blood."

One word of caution is needed here:

> **Faith is not a product of sincerity. Sincerity is a product of faith.**

 **Place a plus mark (+) beside each word that describes sincere prayer. Place a minus sign (–) beside each word that is an opposite of sincere prayer.**

| _____ Genuine | _____ Earnest | _____ Put-on | _____ Fervent |
|---|---|---|---|
| _____ Heartfelt | _____ Artificial | _____ Fake | _____ Serious |

When you pray in sincerity, your faith leads you to pray genuine, heartfelt prayers. You are so serious about your praying that your prayer is earnest and fervent. Sincere prayer is not put-on, fake, or artificial.

## Ask with Perseverance

Perseverance is a very important kind of abiding. Jesus told two parables to impress on us the need to persevere.

---

## Today's Learning Goal

You will understand and begin to practice the principles of asking in sincerity and asking with perseverance.

_"In those days was Hezekiah sick unto death. And the prophet Isaiah the son of Amoz came to him, and said unto him, Thus saith the Lord, Set thine house in order; for thou shalt die, and not live. Then he turned his face to the wall, and prayed unto the Lord, saying, I beseech thee, O Lord, remember now how I have walked before thee in truth and with a perfect heart, and have done that which is good in thy sight. And Hezekiah wept sore. And it came to pass, afore Isaiah was gone out into the middle court, that the word of the Lord came to him, saying, Turn again, and tell Hezekiah the captain of my people, Thus saith the Lord, the God of David thy father, I have heard thy prayer, I have seen thy tears: behold, I will heal thee: on the third day thou shalt go up unto the house of the Lord" (2 Kings 20:1-5)._

_"Epaphras, who is one of you, a servant of Christ, saluteth you, always labouring fervently for you in prayers, that ye may stand perfect and complete in all the will of God. For I bear him record, that he hath a great zeal for you, and them that are in Laodicea, and them in Hierapolis" (Col. 4:12-13)._

_"Being in agony he prayed more earnestly: and his sweat was as it were great drops of blood falling down to the ground" (Luke 22:44)._

Read Luke 11:5-10 and Luke 18:1-8. How would you describe persevering prayer, based on these two parables?

_____

_____

Perseverance in prayer is called importunity in the New Testament. The meaning of this word in Luke 11:8 is *shamelessness*. We are to persist shamelessly in our prayers to God. Jesus' first parable on importunity concerns a man who persistently called for a friend to lend three loaves at midnight. Read Jesus' statement (Luke 11:8) in the margin.

Luke introduced the parable about the wicked judge by telling us that Jesus told us "always to pray, and not to faint." A widow had to badger the judge constantly and shamelessly until he finally granted her legal protection from her opponent. Jesus affirmed that God would act more speedily than the unjust judge, and He ended by asking, "Nevertheless when the Son of man cometh, shall he find faith on the earth?" That is the point of the parable—those who keep asking are the ones who have faith. The opposite of perseverance is fainting or giving up (see Luke 18:1). Requiring perseverance of us is God's way of accomplishing His goals for us.

> ### PERSEVERANCE—
> - makes us sure of what God wants;
> - makes us sure of what we want;
> - trains us to take our eyes off circumstances that may be discouraging;
> - makes us focus on Him;
> - proves and establishes earnestness;
> - demonstrates real faith.

Read another illustration of persistent asking in Matthew 15:21-28. When the Canaanite woman asked Jesus to heal her daughter, He seemed to rebuff her in very surprising ways. At first He ignored her. Then He told her that He was sent only to the Jews. Then in what seemed to be the most cruel stroke of all, He told her, "It is not meet to take the children's bread, and to cast it to dogs." But when she replied, "Truth, Lord: yet the dogs eat of the crumbs which fall from their masters' table," He spoke one of His rare compliments. He told her, "O woman, great is thy faith: be it unto thee even as thou wilt."

Evidently, Jesus recognized this as a woman of faith. Wanting to demonstrate to His disciples what real faith is, Jesus forced her to be persistent. When she was persistent, Jesus praised her faith.

The Bible furnishes other examples of importunate prayer.

 Read 1 Samuel 15:11 in the margin. How did Samuel show perseverance in his prayer?

_____

_____

*"I tell you, even though he will not get up and give him anything because he is his friend, yet because of his persistence he will get up and give him as much as he needs"* (Luke 11:8, NASB).

*"It repenteth me that I have set up Saul to be king: for he is turned back from following me, and hath not performed my commandments. And it grieved Samuel; and he cried unto the Lord all night"* (1 Sam. 15:11).

*"Peter therefore was kept in prison: but prayer was made without ceasing of the church unto God for him"* (Acts 12:5).

*"Ye that make mention of the Lord, keep not silence, and give him no rest, till he establish, and till he make Jerusalem a praise in the earth"* (Isa. 62:6-7).

*"… watching thereunto with all perseverance and supplication for all saints"* (Eph. 6:18).

## Daily Master Communication Guide

Scripture reference:

_____

_____

### What God said to me:

_____

_____

_____

_____

_____

_____

_____

### What I said to God:

_____

_____

_____

_____

_____

_____

_____

Read Acts 12:5 in the margin on page 139. How did the church show perseverance in its prayer for Peter?

_____

When the Lord told Samuel that He regretted making Saul king, "it grieved Samuel; and he cried unto the Lord all night." After Herod imprisoned Peter, "prayer was made without ceasing of the church unto God for him."

Jesus is not the only one in the Bible who commended persistence in prayer. Read Isaiah 62:6-7 and Ephesians 6:18 in the margin on page 139.

Perseverance is not begging. It does not change God. It changes you. As you persist in prayer, your habit of abiding is sharpened. Your faith is proved. Your spiritual senses are given a chance to hear more clearly from God. Perseverance is an important part of God's method of working out His purposes in us.

Write this week's memory verse(s) on a separate sheet of paper.

### Walking in Fellowship with God Today

1. This week you have learned about several attitudes you should have in order to pray according to God's ways. You must ask in an attitude of faith, humility, and sincerity. Turn to prayer guide 9, page 214, and review the meanings of these attitudes as they relate to your praying. Pray today that God will guide you to develop these attitudes so that you can please Him in prayer. As you develop them, you honor Him and your prayers bring Him glory. Do you have a prayer request that you have almost given up on? Review the reasons for perseverance that are given in prayer guide 9. Ask God to guide you in praying for this particular request.
2. As you have your quiet time, complete the Daily Master Communication Guide in the margin.

# DEALING WITH HINDRANCES AND DELAYS

## Temporary Disappointments

At one point in my life I was disappointed that God called me to teach missionaries rather than to be a missionary. The fall of 1974 was a time of particular struggle over that issue. To make matters worse, we were very short of money. We were even unable to pay our daughter's university tuition. We prayed desperately, but the more we prayed, the worse our finances got. Then our daughter was in a minor accident, and our insurance did not cover all of the hospital and doctor bills. Next she had to have a root canal, which cost $300, and we had no dental insurance. We began getting second notices from the university. As the debts got heavier, our prayers became more fervent.

My brokenness was not so much over our inability to pay debts as over the strange delay in the answer to our prayers. I asked the Lord to reveal the reasons for the holdups that characterized my prayer life. This began a reexamination of every aspect of my relationship with the Lord and with others.

A series of circumstances directed my attention especially to my relationship with my wife, Laverne. We had had a good marriage by any earthly standard I knew, but now I undertook with profound seriousness a new probing into the command in Ephesians 5:25-32. I had not realized how important was the husband's responsibility for the holiness of his wife; he should be able to present her to God "without spot or wrinkle," just as Christ felt that concern for His bride, the church. I offered to God the fact that I would "give myself up" for my wife's holiness. I prayed that this new attitude would make her understand something new about God's love by giving her a new understanding of Jesus' love for His church.

One day I casually asked Laverne, "Why do you suppose God won't let me be a missionary?" She answered, "Have you talked to Him lately about it?" I replied that since He had already made my calling clear, I didn't want to talk to Him about rebellion. She reminded me, "Then maybe you should quit teaching in your seminars that He is a Friend, because you can talk to a friend!" I remembered that Jesus wrote the church at Laodicea that if they would open the door to Him, He would come in and dine with them (see Rev. 3:20). I entered our prayer room and invited my Friend to hear why I found mission work so exciting. That hour of prayer convinced me, at long last, that as important as missionaries are, God needs helpers and teachers for them, too.

At the end of November I received a letter from my daughter's university stating, "This is to inform you that a friend [!] who wishes to remain anonymous has paid your daughter's tuition for this semester." The hospital, doctor, and dentist bills were all paid before Christmas. That delay in an answer to prayer reaped spiritual benefits far beyond the cost of the temporary pain.

*Key Idea*
God has a purpose in saying no or in delaying the answer to a prayer request. You must learn to deal adequately with hindrances and delays to prayer.

*This Week's Learning Goal*
You will understand the reasons for hindrances and delays in prayer and will demonstrate cooperation with God that leads to more effective praying.

*Verses to Memorize*
"If I regard iniquity in my heart, the Lord will not hear me" (Ps. 66:18).

"Ye ask and receive not, because ye ask amiss, that ye may consume it upon your lusts" (Jas. 4:3).

*Related Prayer Guide*
Prayer guide 10, "Dealing with Hindrances and Delays," page 215

# Day 1
## God's Responses to Prayer

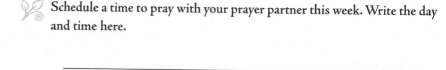 Schedule a time to pray with your prayer partner this week. Write the day and time here.

_____

### Ways God Responds to Prayer Requests

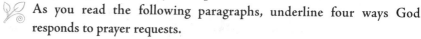 As you read the following paragraphs, underline four ways God responds to prayer requests.

As God considers our petitions, He must thoughtfully weigh the ramifications of our prayers. Throughout the Bible we have already seen many cases in which God answered yes. If God answered every prayer with a yes, however, some of us would become monsters of egocentricity. Sometimes our prayers have implications for other people that are not healthy and wholesome for the progress of God's kingdom. All of God's actions are holy, wise, and loving. If God is consistent with Himself, He cannot encourage wrong qualities in us and others by granting anything that might endanger our growth or the growth of others. Therefore, we sometimes experience disappointment in our prayers when God answers no. Another way God may respond to a prayer is to refuse to hear it altogether. Read Psalm 66:18 in the margin on page 141.

As you studied about perseverance in week 9, you learned that God sometimes has a purpose in delays. He knows your needs. He knows the future. His timetable is always best. God sometimes delays in answering a prayer.

What are four ways God responds to prayer requests?

1. _____  3. _____

2. _____  4. _____

Turn to "Ways God Responds to Prayer Requests" in prayer guide 10, "Dealing with Hindrances and Delays," page 215, to check your answers.

Prayer involves walking in fellowship with God and coping with hindrances and delays. That you have persisted this far in *Disciple's Prayer Life* means that you have already made considerable progress in the most serious of all hindrances to prayer—prayerlessness. However, at times even a veteran prayer warrior faces discouragement. We need to face obstacles to prayer and to deal with them thoroughly if we are to become faithful pray-ers.

Scripture anticipates many problems we have with prayer and directs us in addressing them. The three types of hindrances we will study are sin, wrong motives, and unbelief.

*God sometimes has a purpose in delays.*

## Five Prayer Requests God Did Not Grant

 As you study the following five Bible prayers, try to find out either what was wrong with the request or why the prayer was not answered.

Read Numbers 11:10-15. Moses prayed after the Israelites complained about their food in the wilderness. What did Moses ask for in verse 15?

_____

What do you think might be wrong in this prayer? _____

How many times did Moses say "I" or "me"? _____

Saul had publicly disobeyed God several times and was now threatened by the Philistines. Read about his prayer experience in 1 Samuel 28:3-7. What prevented Saul's prayer from being answered?

_____

Read David's prayer in 2 Samuel 12:13-23. What did David ask for?

_____

Why do you think God did not spare the life of the child?

_____

Read the request of Salome, the mother of James and John, in Matthew 20:20-23. What did she ask for? _____

In your opinion, what prevented this request from being answered?

_____

A prayer experience of Paul is found in 2 Corinthians 12:7-10. What did Paul request?

_____

_____

Even the greatest pray-ers sometimes pray wrongly. "No" was the answer to a number of prayers in the Bible. Moses' prayer to die was outside the Lord's will. God had called Moses to a task. Now when the going got tough, Moses wanted out—by death. Moses used "I" and "me" 13 times, indicating that he had allowed his eyes to get off God and onto self. Selfish motives were part of Moses' problem. Another part of his problem was his unbelief. He did not believe that God could provide meat for the people.

Saul's inquiry about the Philistines camped against him in Shunem was not answered (see 1 Sam. 28:6). He had repeatedly violated God's principles, and God's Word says, "If I regard iniquity in my heart, the Lord will not hear me" (Ps. 66:18). Saul had outwardly obeyed God by putting away all those who had familiar spirits and wizards. God was concerned about what was in Saul's heart. When faced with a delayed answer, Saul immediately sought a medium to tell his future. Saul's failure became a prayer failure and would become for all time a proof of Isaiah's statement that sin separates us from God (see Isa. 59:2 in the margin). Saul's disappointment was self-inflicted due to sin and rebellion against God.

*"Your iniquities have separated between you and your God, and your sins have hid his face from you, that he will not hear" (Isa. 59:2).*

David's prayer request for his son to live was not granted (see 2 Sam. 12:16). God's decision that the child would die had already been given by the prophet Nathan (see 2 Sam. 12:14). David's prayer was not in accord with the expressed will of God. Furthermore, this son was the fruit of adultery. If he had survived, that very fact might have become an occasion for sin—for the enemies of the Lord to blaspheme.

Salome asked Jesus to place her two sons in positions of authority and prominence in His kingdom. She and her sons, who expected Jesus to establish an earthly kingdom, did not understand what they were asking for. Jesus explained that those positions were not His to grant.

Some disappointment in prayer may not indicate that we have prayed wrongly but may indicate spiritual greatness! Paul prayed for his "thorn in the flesh" to be removed. This petition was not granted, but not because he had sinned or had misread God. The thorn was actually given to him "lest I [Paul] should be exalted above measure through the abundance of the revelations." Without the thorn he might not have developed greatness in his humility. With the thorn God was glorified through Paul's achievements in spite of weakness. The Lord told Paul, "My grace is sufficient for thee: for my strength is made perfect in weakness" (2 Cor. 12:7-9). Paul saw the good in what seemed a prayer disappointment. God's strength was shown more clearly in Paul's weakness.

These passages give us hints about how we can accept our disappointments. God is greater than any person. He can bring good from any circumstance for those who love Him and are called for His purposes.

*"We know that all things work together for good to them that love God, to them who are the called according to his purpose" (Rom. 8:28).*

 **Read Romans 8:28 in the margin. As you reflect on your own disappointments in prayer, ask God to use them as growing experiences.**

## Dealing with Disappointments

Disappointments in prayer need not give us a feeling of inferiority. Some of the greatest persons in the Bible occasionally failed in prayer. We can be sure that God's wisdom has assigned a perfect reason whenever a prayer receives a "no" answer. We have seen the examples of Moses, Saul, David, Salome, and Paul.

When a disappointment comes in your prayer life, stop and ask, "God, what do You want to reveal to me through this disappointment?" He may reveal a sin, a wrong motive, or unbelief. He may reveal His desire for further spiritual growth.

Disappointments in prayer can produce bitterness if our eyes remain on our selfish desires. We are warned to be "looking diligently lest any man fail of the grace of God; lest any root of bitterness springing up trouble you, and thereby many be defiled" (Heb. 12:15). The command "Grieve not the holy Spirit of God" is followed by the injunction "Let all bitterness, and wrath, and anger, and clamour, and evil speaking, be put away from you, with all malice" (Eph. 4:30-31). This includes, of course, bitterness and anger against God.

Paul's life is an example worth imitating. When he was disappointed in prayer, Paul believed that God was wiser than he. He maintained his faith in God. He proved that it is possible to experience disappointment in prayer and yet to walk continuously with the Lord. His Christian walk, then, was not interrupted. The disappointment itself led to a new insight: God is wiser than we are!

Disappointment in prayer calls for cooperation with God. Discover the reason for His refusal. Use disappointments as opportunities for growth.

 **How will you face disappointments in prayer in the future? Check one.**
❑ I will become angry at God and hold Him responsible.
❑ I will quit praying.
❑ I will ask God to help me learn and grow from the experience.
❑ I will forget about the past and move on to other things.

 Walking in Fellowship with God Today

Can you remember former prayers? I can remember times when fellowship with God was so high and unhindered that I knew my prayer would be answered. I can also remember prayers that embarrass me when I think of the heavenly host watching. Could I have been that selfish? How could God's glory have become secondary if I was being observed by Elijah and Isaiah?

Does it matter to you whether your prayer is effective? How important to you is prayer? The first key to prayer is belief. The key to dealing with hindrances is to care about the reason for failure in prayer. Sin, wrong motives, and unbelief indicate problems that need to be corrected.

1. Fall on your face before the Lord and settle once for all that He matters supremely and that prayer matters because it indicates your relationship with Him. Ask Him to help you cooperate with Him in dealing with hindrances and disappointments. As you pray, refer to "Ways God Responds to Prayer Requests" and "Stop Signs to Answered Prayer" in prayer guide 10, page 215.

2. As you have your quiet time, complete the Daily Master Communication Guide in the margin.

## Daily Master Communication Guide

SCRIPTURE REFERENCE:

_____

*What God said to me:*

_____

_____

_____

_____

_____

_____

_____

*What I said to God:*

_____

_____

_____

_____

_____

_____

_____

# Day 2
# Sins That Hinder Prayer

Today's Learning Goal
You will understand six types
of sin the Bible identifies that
hinder prayer, and you will
demonstrate a commitment
to avoid them.

*"Behold, the Lord's hand is not
shortened, that it cannot save; neither
his ear heavy, that it cannot hear:
but your iniquities have separated
between you and your God, and your
sins have hid his face from you, that
he will not hear" (Isa. 59:1-2).*

*"If I regard iniquity in my heart, the
Lord will not hear me" (Ps. 66:18).*

*"I will therefore that men pray every
where, lifting up holy hands, without
wrath and doubting" (1 Tim. 2:8).*

In prayer you are growing to be like God. If you make a deliberate move away from
God or one that is counter to His nature, you separate yourself from the source
of answers to your prayers. You have not disqualified God or lessened His ability
to answer prayer. Rather, you have disqualified yourself. You have placed yourself
in a position He cannot bless. Read the warnings of Isaiah and the psalmist in
the margin.

Any sin is serious and hinders prayer, but the Bible names six specific sins in
relation to unanswered prayer—prayer God does not hear or answers no. We
should avoid all sin, but we are wise to give special attention to those the Bible
names as hindering prayer. The sins the Bible mentions as roadblocks are illus-
trated below.

### SIN ROADBLOCKS TO PRAYER

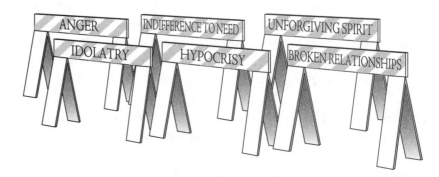

 As you read the following material about these six sins, underline words
and phrases that help you understand them.

## Anger

Read 1 Timothy 2:8 in the margin. God's anger is not like human anger. God's
anger is a holy, unchanging part of His nature. He is eternally angry at sin,
unrighteousness, and injustice. He is never vindictive. He never "gets mad," and He
never loses control of Himself. Even in His anger God is holy.

Human wrath is unholy. It is usually sudden and vindictive. When people
become angry, they often lose control of themselves or hold grudges for a long
time. Our anger hinders our prayers.

 What are examples of unholy anger you can think of?

_____

## Idolatry

When the elders of Israel came to consult Ezekiel, the Lord said, "Son of man,
these men have set up their idols in their heart, and put the stumbling block of
their iniquity before their face: should I be inquired of at all by them?" (Ezek. 14:3).

The idols were in their hearts, and the heart is what God wants (see Prov. 23:26). The Israelites felt that they had kept the second commandment: "Thou shalt not make unto thee any graven image, or any likeness of any thing that is in heaven above, or that is in the earth beneath, or that is in the water under the earth" (Ex. 20:4). They kept physical idols out of their homes and off their altars.

God indicates that He is jealous of your heart. He does not tolerate any competition for your loyalty. Anything you love more than God is an idol in your heart, and it hinders prayer.

 **What are some things that could be modern-day idols of the heart?**

_____

Almost anything can become an idol—money, a job, clothes, another person, television and entertainment, pleasure, leisure time activities.

## Indifference to Need

Indifference to the needs of the weak and helpless is sin. Shutting our ears against need is unlike God, who loves the poor, the oppressed, the widows, the orphans, and the prisoners. Read Proverbs 21:13 in the margin. An open-hearted generosity is like God and wins His heart. He does not hear the prayer of anyone who mistreats or denies help to the needy.

 **According to Proverbs 21:13, if we have not shown compassion and helped people in their need, what will happen to us when we are in need and ask for help?**

_____

If we are indifferent to the cries of the needy, our cries for help will not be heard.

## Hypocrisy

A fourth sin the Bible names that hinders prayer is hypocritical prayer. Praying to be seen by people rather than by God is especially offensive to God. Read in the margin Jesus' instruction in Matthew 6:5. The problem is exactly as Jesus described it: hypocrites want the approval of people rather than of God. They speak to people rather than to God. Consequently, their only reward will be from people.

You are learning much about prayer in this course. God would certainly be pleased for you to help others learn to pray more effectively. You will face the temptation, however, to impress others with your newfound skills of prayer. Reread Matthew 6:5 and pray about this danger.

## Unforgiving Spirit

Failure to forgive others also interferes with your prayers. Read Jesus' words in Mark 11:25, in the margin. Jesus taught more on this subject than any other hindering sin.

"Whoso stoppeth his ears at the cry of the poor, he also shall cry himself, but shall not be heard" (Prov. 21:13).

"When thou prayest, thou shalt not be as the hypocrites are: for they love to pray standing in the synagogues and in the corners of the streets, that they may be seen of men. Verily I say unto you, They have their reward" (Matt. 6:5).

"When ye stand praying, forgive, if ye have aught against any: that your Father also which is in heaven may forgive you your trespasses" (Mark 11:25).

"If ye forgive men their trespasses, your heavenly Father will also forgive you: but if ye forgive not men their trespasses, neither will your Father forgive your trespasses" (Matt. 6:14-15).

"Likewise shall my heavenly Father do also unto you, if ye from your hearts forgive not every one his brother their trespasses" (Matt. 18:35).

"If thou bring thy gift to the altar, and there rememberest that thy brother hath aught against thee; leave there thy gift before the altar, and go thy way; first be reconciled to thy brother, and then come and offer thy gift" (Matt. 5:23-24).

"Ye husbands, dwell with them according to knowledge, giving honour unto the wife, as unto the weaker vessel, and as being heirs together of the grace of life; that your prayers be not hindered" (1 Pet. 3:7).

## Daily Master Communication Guide

SCRIPTURE REFERENCE:

_____

*What God said to me:*

_____

_____

_____

_____

_____

_____

*What I said to God:*

_____

_____

_____

_____

_____

Read the following Scriptures in the margin on page 147. State in your own words what Jesus taught.

Matthew 6:14-15: _____

Matthew 18:35: _____

Jesus' sacrifice of Himself for your sins was so costly that He values a forgiving spirit very dearly. Forgiveness duplicates His character in you. You pay a very high penalty when you refuse to be like Him. If you demonstrate an unforgiving spirit, God does not forgive you.

### Broken Relationships

Allowing broken relationships to exist between yourself and others is very similar to an unforgiving spirit. You are not to allow broken relationships to remain broken. Read Jesus' command in Matthew 5:23-24, in the margin on page 147. If we have not tried reconcile with an offended brother or sister in the body of Christ, we are responsible to make it right. Otherwise, God will not accept our offering.

The sin has to do with destroying the spirit of a close relationship. If a husband disregards his wife, Peter warned that his prayers will be hindered. Read 1 Peter 3:7 on page 147. Any close relationship has the potential of great power in prayer. But close relationships are sensitive, and it is dangerous to allow a fractured relationship to hinder a potentially powerful relationship with the Lord.

Using the words and phrases you underlined, write a definition of each of the six sins listed.

Anger: _____

_____

Idolatry: _____

_____

Indifference to needs: _____

_____

Hypocrisy: _____

_____

Unforgiving spirit: _____

_____

Broken relationships: _____

_____

Turn to "Sin Roadblocks to Prayer" in prayer guide 10, page 215, to check your work.

## ❦ Walking in Fellowship with God Today ❦

1. Look over the sins that block an effective prayer life in "Sin Roadblocks to Prayer" in prayer guide 10, page 215. Which do you consider the most frequent obstacle to your praying? Prayerfully ask God to search your heart for any disagreement with Him that would block your fellowship with Him.
2. As you have your quiet time, complete the Daily Master Communication Guide in the margin on page 148.

## Day 3
# Wrong Motives That Hinder Prayer

### Why Do You Ask?
Your motive for praying may determine whether the request is granted or denied. You must have a proper and pure motive when you ask anything of God.

Read the following questions. Then read "Wrong Motives" in *The Life-Changing Power of Prayer*, pages 101–103, and answer the questions.

1. What is the result when a person elevates personal whims above the needs of others?

_____

_____

2. When can a prayer for self not be selfish? _____

_____

_____

3. What are two examples of prayers for self that were not selfish?

_____

_____

*Today's Learning Goal*
You will understand the effect of wrong motives on prayer and will demonstrate your willingness to check your own motives for asking.

4. Read the following Scriptures in the margin on page 151. What does each say about the flesh and our craving for evil things?

1 Corinthians 10:6: _____

Romans 13:14: _____

Galatians 5:17: _____

5. When can you be most sublimely human?

_____

1. The result is a separation from the larger goals of the body of Christ and the work of His kingdom. 2. Prayer for self is not selfish when you are deeply involved in advancing the kingdom, in fulfilling God's will, or in meeting others' needs. 3. Paul's prayers for boldness and for the chance to travel to a church that needed him were not selfish. Hannah's prayer for a son she could give to the Lord's service was not selfish. 4. We should not crave evil things like the Israelites at Taberah (see 1 Cor. 10:6). We should not make provision to give in to our lusts (see Rom. 13:14). The flesh stands in direct opposition to the Spirit (see Gal. 5:17). 5. You can be most sublimely human when the spiritual nature is in control and dominates your entire being.

## Wrong Reasons

Read James 4:3 in the margin on page 151. In context James identified selfish lust as a wrong motive. Lust is not only an intense sexual desire but also an intense craving for other things. If God were to grant the answers to some of your prayers, the answers themselves would become occasions for sin.

Like Salome, James, and John, whom you studied yesterday, we often do not realize all our requests entail. This is especially true when they derive from selfish motives. Some of our wrong requests can harm others or damage the Kingdom.

How does God answer a prayer asked with wrong motives? Check the correct answer.
❑ 1. Always yes
❑ 2. Always no
❑ 3. Sometimes yes, sometimes no

Unless you carefully read your assignment in *The Life-Changing Power of Prayer*, you may have answered 2. In most cases God refuses to answer a prayer asked with the wrong motivation. He knows what is best for us, so He must often refuse to grant our request.

In the case of Israel at Taberah, however, God granted a request asked with evil motives. The consequences were far from what Israel expected. God's anger burned, and He consumed some of them with fire (see Num. 11:1). He sent meat to eat—a tremendous flock of quail. But "while the flesh was yet between their teeth, ere it was chewed, the wrath of the Lord was kindled against the people, and the Lord smote the people with a very great plague" (Num. 11:33).

When you ask a request with wrong and selfish motives, God usually answers no. Sometimes He answers yes. You can be assured, however, that the consequences of that answer will be most unpleasant. You should have checked 3.

### Pure Motives

The opposite of wrong motives is pure motives. The only purity acceptable to God is the purity of the Lord Jesus Christ in you. You need to have the mind of Christ (see Phil. 2:5). To do that, you must know Him very well indeed. You must so immerse yourself in His life and character that you begin to think as He thinks. You can ask, *If Jesus were in this situation, what would He ask?*

God-pleasing prayer is not asking, *How can I get God to do what I want?* Rather, it is asking, *If I could have God's way, I would ask …* Consider asking, *If God put words in my mouth for this situation, what would He say?* Jesus said, "My meat is to do the will of him that sent me, and to finish his work" (John 4:34). Later He would say, "I came down from heaven, not to do mine own will, but the will of him that sent me" (John 6:38). When you are as consumed with a desire to accomplish God's will, as Jesus was, your motives will be pure.

*"Now these things were our examples, to the intent we should not lust after evil things, as they also lusted" (1 Cor. 10:6).*

*"Put ye on the Lord Jesus Christ, and make not provision for the flesh, to fulfill the lusts thereof" (Rom. 13:14).*

*"The flesh lusteth against the Spirit, and the Spirit against the flesh: and these are contrary the one to the other: so that ye cannot do the things that ye would" (Gal. 5:17).*

*"Ye ask, and receive not, because ye ask amiss, that ye may consume it upon your lusts" (Jas. 4:3).*

### ✿ Walking in Fellowship with God Today ✿

1. Review James 4:3, one of your memory verses for this week. Examine your daily and weekly prayer lists (see pp. 224–25) and check what you are asking. Is there any item that should be crossed off or changed because it is prompted by a wrong motive? Ask God to make you want what He wants. Give Him your will and pray, "If I could have Your way, I would ask …" On a separate sheet of paper write a commitment of your desire to develop and pray from pure motives.

2. As you have your quiet time, complete the Daily Master Communication Guide in the margin on page 150.

# Day 4
# Unbelief Hinders Prayer

### Opposites of Praying in Faith

In week 9 you learned that faith is indispensable to prayer. Turn to pages 135–36 and briefly review what you studied about praying in faith.

Faith is an attitude that is necessary for a prayer warrior. A lack of faith or unbelief hinders prayer.

*Today's Learning Goal*
You will understand ways to overcome unbelief in prayer and to demonstrate your faith in God.

✿ On the following page are listed some aspects of praying in faith. Under each write an attitude or action that would indicate a lack of faith or that would be an opposite of faith.

1. Asking without doubt in your heart:

_____

2. Believing that the things you ask will come to pass:

_____

3. Reflecting God's character of constancy:

_____

4. Recognizing God's authority and power to answer:

_____

5. Having confidence in God's care and purposes for your life:

_____

6. Claiming a Bible promise and holding God to His Word:

_____

Opposites might include: 1. doubt, disbelief, questioning; 2. wavering, doubting, not believing; 3. inconsistent, fickle, variable, double-minded; 4. questioning God's ability to answer the request by words or by actions; 5. believing or acting as if God does not have your best interest at heart, believing that God does not care; 6. not claiming Bible promises, not believing that the promises are for you, doubting God's willingness to keep His promises.

### The Tragedies of Unbelief

Read these Scripture passages and describe what did *not* happen due to lack of faith or unbelief.

Hebrews 3:7-19: _____

Matthew 13:53-58: _____

Matthew 17:14-21: _____

The writer of Hebrews stated that the first generation of Jews delivered in the exodus could not enter the promised land because of its unbelief. The people in Jesus' hometown were "offended in him" because they thought He was just an ordinary carpenter's son. As a result of their unbelief, Jesus "did not many mighty works there." Jesus' disciples were confronted by a need to heal a spirit-possessed boy. Because of their unbelief, they were unable to heal him.

Read "Lack of Faith" in *The Life-Changing Power of Prayer*, **pages 104–6, and respond to the following questions.**

How does James 1:5-8 describe someone who asks in unbelief?

_____

What do you get in God's kingdom? Not what you earn but _____

_____

What are two causes of unbelief? _____

_____

James described the one who asks in unbelief as wavering like a wave of the sea, as double-minded and unstable. In God's kingdom you get what you believe. The believing is the receiving. Without the believing there is no receiving. Two causes of unbelief are:
1. Fearing that God does not want to give
2. Fearing that what you are asking for is too great or too difficult

## Overcoming Unbelief

*Concentrate on Christ and His message.* One of the greatest facilitators to belief is the message of Christ. Read Romans 10:17 in the margin. This is an extremely crucial verse in understanding how faith develops. Faith in Christ is our means of access to the throne of God. Paul said, "We have boldness and access with confidence by the faith of him" (Eph. 3:12). He overcame every trial and every temptation and even defeated death itself. Death is the final and greatest threat any of us face— and yet Jesus conquered death. In doing so, He triumphed over all of the rulers of hell (see Col. 2:15 in the margin). He defeated Satan's highest efforts. He triumphed over the most that hell could offer. He has done everything possible to help us believe. The greatest secret to faith is concentrating on Him and putting our attention on His message.

*"Faith cometh by hearing, and hearing by the word of God" (Rom. 10:17).*

*"Having spoiled principalities and powers, he made a shew of them openly, triumphing over them in it" (Col. 2:15).*

Summarize in your own words one of the best ways to overcome unbelief.

_____

_____

Read the following verses in the margin and describe other resources that may help you overcome unbelief.

Hebrews 3:13-14: _____

_____

*"Exhort one another daily, while it is called To-day; lest any of you be hardened through the deceitfulness of sin. For we are made partakers of Christ, if we hold the beginning of our confidence stedfast unto the end" (Heb. 3:13-14).*

*"Howbeit this kind goeth not out but by prayer and fasting" (Matt. 17:21).*

Matthew 17:21: _____

_____

*Exhort one another daily.* Faith is an attitude; so is unbelief. Others can influence your attitudes. The writer of Hebrews encourages Christians to help one another avoid the hardness of heart that can come by the deceitfulness of sin. Stand by your fellow Christians. Encourage them in their faith. Pray together in faith. Hold one another accountable for maintaining an attitude of faith.

Meditate on the meaning of Hebrews 3:13-14 and record your thoughts.

_____

_____

_____

_____

*Hold on to your confidence in Christ.* When you became a Christian, you placed your faith in Christ. You had confidence in Him and what He did for you on the cross. You believed that He could and would save you. The writer of Hebrews calls you to hold on to that same confidence steadfastly. Do not let it go.

*Pray and fast.* The disciples could not cast out the evil spirit that possessed the boy. Jesus told them that their problem was unbelief. Faith the size of a mustard seed is enough to move mountains. Jesus commended prayer and fasting for this kind of faith. We will look at fasting in more detail in week 13.

### Walking in Fellowship with God Today

Long ago I discovered a prayer that changed my style of thinking. I pray it every morning: "Lord, open my eyes to see spiritual reality and open my ears to hear Your voice." The greatest obstacle to belief in our day is a determined teaching that things that cannot be verified by observation cannot be real. This is a refusal to accept the spiritual as real. Unbelief is basically an inability to think in spiritual terms. I hope that 10 weeks of *Disciple's Prayer Life* have already removed some of the obstacles to your thinking in spiritual terms.

1. Throughout the day thank God for your growth in thinking spiritually. Ask Him to open your eyes to see spiritual reality and to open your ears to hear His voice. As you pray, refer to "Two Causes of Unbelief" and "Overcoming Unbelief" in prayer guide 10, page 215.

2. As you have your quiet time, complete the Daily Master Communication Guide in the margin.

## Daily Master Communication Guide

SCRIPTURE REFERENCE:

_____

*What God said to me:*

_____

_____

_____

_____

_____

_____

*What I said to God:*

_____

_____

_____

_____

_____

_____

Day 5
# Delayed Prayers

## Your "Unanswered" Prayers

Prayers offered at one point in life may not be answered until years later. Delayed answers, like "no" answers, can be occasions of disappointment or even bitterness. Understanding the ways God uses delayed prayers may help you in your prayer life.

 **On a separate sheet of paper write the heading** *Delayed Prayer Requests.* **List as many requests as possible that you have prayed or are currently praying for that have yet to be answered. This will take some time and thought.**

**Referring to "Stop Signs to Answered Prayer" in prayer guide 10, page 215, evaluate your requests to see if they have gone unanswered due to sin, wrong motives, or unbelief. If so, write the reason beside the request.**

The answers to the remaining requests you listed have been delayed for a purpose, as well. Let's look at some biblical prayers that had delayed answers.

## Zacharias and Elisabeth

Apparently, this was the prayer experience of John the Baptist's parents. When the angel Gabriel announced to Zacharias that he and Elisabeth would have a son, Gabriel began the announcement by saying, "Fear not, Zacharias: for thy prayer is heard" (Luke 1:13). Luke wrote, "They had no child, because that Elisabeth was barren, and they both were now well stricken in years" (Luke 1:7). The circumstances indicate that Zacharias's petition must have been made many years before. Likely, in their advanced years Elisabeth and Zacharias had stopped praying for a child.

 **Read Luke 1:5-25,57-66. In your opinion, why did God delay in answering their prayer for a child?**

_____

_____

The answer was delayed for reasons in God's wisdom. We cannot know exactly what those reasons may have been; however, Luke tells us that "they were both righteous before God, walking in all the commandments and ordinances of the Lord blameless" (Luke 1:6). Perhaps the purpose was to show God's power in a humanly impossible situation. When they prayed for a son, God deemed their character as being fit to parent the man who would be given the highest and holiest task any human being had previously been entrusted with: preparing the way for the coming Messiah.

*Answers are delayed for reasons in God's wisdom.*

Zacharias and Elisabeth were uniquely qualified to become the parents of John the Baptist. God chose them, and from His standpoint their prayer was answered as soon as they prayed. But the timing of the birth of their son had to wait. This birth needed to occur just prior to that of Jesus.

Luke said that Zacharias and Elisabeth were "righteous before God" (Luke 1:6). No bitterness or recrimination had crept into their lives. They had accepted with grace what seemed to be a "no" answer. Zacharias, shocked by the angel's words, said, "Whereby shall I know this? for I am an old man, and my wife well stricken in years" (Luke 1:18). He no longer expected the prayer to be answered, and yet he continued faithfully serving the Lord. He and Elisabeth continued to abide in their relationship with God despite delays in their prayer.

## Daniel

Daniel also experienced a delay in the answer to his prayer.

 Read Daniel's experience in Daniel 10:2-14 and answer these questions.

How long was the answer to Daniel's request delayed? _____

What do you think Daniel was asking God about (see vv. 12,14)?

_____

Why was the answer to Daniel's prayer delayed?

_____

When Daniel experienced terrifying visions, he prayed for understanding and humility before God. The answer was delayed for three weeks. Read in the margin the angel's words when he finally appeared to Daniel.

Evil forces such as demonic powers can be the agents of delay. We learn from this incident that if evil attempts a delay, God intervenes. We can be assured that God had a timing the evil force could not alter. God would not have allowed Daniel to be pressured too much by the delay.

Daniel exhibited the same characteristics Zacharias and Elisabeth did in delay: he maintained his faith, even in "mourning three full weeks" (Dan. 10:2). He remained faithful to God, and he fasted before the Lord while he awaited the answer (see Dan. 10:3). Daniel abided in the Lord.

*"Fear not, Daniel: for from the first day that thou didst set thine heart to understand, and to chasten thyself before thy God, thy words were heard, and I am come for thy words. But the prince of the kingdom of Persia withstood me one and twenty days; but, lo, Michael, one of the chief princes, came to help me" (Dan. 10:12-13).*

## Facing Delays by Abiding

 Read "Not Abiding" in *The Life-Changing Power of Prayer,* **pages 106–9. How will abiding help you continue praying when the answer seems slow in coming?**

_____

_____

God's timing is measured according to His wisdom. Our faith is measured according to who He is. Abiding indicates a deep relationship with God—a relationship with a deep root system. Your spiritual root system is developed by "much prayer, much attention to the biblical directives, and much cleaving to the Lord." However, a deep root system—a deep relationship with God—can endure long periods of drought if necessary. One of the best ways to cope with delays is to continue abiding in Christ.

Something remarkable about Daniel, Zacharias, and Elisabeth is that their faith did not depend on the coming of the answer. Their fellowship with the Lord was pleasing to Him. They practiced abiding. The angel said that Daniel was "greatly beloved" (Dan. 10:19), and Luke said that Zacharias and Elisabeth were "righteous before God" (Luke 1:6). God selected these people of high character and godliness to demonstrate that His timetable need not affect our faith. We are faithful to Him not because of His gifts but because He is our God.

 Assume that one of your Christian friends has come to you with a problem. He has prayed for a matter a long time without receiving an answer to the prayer. He is frustrated, disappointed, and discouraged. Using your study this week, write on a separate sheet of paper the steps you would take to help him. Bring your list of steps to your group session this week.

Write this week's memory verse(s) on a separate sheet of paper.

 Walking in Fellowship with God Today

The most important reason for delayed answers to prayer is that the process of waiting develops in us the character trait of perseverance. Abiding is not an involuntary habit. It does not require intelligence or training. Abiding is an act of the will.

One test of your abiding is delayed answers. If all answers were instantaneous, Christianity would become little more than a magic show. What was important in the lives of such Bible pray-ers as Joseph, Daniel, Jesus, and Paul is not that God eventually took care of them but that their circumstances indicated that each was a certain kind of person. They continued to abide regardless of external circumstances.

1. Tell God today that you understand that His plan for you cannot be different from that of the Bible characters. Commit to Him your willingness to become a faithful, persevering prayer warrior.
2. As you have your quiet time, complete the Daily Master Communication Guide in the margin.

*Daily Master Communication Guide*

SCRIPTURE REFERENCE:

_____

*What God said to me:*

_____

_____

_____

_____

_____

_____

*What I said to God:*

_____

_____

_____

_____

_____

_____

# ASKING FOR YOURSELF AND OTHERS

## Key Idea
The fervent prayer of a righteous person on behalf of self and others, though difficult, is a holy privilege that bring results.

## This Week's Learning Goal
You will understand ways to pray more effectively for yourself and others, and you will demonstrate a commitment to pray for others.

## Verses to Memorize
"Be careful for nothing; but in every thing by prayer and supplication with thanksgiving let your requests be made known unto God" (Phil. 4:6).

"Our Father which art in heaven, hallowed be thy name. Thy Kingdom come. Thy will be done in earth, as it is in heaven. Give us this day our daily bread. And forgive us our debts, as we forgive our debtors. And lead us not into temptation, but deliver us from evil: for thine is the kingdom, and the power, and the glory, for ever" (Matt. 6:9-13).

## Related Prayer Guide
Prayer guide 11, "Asking for Yourself and Others," page 216

## Prayer Helped!

Jim was on the phone. "T. W., is this Music in Missions day?" While taking that course in seminary, Jim had been overwhelmed by some of the answers to prayer that had come as the class prayed. I told him that Thursday was indeed the day for the class. Jim then shared a heart-breaking prayer request. In February of that year his city had experienced an outbreak of Reye's Syndrome, a children's disease that is often fatal. Eleven children had been struck by the disease; nine of them had died.

The disease struck Laura, a 10-year-old member of the church Jim pastored. She had started attending the church's Vacation Bible School the previous summer. Six weeks prior to her illness Laura had accepted Christ as her Savior. Now she was in a coma. I promised Jim that the class and I would pray. Presenting to the Lord Laura's faith and witness, we asked Him to raise her up quickly. Friday she was much improved, and on Saturday she opened her eyes and saw her father in the room with her. She spoke: "Jesus saved me!" That afternoon the doctors assured her father that his daughter was going to live. Two Sundays later Laura's entire family accepted Christ.

On Wednesday, April 3, 1974, the *North Hills News Record* carried on page 1 the headline "Prayer Helped." The article recounted Laura's amazing recovery from Reye's Syndrome.

# Day 1
## Model Prayer Requests

Schedule a time to pray with your prayer partner this week. Write the day and time here.

_____

As you complete each of the following reviews, place an X in each box.

❑ Using prayer guide 1, page 205, review the reasons God answers prayer. Which reason do you use most often? _____

❑ Using prayer guide 9, page 214, review the eight principles of asking. Which principle do you have the most difficulty with? _____

❑ Turn to page 126 and read again "God Invites Asking."

This week you will study all kinds of prayers for yourself and others. You will not be able to pray these requests every day, but you will be able to use them as guides to asking for years to come. Later in the week you will use "Weekly Prayer List" on page 225 to pray for others. Prepare at least five copies of this list to use later this week, following the instructions in "Weekly Intercession," page 223.

### Prayers of Petition

Read "Prayers of Petition" in *The Life-Changing Power of Prayer*, **pages 62–64.** What three attitudes in prayer are implied by the words used in Matthew 7:7-8 (in the margin)?

*Ask* suggests _____

*Seek* suggests _____

*Knock* suggests _____

Week 9 taught the importance and the principles of asking. Matthew 7:7-8 points out the need for the attitudes of dependence, earnestness, and persistence. We also need to ask specifically. Without a specific request, a general request receives a general answer. We can be guided to ask more clearly by the examples of asking we find in the Bible.

### Model Prayers

Consider the prayer Jesus taught the disciples in Matthew 6:9-13, in the margin on page 158, as a model prayer. According to this model, what kinds of things are Jesus' disciples to ask for?

Verse 10: _____

Verse 11: _____

*Today's Learning Goal*
You will understand the need to focus prayer requests more on spiritual than physical needs, and you will demonstrate your concern for the spiritual welfare of others.

*"Ask, and it shall be given you; seek, and ye shall find; knock, and it shall be opened unto you: for every one that asketh receiveth; and he that seeketh findeth; and to him that knocketh it shall be opened" (Matt. 7:7-8).*

"For this cause I bow my knees unto the Father of our Lord Jesus Christ, of whom the whole family in heaven and earth is named, that he would grant you, according to the riches of his glory, to be strengthened with might by his Spirit in the inner man; that Christ may dwell in your hearts by faith; that ye, being rooted and grounded in love, may be able to comprehend with all saints what is the breadth, and length, and depth, and height; and to know the love of Christ, which passeth knowlcdge, that ye might be filled with all the fulness of God" (Eph. 3:14-19).

"For this cause we also, since the day we heard it, do not cease to pray for you, and to desire that ye might be filled with the knowledge of his will in all wisdom and spiritual understanding; that ye might walk worthy of the Lord unto all pleasing, being fruitful in every good work, and increasing in the knowledge of God; strengthened will all might, according to his glorious power, unto all patience and longsuffering with joyfulness; giving thanks unto the Father, which hath made us meet to be partakers of the inheritance of the saints in light" (Col. 1:9-12).

"This I pray, that your love may abound yet more and more in knowledge and in all judgment; that ye may approve things that are excellent; that ye may be sincere and without offence till the day of Christ; being filled with the fruits of righteousness, which are by Jesus Christ, unto the glory and praise of God" (Phil. 1:9-11).

Verse 12: _____

Verse 13: _____

Pause and pray through this prayer for yourself. Make each request specific for your situation.

Read Jesus' prayer to the Father in John 17. Not all of the verses contain requests. In verse 5 Jesus made a personal request: "Glorify thou me with thine own self with the glory which I had with thee before the world was." This was a unique request that only He could pray. What did Jesus request for His disciples?

Verse 11: _____

Verse 15: _____

Verse 17: _____

Verse 21: _____

Verse 24: _____

Read Ephesians 3:14-19 in the margin. Pray these verses for a friend so that—
   • he or she is strengthened in the inner person (see v. 16);
   • Christ dwells in his or her heart through faith (see v. 17);
   • he or she is able to comprehend Christ's love (see v. 18-19);
   • he or she is filled to all the fullness of God (see vv. 18-19).

Read another of Paul's prayers in Ephesians 1:15-23 and list at least three things he asked for.

Verse 17: _____

Verse 18: _____

Verse 19: _____

In his prayer for the Christians in Colossians 1:9-12, in the margin, what did Paul ask for?

Verse 9: _____

Verse 10: _____

Verse 11: _____

In Philippians 1:9-11, in the margin on page 160, Paul prayed that—

Verse 9: _____

Verse 10: _____

Verse 11: _____

Check your work with the lists in "Model Prayer Requests" in prayer guide 11, "Asking for Yourself and Others," page 216.

## Emphasize the Spiritual

Look over the topics listed in the preceding model prayers. How many were for spiritual matters? _____ How many were for material needs or changes? _____

The prayers of Jesus and Paul indicate that they gave first priority to prayer for spiritual change. Their concern for spiritual matters far exceeded requests for material needs. Of the 25 or more requests in these prayers, only 1 is for material or physical concerns—the request for daily bread. This does not mean that we should not pray about physical or material concerns. However, it indicates that the emphasis of our praying ought to be on spiritual concerns. Our prayers should ask first for the glory of God and for His purposes to be accomplished. Jesus taught us to begin our prayers by asking that God's name be hallowed, that His kingdom come, and that His will be done on earth. These subjects take precedence over all else we might ask.

Much of our praying is crisis praying. In His great prayer in John 17 Jesus is at the most somber and difficult moment of His life. Yet His prayer is a majestic monument of untroubled love. He asked for only a few things, but He repeated their importance again and again. He prayed for great, sweeping issues—issues whose weight and importance could not even be perceived by those with Him.

### Walking in Fellowship with God Today

1. Make a point to increase the number of spiritual petitions you present to the Lord. Pray about your role in the Kingdom. What about the Kingdom, to your knowledge, needs prayer? Pray for leaders in the work of the Kingdom. Pray for unity in the body of Christ.
2. Look again in "Model Prayer Requests" in prayer guide 11, page 216, at Paul's prayers for believers at Ephesus, Colossae, and Philippi. Single out four Christians in your *Disciple's Prayer Life* group and pray for those spiritual changes in their lives. If you want to, be more specific in your requests and write the persons' names and your requests for them on a separate sheet of paper. Pray for these four persons once each week for the remainder of this course.
3. As you have your quiet time, complete the Daily Master Communication Guide in the margin.

## Daily Master Communication Guide

SCRIPTURE REFERENCE:

_____

*What God said to me:*

_____
_____
_____
_____
_____
_____
_____

*What I said to God:*

_____
_____
_____
_____
_____
_____
_____

You will be able to list your personal prayer needs after studying biblical examples of personal petitions.

*"It came to pass in those days, that he went out into a mountain to pray, and continued all night in prayer to God. And when it was day, he called unto him his disciples: and of them he chose twelve, whom also he named apostles" (Luke 6:12-13).*

*"David inquired of the Lord, saying, Shall I go and smite these Philistines? And the Lord said unto David, Go, and smite the Philistines, and save Keilah. And David's men said unto him. Behold, we be afraid here in Judah: how much more then if we come to Keilah against the armies of the Philistines? Then David inquired of the Lord yet again. And the Lord answered him and said, Arise, go down to Keilah: for I will deliver the Philistines into thine hand" (1 Sam. 23:2-4).*

*"He said, O Lord God of my master Abraham, I pray thee, send me good speed this day, and shew kindness unto my master Abraham. Behold, I stand here by the well of water; and the daughters of the men of the city come out to draw water: and let it come to pass, that the damsel to whom I shall say, Let down thy pitcher, I pray thee, that I may drink; and she shall say, Drink, and I will give thy camels drink also: let the same be she that thou hast appointed for thy servant Isaac; and thereby shall I know that thou hast shewed kindness unto my master" (Gen. 24:12-14).*

# Day 2
# Personal Prayer Requests

## Three Areas of Personal Requests

You should petition God for your personal needs, as Jesus taught His disciples in the Model Prayer (see Matt. 6:9-13). After praying for God's honor and kingdom, Jesus authorized a series of personal requests:

- For daily food
- For forgiveness of sins
- For deliverance from temptation

These represent three large areas God is interested in—our physical needs, restoration to fellowship with Him if we break it, and protection from forces beyond our control. *Temptation* can refer either to an enticement to sin or to a trial. Because we are specifically promised deliverance from anything God allows us to be tempted with (see 1 Cor. 10:13), we can and should ask God for deliverance.

 **Yesterday you prayed for yourself the Model Prayer in Matthew 6:9-13. Pray for yourself the three requests listed above. Write your requests so that they are specific. Which request seems more important to you today? Why?**

_____

_____

## Ask for Guidance

Jesus not only told us to ask about personal needs, but He also did that Himself. He often prayed for guidance. The night before He chose the twelve disciples, He spent the entire night in prayer (see Luke 6:12-13 in the margin). When the time came to expand His Galilean ministry beyond Capernaum, Jesus arose early in the morning and prayed in a "solitary place" (see Mark 1:35-39). Jesus' prayers demonstrate that divine guidance is available through prayer.

We have other examples of biblical characters seeking God's guidance.

 **Read 1 Samuel 23:2-4 in the margin. What guidance did David seek?**

_____

**Read Genesis 24:12-14 in the margin. What guidance did Abraham's servant, Eliezer, seek in prayer?**

_____

**In what areas do you personally need guidance at the present time?**

_____

## Ask for Wisdom

Another similar personal petition often found in Scripture is for wisdom. Asking for wisdom is appropriate. Read James 1:5 in the margin.

 In 1 Kings 3:9-12, in the margin, who asked for wisdom? _____

In Romans 16:19, in the margin, who wanted the Romans to be wise?

_____

In Matthew 10:16, in the margin, who wanted wisdom for those sent out?

_____

What special need for wisdom do you have at this time?

_____

_____

## Other Personal Requests

In the Bible most personal requests bring great benefit for God's work, even if they seem to pertain only to the person asking.

 **Read the following Scriptures and write what each person petitioned.**

Abram (Gen. 15:2-6): _____

Hannah (1 Sam. 1:10-11): _____

Zacharias (Luke 1:13): _____

Hezekiah (2 Kings 20:1-3): _____

Peter (Acts 9:36-42): _____

All of the requests above were for material or physical changes, but each answer had great spiritual results. Abram prayed for a son, and the answer to that prayer, Isaac, became a very important ingredient in God's creation of the chosen people. Hannah's prayer for a son produced a pivotal figure in Israel's history, Samuel. The last of the judges, Samuel was also a prophet prefiguring many of the later great prophets of Israel. Zacharias's prayer for a son was answered with the birth of John the Baptist, the forerunner of Christ. Although these prayers seem to be personal and private, God was guiding their utterance because of what each prayer ultimately produced for His purposes.

Other seemingly personal requests in the Bible follow the same pattern of producing unexpected benefits for God's purposes. In a mortal illness Hezekiah

*"If any of you lack wisdom, let him ask of God, that giveth to all men liberally, and upbraideth not; and it shall be given him" (Jas. 1:5).*

*"Give therefore thy servant an understanding heart to judge thy people, that I may discern between good and bad: for who is able to judge this thy so great a people? And the speech pleased the Lord, that Solomon had asked this thing. And God said unto him, Because thou hast asked this thing, and hast not asked for thyself long life; neither hast asked riches for thyself, nor hast asked the life of thine enemies; but hast asked for thyself understanding to discern judgment; behold, I have done according to thy words: lo, I have given thee a wise and an understanding heart; so that there was none like thee before, neither after thee shall any arise like unto thee" (1 Kings 3:9-12).*

*"Your obedience is come abroad unto all men. I am glad therefore on your behalf: but yet I would have you wise unto that which is good, and simple concerning evil" (Rom. 16:19).*

*"Behold, I send you forth as sheep in the midst of wolves: be ye therefore wise as serpents, and harmless as doves" (Matt. 10:16).*

## Daily Master Communication Guide

SCRIPTURE REFERENCE:

_____

_____

*What God said to me:*

_____

_____

_____

_____

_____

_____

_____

*What I said to God:*

_____

_____

_____

_____

_____

_____

_____

prayed to live. He survived, and later Manasseh was born to him. Although Manasseh was a very wicked king, his succession to the throne preserved the royal Davidic line for the coming of the Messiah.

Peter's prayer for Dorcas's resurrection brought about the conversion of many people in Joppa, so that the church grew. No doubt Dorcas continued to minister to the needs of others as she had prior to her death. Personal, private prayers of godly people are likely to yield great results for the kingdom of God.

To list all of the personal prayers you might make would be pointless. Different people and different circumstances call for different specific requests. Remember, however, that the Bible commends personal prayer. The tone of the whole Bible is that God uses the personal prayers of godly people to accomplish greater ends than the pray-er might expect.

### ❧ Walking in Fellowship with God Today ❧

1. Personal requests should grow from a personal relationship with God. Try to envision how God sees your requests. Think of two personal requests you have recently made or could make today. Prayerfully trace what would happen to advance the Kingdom or to honor God if those requests were granted. Learn to say, "Thy Kingdom come in the granting of [personal request]."
2. As you have your quiet time, complete the Daily Master Communication Guide in the margin.

## Day 3
## Asking for Others

Read "Prayers of Intercession" in *The Life-Changing Power of Prayer*, pages 58–61. List biblical examples of persons who prayed for others. Write the name of the pray-er, one(s) prayed for, and Scripture reference.

| Pray-er | Prayed For | Scripture Reference |
|---------|-----------|---------------------|
|         |           |                     |
|         |           |                     |
|         |           |                     |
|         |           |                     |
|         |           |                     |

Do you agree or disagree with the following statement? "Intercessory prayer … reaches its highest power and its highest goal when it is intended to bring the kingdom and accomplish the will of God." ❑ Agree ❑ Disagree Why?

_____

_____

Praying for others is often referred to as intercessory prayer. If we are to love others as we love ourselves, we should pray for others as we pray for ourselves. We have seen that Jesus prayed for His disciples in John 17. An especially poignant prayer is His prayer for Simon at the Lord's Supper. After telling the disciples that Satan had asked permission to sift them like wheat, Jesus then told Simon, "But I have prayed for thee, that thy faith fail not: and when thou art converted, strengthen thy brethren" (Luke 22:32). This prayer made possible Peter's great courage before the Sanhedrin in Acts 4:8-12. The Sanhedrin "saw the boldness of Peter and John" and "took knowledge of them, that they had been with Jesus" (Acts 4:13)!

Other examples you should have listed include Jesus' prayers for us (see Heb. 7:25; 9:24; Rom. 8:33-34), the Jerusalem church's prayer for Peter (see Acts 12:5), and Paul's prayers for the churches of his day (see Eph. 1:15-20; Col. 1:9-11; Phil. 1:9; 1 Thess. 3:10-13; 2 Thess. 1:11). You may have also noticed the prayers implied by Paul's requests of the churches at Thessalonica, Rome, Ephesus, Colossae, and Philippi.

Intercessory prayer reaches its highest potential when it is intended to further the kingdom of God and to accomplish His will. This is in keeping with our focus in day 1 on seeing from a spiritual perspective. Yet God's will includes not only our spiritual needs but also every other need we have. Biblical examples and instruction reveal several groups of people we need to pray for in special ways.

## Pray for Friends and Acquaintances
We have Paul's example to follow in praying for friends and acquaintances.

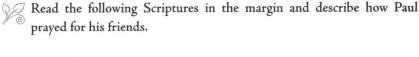 **Read the following Scriptures in the margin and describe how Paul prayed for his friends.**

2 Timothy 1:3: _____

Philemon 4: _____

2 Timothy 1:16: _____

Turn to your weekly prayer lists (see p. 225) for friends and associates. Add names and requests for persons you want to add to these two lists.

## Pray for Your Enemies
Read Luke 6:28; Luke 23:34; and 2 Timothy 4:16 in the margin. Perhaps in earlier weeks you have already forgiven someone who has harmed you. Such persons still need your prayers. Select a day of the week to pray specifically for enemies.

Turn to your weekly prayer list (see p. 225) for enemies. List the names or initials and requests you want to pray for regularly.

Stop and pray for forgiveness of enemies and for spiritual changes to occur in their lives.

(see p. 225)

*Today's Learning Goal*
You will understand and begin to follow the pattern of persons in Scripture by praying for friends, enemies, civil authorities, your nation, and the sick.

*"I thank God, whom I serve from my forefathers with pure conscience, that without ceasing I have remembrance of thee in my prayers night and day"* (2 Tim. 1:3).

*"I thank my God, making mention of thee always in my prayers"* (Philem. 4).

*"The Lord give mercy unto the house of Onesiphorus; for he oft refreshed me, and was not ashamed of my chain"* (2 Tim. 1:16).

*"Bless them that curse you, and pray for them which despitefully use you"* (Luke 6:28).

*"Father, forgive them; for they know not what they do"* (Luke 23:34).

*"At my first answer no man stood with me, but all men forsook me. I pray God that it may not be laid to their charge"* (2 Tim. 4:16).

*"I exhort therefore, that, first of all, supplications, intercessions, and giving of thanks, be made for all men; for kings, and for all that are in authority; that we may lead a quiet and peaceable life in all godliness and honesty"* (1 Tim. 2:1-2).

*"Seek the peace of the city whither I have caused you to be carried away captives, and pray unto the Lord for it: for in the peace thereof shall ye have peace"* (Jer. 29:7).

*"Is any sick among you? let him call for the elders of the church; and let them pray over him, anointing him with oil in the name of the Lord: and the prayer of faith shall save the sick, and the Lord shall raise him up; and if he have committed sins, they shall be forgiven him. Confess your faults one to another, and pray one for another, that ye may be healed. The effectual fervent prayer of a righteous man availeth much" (Jas. 5:14-16).*

*"When Jesus was entered into Capernaum, there came unto him a centurion, beseeching him, and saying, Lord, my servant lieth at home sick of the palsy, grievously tormented. When Jesus heard it, he marvelled, and said to them that followed, Verily I say unto you, I have not found so great faith, no, not in Israel" (Matt. 8:5-6,10).*

*"Behold, a woman of Canaan came out of the same coasts, and cried unto him, saying, Have mercy on me, O Lord, thou son of David; my daughter is grievously vexed with a devil. Then Jesus answered and said unto her, O woman, great is thy faith: be it unto thee even as thou wilt. And her daughter was made whole from that very hour" (Matt. 15:22,28).*

*"When Jesus saw their faith, he said unto the sick of the palsy, Son, thy sins be forgiven thee" (Mark 2:5).*

*"A woman having an issue of blood twelve years, which had spent all her living upon physicians, neither could be healed of any. And he said unto her, Daughter, be of good comfort: thy faith hath made thee whole; go in peace" (Luke 8:43,48).*

## Pray for Civil Authorities

Paul, instructing Timothy in conducting public worship, listed some who should be in our prayers. Read his words in 1 Timothy 2:1-2, in the margin on page 165. Jeremiah sent a message from the Lord to the captives who were taken to Babylon. Read Jeremiah 29:7 in the margin on page 165. We are to pray for all people, especially for civil authorities.

 Turn to your weekly prayer list (see p. 225) for authorities. Add the persons you want to pray for regularly. Include persons such as your president or head of state, legislative representatives, judges, governor, mayor, and other officials. Pay attention to the news about these individuals so that you can pray more specifically for them.

Stop and pray for the ones you have listed as Paul told Timothy to pray.

## Pray for Your Nation

In our nation a great need is for national spiritual awakening or spiritual renewal. We need to return to the fear of God and obedience to Christ. The love of sin and the hardness of many hearts toward God is an alarming national disaster. Many Christians are praying for spiritual awakening in America. The church must pray for its own cleansing and for our nation to be renewed spiritually.

A great promise to use in prayer for your nation is 2 Chronicles 7:14. In week 4, day 5 you were asked to record this promise and its conditions on the chart "Bible Promises." Turn to that chart on page 221 and review this promise.

This promise was given in Solomon's day in preparation for a future time when Israel would need it. The promise is also available for us in our day.

 Pause and consider the possibility of enlisting other individuals and groups to pray for your country's spiritual renewal. What could you do to stimulate others to pray for your fellow citizens?

_____

On a daily or weekly prayer list (see pp. 224–25), begin listing specific requests you can pray for the spiritual awakening of your nation. Bring this list with you to your group session.

## Pray for the Sick

Read James 5:14-16 in the margin. The numerous examples of healing and miraculous works in Jesus' ministry are instructive. Certain outstanding virtues on the part of the petitioners emerge in different cases—faith, discernment of authority, earnestness, persistence, and humility.

 In the following passages, in the margin on this page, discover who responded with faith that produced healing.

Matthew 8:5-6,10: _____

Matthew 15:22,28: _____

Mark 2:5: _____

Luke 8:43,48: _____

Because the sick may need to be prayed for daily, add them to your temporary daily prayer list (see p. 224). Pause to pray for them.

❦Walking in Fellowship with God Today ❦

1. The appeal in 1 Timothy 2:1-2 is made to Timothy as the leader of a church. The church is to pray for "kings and all who are in authority." Pray that every prayer group in which you participate might undertake praying for the civil authorities in your nation.
2. Pray that according to 2 Chronicles 7:14, a concert of prayer by godly people may be raised up to pray for your state and the nation. Include the following in your prayers: God's purposes for your church and denomination and their influence on the nation; a cleansing of the media and their influence; and the elevation of godly men and women in leadership, both in government and in church.
3. As you have your quiet time, complete the Daily Master Communication Guide in the margin.

## Day 4
## Praying for the Lost

**Your Heart's Desire**
🌿 How frequently do you pray specifically for a lost person by name?
❑ At least daily          ❑ Twice or more a week
❑ Once a week           ❑ Less than once a week

The frequency with which you pray for the lost may indicate how much compassion you have for the lost. It may indicate whether you believe that prayer can have an effect on the lost person's life. It may indicate what you believe about hell and the lost person's destiny.

Paul's "heart's desire and prayer" for his fellow Jews was for their salvation (see Rom. 10:1). He so reflected the mind of Christ that his heart became like God's heart. The essence of all prayer is agreeing with God. He does not want any person to die without accepting His Son's sacrifice for the purpose of salvation. God desires that all come to repentance (see 2 Pet. 3:9 in the margin, p. 168). The more we pray, the more we think as God thinks. As a faithful prayer warrior, you will want to cultivate a compassion for the lost that wants "all men to be saved, and to come unto the knowledge of the truth" (1 Tim. 2:4), just as God does.

*Daily Master Communication Guide*

SCRIPTURE REFERENCE:

_____

*What God said to me:*

_____
_____
_____
_____
_____
_____
_____
_____

*What I said to God:*

_____
_____
_____
_____
_____
_____
_____

*Today's Learning Goal*
You will understand five steps in praying for the lost and will demonstrate your compassion for the lost by praying for them.

*"The Lord is not slack concerning his promise, as some men count slackness; but is longsuffering to us-ward, not willing that any should perish, but that all should come to repentance" (2 Pet. 3:9).*

Praying for the lost involves beseeching God not only for their initial acceptance of Christ's salvation but also for an atmosphere of spiritual growth for new converts.

## Seeing God's Point of View

When we are concerned for the lost, in prayer we try to see God's point of view. If we are submitted to Christ's lordship, are filled and guided by the Holy Spirit, and earnestly seek God's mind and heart, He prompts our prayer by helping us mentally "see" what He sees. We then apply our faith and action to bring into reality the God-given vision. We ask God for what He wants to give, and we rejoice in the vision of the completed answer to our request.

A helpful prayer exercise is to visualize a lost person receiving Christ, being baptized, and finally becoming a glorious light for the Lord by contributing notably to the life of the church.

Close your eyes and visualize yourself presenting to God at His judgment seat a lost person you brought to Christ. Write the name of the person you visualized: _____. Think of what you would say to God and what He would say to you. Write the dialogue on a separate sheet of paper.

---

### FIVE STEPS IN PRAYING FOR THE LOST
1. Cultivate a genuine concern and love for the lost.
2. Discover specific persons in your circles of relationship who are lost.
3. Pray appropriately and in detail for these specific persons.
4. Persist in prayer.
5. Thank God for each step He takes in moving them to salvation.

---

## Step 1: Cultivate Genuine Concern

Christian history is replete with men and women whose burning hearts so yearned for the salvation of the lost that they sacrificed health, comfort, and even family to gain for God those Christless souls He longed for. David Brainerd agonized so intensely in prayer for the Indians in New England that he is described as one who "wept himself to death." He had to leave his missionary work because of tuberculosis. John Knox prayed, "Give me Scotland or I die!" As a missionary to India, William Carey agonized for seven years before he saw his first convert.

Ask God to impress on you the penalty of being lost. As Christians grow older, their security in the hands of God sometimes does the opposite of what it should do: it leads to a comfortable indifference to the awesome eternity of hell instead of a grateful acknowledgment of our salvation in the form of witnessing. Ask God to increase your horror of hell and to give you a renewed vision of Christ suffering your own judgment.

*Prayer for the lost should be specific prayer.*

## Step 2: Discover Specific Persons

Prayer for the lost should be specific prayer. It should include prayer for specific individuals and specific requests for those individuals.

---

On the lines below write the names of lost persons in the relationships named. Select persons who are closest to you at this time.

Relative: _____

Friend: _____

Business or social acquaintance: _____

Add these names to one of your prayer lists (pp. 224–25). Which of these three individuals do you think is closest to making a decision for Christ?

_____

Which do you think is farthest from being ready to accept Christ?

_____

## Step 3: Pray

In your prayers for these persons, remember that you can impact only God's side of the relationship; you cannot touch anything God would not touch. God leaves the will free. Anyone who accepts salvation must decide to do so. God does not force the person.

Pray the following requests for each person you listed above. Check the boxes below when you have prayed as indicated.
- ❑ "Lord, bring effective witnesses, including me, across their paths."
- ❑ "Savior, arrange circumstances in their lives so that the details of their lives will point them to Christ."
- ❑ "Lord, send Your Holy Spirit in great power to convict them of their sin and lostness."
- ❑ "Father, cause them to understand through Your Holy Spirit that Jesus is adequate for their salvation from sin."

## Step 4: Persist in Prayer

Remember that God honors importunity, or persistence. Keep in mind that delayed answers are sometimes tests of your faith. Ask God to reveal new ways to pray for the lost persons—such as using their needs to point to Christ's sufficiency or prodding their memories with Scriptures they have heard. Pray for specific individuals who may be able to influence their lives for Christ. Pray without wavering.

## Step 5: Thank God

Ask God to sensitize you to the progress your target persons are making toward salvation. Regularly thank Him for progress that may not be outwardly visible. My wife and I once knew a lost man who became meaner when we started praying for him. We were elated! This indicated that the Holy Spirit was convicting him of his sin. He was experiencing the normal reaction of natural flesh to the Holy Spirit's work.

## Daily Master Communication Guide

SCRIPTURE REFERENCE:

_____

*What God said to me:*

_____

_____

_____

_____

_____

_____

*What I said to God:*

_____

_____

_____

_____

_____

_____

**Broaden Your Vision for the Lost**

As you pray for the lost, don't forget God's broader vision for the lost who are spread over His big world. Make a point to pray for each of the following.

- For God to remind missionaries of their original call as Christ's ambassadors. If you can, name specific missionaries you have met or heard.
- For God to quicken the hearts of lost persons in the paths of missionaries and to give missionaries sensitivity to the lost in meeting their needs, relating to them, and drawing them to Christ
- For God to enlarge the evangelistic vision of your own church and to equip witnesses in it
- For God to give you a greater burden for the lost and skill and sensitivity in witnessing

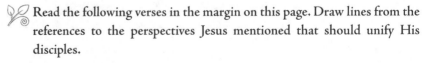 **Walking in Fellowship with God Today**

1. As you go through the day, continually remind God of the three persons you named in step 2. Also pray for the four items in step 3 and the four items in "Broaden Your Vision for the Lost." Refer to "Five Steps in Praying for the Lost" and "Broaden Your Vision for the Lost" in prayer guide 11, page 216, as you pray.
2. Pray that your pastor will be led to concentrate on your church's outreach, that he will have a burden for the lost, and that he will lead church members to have that same burden.
3. As you have your quiet time, complete the Daily Master Communication Guide in the margin on page 169.

# Day 5
# Praying for Other Christians

In Jesus' prayer in John 17 He was concerned about His followers. Jesus prayed for the spiritual needs of His disciples, those who would be leaders in promoting the kingdom of God. For His disciples He requested (1) unity; (2) preservation and deliverance; and (3) sanctification, or holiness.

## Unity

Jesus prayed that His disciples would be one. The great unity He wanted had been disrupted that night by a quarrel among the disciples about which of them would be the greatest (see Luke 22:24-27). In John 17 Jesus asked for that unity four times from four perspectives.

Read the following verses in the margin on this page. Draw lines from the references to the perspectives Jesus mentioned that should unify His disciples.

---

*Today's Learning Goal*

You will understand and follow Jesus' example by praying for the unity, preservation, and sanctification of Christians.

*"Now I am no more in the world, but these are in the world, and I come to thee. Holy Father, keep through thine own name those whom thou hast given me, that they may be one, as we are" (John 17:11).*

*"That they all may be one; as thou, Father, art in me, and I in thee, that they also may be one in us: that the world may believe that thou hast sent me" (John 17:21).*

*"The glory which thou gavest me I have given them; that they may be one, even as we are one" (John 17:22).*

*"I in them, and thou in me, that they may be made perfect in one; and that the world may know that thou hast sent me, and hast loved them, as thou hast loved me" (John 17:23).*

---

| John 17:11 | They had the same glory. |
| John 17:21 | They had the same relationship to the Father. |
| John 17:22 | They had the same witness to the world. |
| John 17:23 | They had the same name. |

Jesus prayed for the unity of His disciples from the standpoint of the name He had given them (v. 11), from the standpoint of His own perfect unity with the Father (v. 21), from the standpoint of the glory He had given them (v. 22), and from the standpoint of what their unity would witness to the world (v. 23). Something so significant to Jesus ought to be a part of our prayers, too.

 **Reread the four verses in John 17 related to unity (11,21-23) and pray for a spirit of unity in your church.**

## Preservation and Deliverance

Jesus prayed for the preservation and deliverance of believers. Twice in His High Priestly prayer Jesus prayed for the preservation of His disciples.

 **Read the following two verses in the margin. Write similar prayer requests that you might pray for believers today.**

John 17:11: _____

_____

John 17:15: _____

_____

While with them, Jesus kept and guarded His followers. In His absence the disciples would need God's protection. His prayer examples might lead you to pray prayers like these for other Christians: "Father, keep _____ and protect them through Your name." "Father, keep and protect _____ from evil."

 **Read Luke 22:24-34. What occurred among the disciples just before Jesus went to Gethsemane to pray?**

_____

The disciples quarreled among themselves the night before Jesus was to die. He told Simon Peter that Satan had asked permission to tempt them. The pronoun *you* in Luke 22:31 is plural. Satan had asked permission to tempt all of them. The disciples' temporary lapses that night were not a fall. The answer to Jesus' prayer can be read in the pages of Acts. These men, with others, brought many in Jerusalem, Judea, Samaria, and the "uttermost part of the earth" to Christ in the years following. Jesus' prayers for protection and deliverance were answered.

*"Now I am no more in the world, but these are in the world, and I come to thee. Holy Father, keep through thine own name those whom thou hast given me, that they may be one, as we are" (John 17:11).*

*"I pray not that thou shouldest take them out of the world, but that thou shouldest keep them from the evil" (John 17:15).*

*"I beseech you, brethren, for the Lord Jesus Christ's sake, and for the love of the Spirit, that ye strive together with me in your prayers to God for me; that I may be delivered from them that do not believe in Judaea; and that my service which I have for Jerusalem may be accepted of the saints" (Rom. 15:30-31).*

*"… that we may be delivered from unreasonable and wicked men: for all men have not faith" (2 Thess. 3:2).*

*"The Lord make you to increase and abound in love one toward another, and toward all men, even as we do toward you: to the end he may stablish your hearts unblameable in holiness before God, even our Father, at the coming of our Lord Jesus Christ with all his saints" (1 Thess. 3:12-13).*

## Daily Master Communication Guide

SCRIPTURE REFERENCE:

_____

*What God said to me:*

_____

_____

_____

_____

_____

_____

*What I said to God:*

_____

_____

_____

_____

_____

_____

_____

Prayers for deliverance characterized some important prayers of the later New Testament. Paul asked the Roman and the Thessalonian churches to pray for him to be delivered. Read the following Scriptures in the margin on page 171. What did Paul seek deliverance from?

Romans 15:30-31: _____

2 Thessalonians 3:2: _____

Assume that you are praying for a home missionary who is working in a dangerous area of the capital. How could you rephrase these requests into prayers for this missionary?

_____

_____

You could pray for the person's protection and deliverance from those who do not believe and from those who are unreasonable and wicked. Praying for the preservation and deliverance of Christian workers who live and work in difficult areas is an important ministry of intercession.

### Sanctification

Jesus also prayed for the sanctification of His disciples. Jesus prayed that they be sanctified in the truth (see John 17:17). *Sanctified* means *made holy*, and *holy* means *set apart.* This is another grand petition. We are to be set apart in the truth. Since truth is purity, no impurity from the world should be allowed into the hearts of people who have been set apart in this way. In Paul's prayers he also asked for the sanctification of his spiritual children. Read his prayer for the Thessalonians in the margin on page 171 (1 Thess. 3:12-13). Today we should pray for holiness and sanctification in churches and Christians we know.

 On a separate sheet of paper write a prayer request for the sanctification of a Christian brother or sister and bring it with you to the group session.

Write this week's memory verse(s) on a separate sheet of paper.

### Walking in Fellowship with God Today

1. Name to the Lord things you and your immediate family need preservation from, like temptation, worldliness, deception, and misunderstanding. Refer to "Praying for Other Christians" in prayer guide 11, page 216, as you pray.
2. Pray for Christian workers in dangerous areas.
3. Pray for believers in Islamic, Jewish, and Communist countries.
4. Pray for the unity and sanctification of the believers in your church.
5. As you have your quiet time, complete the Daily Master Communication Guide in the margin.

# [week 12]
# PRAYING FOR MISSIONS

## Breakthrough Praying

Don and Vi Orr became Southern Baptists' first music missionaries. Don taught a School of Missions in my church on his first furlough. The accounts of the persecution he experienced in Colombia prompted serious prayer by our church and by my wife and me.

While the Orrs were on their second furlough, I learned that the severe persecution had continued. On the third furlough, however, they shared with me a phenomenal breakthrough that had occurred in Colombia. A civic production of *Messiah* had earned for Colombian Baptists their first mention in a national newspaper. Civic authorities and Catholic leaders were now treating Baptists with considerable respect. My prayers increased with pleas for the effectiveness of their witness. Letters told of large-scale movements of Colombian people toward salvation. Prayer became joyous as I began to see long-delayed answers to earlier prayers.

Shortly before their third furlough a series of physical difficulties began. An old knee injury required fusion of Don's knee. Various back and bone problems also began plaguing him. Later, Vi suffered a series of illnesses. While the external difficulties were largely past, Satan seemed to attack the couple through their bodies. My wife and I prayed much as Don went through 13 major operations. We prayed not only for their physical health and their witness but also for their encouragement.

Don's mighty courage and Vi's persistent dedication paid off far beyond their investment in Colombia. The music-missionary force grew from those two to about one hundred, many of them inspired by the Orrs' pioneering and unparalleled persistence. Somehow the work never grew easy and comfortable for Don and Vi, although they never mentioned anything but the joys and rewards. Various attacks and difficulties plagued their work, their home, or their bodies until the very end of their missionary careers. Much prayer supported them all through their trials. They were destined to be overcomers throughout a long and difficult ministry.

In 1985 Don and Vi Orr completed their service and retired to a long and much-needed rest. New Christians in Colombia, churches strengthened by their hard work, and a whole new kind of work force on the mission field—all of these are tributes to what widespread prayer can accomplish, even at times when the pray-ers were not aware of the full accomplishment God was working through their prayers.

## Key Idea
You can agree with God in His great compassion for all of the world's people and can participate in Christ's mission by supporting missions through intercessory prayer.

## This Week's Learning Goal
You will understand ways to participate in world evangelization through prayer and will demonstrate a commitment to pray knowledgeably for home and world missions needs.

## Verses to Memorize
"The harvest truly is plenteous, but the labourers are few; pray ye therefore the Lord of the harvest, that he will send forth labourers into his harvest" (Matt. 9:37-38).

"Brethren, pray for us, that the word of the Lord may have free course, and be glorified, even as it is with you" (2 Thess. 3:1).

## Related Prayer Guide
Prayer guide 12, "Praying for Missions," page 217

# Day 1
## Calling and Sending

*Today's Learning Goal*
You will understand the process of calling and sending missionaries so that you can pray more effectively for missions.

 Schedule a time to pray with your prayer partner this week. Write the day and time here.

_____

This week your prayers for the world should expand your vision as you try to view the world from God's perspective. God is interested in all the world, in all He created, from the farthest star to the tiniest baby. God's greatest concern is that people everywhere hear about and respond to His Son's death and resurrection for their redemption. You too need that world vision and concern.

### The Sent Ones

*"It is enough for the disciple that he be as his master, and the servant as his lord" (Matt. 10:25).*

*"He that heareth you heareth me; and he that despiseth you despiseth me; and he that despiseth me despiseth him that sent me" (Luke 10:16).*

Focus your attention first on missionaries, the sent ones. The word *mission* comes from a Latin word that means *to send*, and the word *apostle* comes from a Greek word meaning *one sent*. Jesus was the first great Sent One (see Heb. 3:1). When He designated His disciples as apostles, He implied that they would also be sent ones (see Luke 6:13). Mark, in fact, wrote that "he ordained twelve … that he might send them forth to preach" (Mark 3:14). Paul called himself an apostle; today he is considered the first Christian missionary.

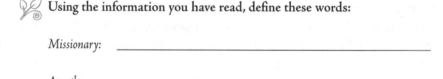 Using the information you have read, define these words:

Missionary: _____

Apostle: _____

*"As thou hast sent me into the world, even so have I also sent them into the world" (John 17:18).*

*"Then said Jesus to them again, Peace be unto you: as my Father hath sent me, even so send I you" (John 20:21).*

*"Jesus came and spake unto them, saying, All power is given unto me in heaven and in earth. Go ye therefore, and teach all nations, baptizing them in the name of the Father, and of the Son, and of the Holy Ghost: teaching them to observe all things whatsoever I have commanded you: and, lo, I am with you alway, even unto the end of the world. Amen" (Matt. 28:18-20).*

Jesus, the great Sent One, also sent others. He sent the twelve through Galilee to preach the good news of the Kingdom (see Matt. 10:5). Later in Perea He sent 70 more to go ahead of Him and prepare the way for His coming (see Luke 10:1). Their sending was very similar to His own. Read in the margin His words to the twelve (Matt. 10:25). He had been sent; now He was sending them. They were to be like Him, just as they were sent by Him. Read in the margin what He told the 70 (Luke 10:16). Being sent identifies those sent with the sender.

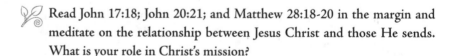 Read John 17:18; John 20:21; and Matthew 28:18-20 in the margin and meditate on the relationship between Jesus Christ and those He sends. What is your role in Christ's mission?

_____

In one sense, all Christians are apostles or missionaries—sent ones—sent out by the great Sent One. All Christians become part of Christ's mission effort in the world. Your task as a Christian is to discover the part of that mission He intends for you to do and where you are to do it.

This week as we consider praying for missionaries, keep in mind two concepts. First, since we are all called to be involved in Christ's mission, we are part of His kingdom's advance by praying for all Christians. Second, some people sense a special calling to vocational service as a missionary. Missionaries are persons sent to other areas or countries to perform special tasks in God's kingdom work.

## Pray for Sending

 Read Matthew 9:35-38 in the margin. Jesus was speaking to the disciples, but we too should follow this command. What did Jesus command?

_____

Jesus issued a call to pray for workers for God's harvest. Multitudes of people need to be led to the Good Shepherd, Jesus Christ. We will not all serve God as career missionaries, but through prayer every Christian can be a significant part of the missionary enterprise.

Constantly sensitive to the needs of people for God, Jesus often used the picture of a harvest to describe them. Read John 4:35 in the margin. Jesus saw ripe fields of needy people as a call to prayer to the Lord of the harvest; should not we? What do we ask the Lord of the harvest for? Pray—

+ for the youth and adults of your church to be sensitive to the call of the Holy Spirit to missionary service;
+ for your children to be called into the harvest;
+ for college and seminary students to learn God's specific plans for their lives;
+ for evangelists and pastors God may call to places of greater need;
+ about your involvement in the harvest.

 Stop and pray for God to call forth laborers. Pray for specific individuals the Lord may bring to mind. Write their names in the margin.

## The Senders

The church became a sending agency early in its history. God and the church are the senders of missionaries. In the Bible, as is the case today, missionaries were sent forth by the Holy Spirit and by a group of believers who affirmed that the Spirit had called those to be sent.

 Read in the margin the account of a "missionary commissioning service" in Acts 13:1-4. What role did each of the following have in this event?

Prophets and teachers: _____

Saul and Barnabas: _____

The church at Antioch: _____

The Holy Spirit: _____

"Jesus went about all the cities and villages, teaching in their synagogues, and preaching the gospel of the kingdom, and healing every sickness and every disease among the people. But when he saw the multitudes, he was moved with compassion on them, because they fainted, and were scattered abroad, as sheep having no shepherd. Then saith he unto his disciples, The harvest truly is plenteous, but the labourers are few; pray ye therefore the Lord of the harvest, that he will send forth labourers into his harvest" (Matt. 9:35-38).

"Say not ye, There are yet four months, and then cometh harvest? Behold, I say unto you, Lift up your eyes, and look on the fields; for they are white already to harvest" (John 4:35).

"There were in the church that was at Antioch certain prophets and teachers; as Barnabas, and Simeon that was called Niger, and Lucius of Cyrene, and Manaen, which had been brought up with Herod the tetrarch, and Saul. As they ministered to the Lord, and fasted, the Holy Ghost said, Separate me Barnabas and Saul for the work whereunto I have called them. And when they had fasted and prayed, and laid their hands on them, they sent them away. So they, being sent forth by the Holy Ghost, departed unto Seleucia; and from thence they sailed to Cyprus" (Acts 13:1-4).

## Daily Master Communication Guide

SCRIPTURE REFERENCE:

_____

_____

### What God said to me:

_____

_____

_____

_____

_____

_____

### What I said to God:

_____

_____

_____

_____

_____

_____

This is an interesting and important scene. Some suggest that this was the beginning of the Christian missionary movement. Five men served as prophets and teachers—leaders—in the church at Antioch. We do not know for sure whether the whole church was ministering to the Lord and fasting or if only the five leaders were meeting together. We do know that the Holy Spirit asked that the church set apart Saul (Paul) and Barnabas for mission service. The language of Acts 13: 2-3 implies that Saul and Barnabas may have felt the missionary call first. Then in prayer the church at Antioch responded and sent them on their way.

What two parties were involved in appointing and sending out these missionaries?

_____

What part did prayer have in sending out these first missionaries from Antioch?

_____

The Holy Spirit called out His servants during a prayer meeting. The church sent out the first missionaries with prayer. Prayer was a responsibility and privilege of the sending church.

Has the Holy Spirit called missionaries to go out from your church? ❑ Yes ❑ No If so, how and when do you and your church family pray for these?

_____

Stop and pray that your church will be concerned about calling out and sending missionaries and that it will increase prayer for them. What can you do to influence this necessity?

_____

### Walking in Fellowship with God Today

1. Think about the harvest and the need for laborers. When you come into contact with people at work, at school, or during leisure time, recall that the fields are ready for harvest. As you read the newspaper or watch the news, think about the masses of people who need to know Christ. Pray throughout the day that God will call forth a large work force to bring in the harvest. Refer to "Praying for Laborers" in prayer guide 12, "Praying for Missions," on page 217 as you pray.

2. As you have your quiet time, complete the Daily Master Communication Guide in the margin.

# Day 2
## Paul's *A* to *F* Prayer Requests

**Six Prayer Requests for Missionaries**

Paul was a first-century missionary. While he was on his mission field starting new churches, preaching, and teaching, he had special needs for which he desired prayer. In his letters to various churches he requested prayer for certain needs.

 Read each of the following verses in the margin to find the prayer Paul requested for himself. Beside each reference write in your own words what Paul wanted people to pray for.

1. Romans 15:31a: _____

2. Romans 15:31b: _____

3. Ephesians 6:19: _____

4. Colossians 4:2-3: _____

5. Colossians 4:4: _____

6. 2 Thessalonians 3:1: _____

Paul requested prayer: 1. that he be delivered from unbelievers, 2. that his service be accepted by the saints, 3. that he speak boldly to make the gospel known, 4. that opportunities be opened for witnessing, 5. that he make the message clear and easy to understand, and 6. that the Word of the Lord have free course and be glorified.

 Below are six key words that relate to Paul's requests. They can help you remember six things to pray for when interceding for missionaries and others who work as Paul did. See if you can pair one of these key words with each request above. Write the number of the request beside the key word below that best matches it.

_____ Acceptance by coworkers—other believers

_____ Boldness in witnessing

_____ Clarity in communicating

_____ Deliverance from evil

_____ Extension of the ministry

_____ Fruitfulness in spiritual endeavors

Turn to prayer guide 12, page 217, to check your answers. Try to memorize Paul's requests from *A* to *F.* Use these requests when you pray for missionaries, evangelists, pastors, and other Christian workers.

Today let's take a closer look at four of these requests.

*Today's Learning Goal*

You will understand the content of prayers Paul requested for himself and will use those requests to pray for missionaries.

*"… that I may be delivered from them that do not believe in Judaea; and that my service which I have for Jerusalem may be accepted of the saints" (Rom. 15:31).*

*"… for me, that utterance may be given unto me, that I may open my mouth boldly, to make known the mystery of the gospel" (Eph. 6:19).*

*"Continue in prayer, and watch in the same with thanksgiving; withal praying also for us, that God would open unto us a door of utterance, to speak the mystery of Christ, for which I am also in bonds" (Col. 4:2-3).*

*"… that I may make it manifest, as I ought to speak" (Col. 4:4).*

*"Brethren, pray for us, that the word of the Lord may have free course, and be glorified, even as it is with you" (2 Thess. 3:1).*

*"… for me, that utterance may be given unto me, that I may open my mouth boldly, to make known the mystery of the gospel, for which I am an ambassador in bonds: that therein I may speak boldly, as I ought to speak" (Eph. 6:19-20).*

## Daily Master Communication Guide

SCRIPTURE REFERENCE:

_____

_____

### What God said to me:

_____

_____

_____

_____

_____

_____

### What I said to God:

_____

_____

_____

_____

_____

_____

### Acceptance

Paul wanted to be accepted by the saints in Jerusalem. All Christians are saints, or holy ones, for each has been sanctified (see Heb. 10:10). Christian workers today need prayer that they will be received well by the believers already in the place where they minister.

 **Church planters often face some of their greatest resistance from existing churches. Choose someone you are familiar with who is starting a new church and pray for an open door in that work.**

### Boldness

Read in the margin on page 177 Paul's request of the Ephesian church in Ephesians 6:19-20. Speaking boldly in a second language, in a strange culture, and in threatening circumstances is not easy. Paul knew that he needed to ask for prayer.

Simon Peter also knew that he needed to ask for prayer. After the Sanhedrin commanded the apostles "not to speak at all nor teach in the name of Jesus" (Acts 4:18), the apostles and the church prayed, "Now, Lord, behold their threatenings: and grant unto thy servants, that with all boldness they may speak thy word" (Acts 4:29). The answer to this prayer can be the answer for any time in Christian history: "When they had prayed, the place was shaken where they were assembled together; and they were all filled with the Holy Ghost and they spake the word of God with boldness" (Acts 4:31). The bold proclamation was an answer to prayer that transformed Jerusalem.

Many churches are becoming more and more involved in volunteer missions efforts away from their hometowns. The need for such involvement and support is great. Some Christians, however, seem to be more bold in their witness away from home than in their own communities.

 **Pray for the bold witness of your church's members in local missions efforts. What area of your community needs an especially bold witness?**

_____

**Read again Ephesians 6:19 on page 177. Pray for your own boldness.**

### Extension

You have probably prayed often for missionaries and for missions advance. Your prayers need to include requests for the spiritual battles missionaries are fighting. Paul's pleas help us determine how to pray. He requested the Colossian Christians to "continue in prayer; … withal praying also for us, that God would open unto us a door of utterance" (Col. 4:2-3). The first thing a missionary needs is an open door. Many things may block that door—resistant attitudes; legal maneuvering; visa renewals; or technical difficulties, such as conflicts in travel plans. One thing we can infer from Paul's request is that open doors depend largely on prayer.

 **Select a missionary you know or a country in which missions work is being carried out. Stop and pray for doors to open in that work.**

## Fruitfulness

Paul asked the church at Thessalonica to "pray for us, that the word of the Lord may have free course, and be glorified, even as it is with you" (2 Thess. 3:1). A missionary goes to spread the gospel. This can be effective only through the power and work of the Holy Spirit. We have the privilege to pray for the Holy Spirit to prepare the way for the reception of His Word, to provide channels and means for its proclamation, and to empower those proclaiming the Word. The very speed at which the word spreads depends in large measure on our prayers.

*We have the privilege to pray for the Holy Spirit to prepare the way for the reception of His Word, to provide channels and means for its proclamation, and to empower those proclaiming the Word.*

International missionaries are starting new churches at an unprecedented rate. Pray for the fruitfulness of their work.

### Walking in Fellowship with God Today

As you pray today, refer to "Paul's *A* to *F* Prayer Requests" in prayer guide 12, page 217. As you repeatedly pray Paul's prayer requests every day this week, learn them well enough that you can stop referring to the list in prayer guide 12.

1. Pray all six of Paul's prayer requests for your pastor.
2. Choose a country and pray Paul's prayer requests for all of the missionaries and national leaders who work there. Pray for all of the Christians in that country. For example: Pray for the Christians in Brazil that "the word of the Lord may have free course and be glorified."
3. Pray Paul's prayer requests for two home missionaries you know or for the missionaries in two states you select.
4. As you have your quiet time, complete the Daily Master Communication Guide in the margin on page 178.

# Day 3
# Four Missions Imperatives

---

### MISSIONS IMPERATIVES
1. All people need the salvation God has provided.
2. God wants all people to repent and be saved.
3. God's plan requires people to go and preach the gospel to all nations.
4. All humankind must acclaim the glory of God.

### PRAYERS BASED ON MISSIONS IMPERATIVES
1. Pray that the lost will hear the gospel.
2. Pray that the lost will repent and believe.
3. Pray that missionaries will go.
4. Pray that God will be glorified.

---

*Today's Learning Goal*
You will understand four missions imperatives and will demonstrate persistence in praying for God's kingdom to come on earth.

## Imperative 1: All People Need the Salvation God Has Provided

The realization of the ancient Jewish longing for all nations to know God was

*"Repentance and remission of sins should be preached in his name among all nations, beginning at Jerusalem" (Luke 24:47).*

*"Ye shall be witnesses unto me both in Jerusalem, and in all Judea, and in Samaria, and unto the uttermost part of the earth" (Acts 1:8).*

*"I will have mercy upon her that had not obtained mercy; and I will say to them which were not my people, Thou art my people; and they shall say, Thou art my God" (Hos. 2:23).*

*"Be it known therefore unto you, that the salvation of God is sent unto the Gentiles, and that they will hear it" (Acts 28:28).*

*"Declare his glory among the heathen, his wonders among all people" (Ps. 96:3).*

*"They shall speak of the glory of thy kingdom, and talk of thy power; to make known to the sons of men his mighty acts, and the glorious majesty of his kingdom" (Ps. 145:11-12).*

made fully possible in the work of Jesus. With His redemptive work finished, the awesome need of all people for salvation was met at long last. Salvation was now universally available. Read in Luke 24:47, in the margin, what Jesus told His disciples as He neared the time of His departure from the earth. Now read His words to the disciples just before He ascended (Acts 1:8 in the margin). The disciples bore witness to Jesus' death and resurrection.

What is the missionary message for which we pray for all to hear? Jesus told Paul that He was to go to the Gentiles "to open their eyes, and to turn them from darkness to light, and from the power of Satan unto God, that they may receive forgiveness of sins, and inheritance among them which are sanctified by faith that is in me" (Acts 26:18). We might quote this commission when we pray for our missionaries today. Our prayer must be that the gospel will reach all people.

 Why do you think lost people need the salvation God has to offer? Check all that apply.
❑ Sinful people will suffer eternally in hell without it.
❑ Lost people live their lives in spiritual darkness.
❑ Lost people live in bondage to sin and Satan's power.
❑ People need to find forgiveness of sin and cleansing of the heavy load of guilt they carry.

Sometimes we have a tendency to forget about the terrible destiny that awaits those who are "dead in trespasses and sins" (Eph. 2:1). Each reason above is a good reason people need God's salvation. If you cannot sincerely pray for the lost to be saved, then you may need to pray first for God to reveal clearly to you the destiny of those without Christ. Pray for God to give you compassion for the lost.

 Stop and pray that the lost will hear the gospel.

### Imperative 2: God Wants All People to Repent and Be Saved

This is why the way of redemption was provided. God yearns for a people for Himself, and He wants all people to claim Him as their God. Read in the margin the Lord's words in Hosea 2:23. The last Jewish rejection of Christ by the Roman Jews, recorded in the Book of Acts, led to Paul's announcement in Acts 28:28. Read that verse in the margin. God's desire is a people for Himself. He is always reaching out for them. Missionaries, God's messengers, are working to fulfill that desire of the Lord, ever reaching farther and farther "to the uttermost part of the earth" (Acts 1:8). We must pray for God's desire that all will come to Jesus in repentance and faith.

Stop and pray that the lost will repent and believe.

### Imperative 3: God's Plan Requires People to Go and Preach the Gospel to All Nations

The progression of God's plan can be carried out only as missionaries and others preach Christ to all nations. In His great discourse on the end times Jesus prophesied, "This gospel of the kingdom shall be preached in all the world for a witness unto all nations; and then shall the end come" (Matt. 24:14). Although the Bible has been translated into the major languages of the world, it still does not exist in thousands of dialects and languages. The majority of the world's peoples are not Christians. God's plan requires that means be provided by which they can come to Him.

By nations Jesus most likely did not mean centralized governments. He was probably referring to cultural groups, or peoples. Of the 13,975 ethno-linguistic peoples in the world today, about 7,460 peoples are unreached. These groups make up more than half of the global population. Among these unreached groups, 2,900 ethno-linguistic peoples have little or no access to the gospel. Known as World A peoples, these groups compose 30 percent of the global population. Our Christian mission efforts must expand at a much more rapid rate if millions of lost people are to find Christ before they die. All Christians must pray for missionaries to carry the gospel to all nations.

 Stop and pray that missionaries will go. You may want to pray specifically for the following.
- Church planters who can help start new churches and disciple believers
- Evangelists who can preach the gospel
- Teachers who can help train others to spread the gospel
- Christian groups in other cultures and nations who can develop and send missionaries to their own people around the world
- Bible translators who can help provide the Bible in a language people can read and understand

## Imperative 4: All Humankind Must Acclaim the Glory of God

Often the Old Testament saints were zealous for other nations to recognize the glory of the only God. Read the psalms in the margin on page 180. All who know God want others to know Him. This is a missionary purpose.

In some parts of the world today, stone, wooden, or metal idols are glorified. In much of the Western world the idols are wealth, power, and position. The Jewish mind characteristically despised any false idol (see Isa. 44:9-20; Hab. 2:19). Likewise, Christians want to say with Elijah, "If the Lord be God, follow him; but if Baal, then follow him" (1 Kings 18:21). Our instinctive spiritual nature wants to hear all humankind cry, as did the Israelites, "The Lord, he is the God; the Lord, he is the God" (1 Kings 18:39). We must pray for God's peculiar and private glory, as shown in Jesus Christ, to be recognized and praised in all parts of His world.

Have you been acknowledging God's glory as a basis for your prayers (see week 1)? One thing that will happen when you pray is that God may call or lead you to be personally and actively involved in answer to the prayer. For instance:
- You pray that the lost will hear the gospel, and God leads you to contribute money to a Bible society, the Gideons, or a Bible-translation organization.
- You pray that the lost will repent and believe, and God leads you to share Christ with a lost neighbor or coworker.
- You pray that missionaries will go, and God leads you to volunteer for a mission trip that will conduct evangelistic crusades in a foreign country.

*Daily Master Communication Guide*

SCRIPTURE REFERENCE:

_____

*What God said to me:*

_____

_____

_____

_____

_____

_____

_____

*What I said to God:*

_____

_____

_____

_____

_____

_____

_____

• You pray that God will be glorified, and He gives you an opportunity to help a new Christian learn ways to exalt and magnify his or her newfound Lord.

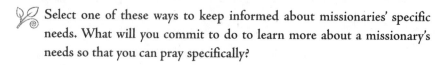 Does God want you to do something specific in answer to these four prayers or in fulfillment of the missions imperatives? Pray about what He might lead you to do personally. Take a few minutes to describe to Him your willingness to obey.

## Walking in Fellowship with God Today

1. Refer to "Prayers Based on Missions Imperatives" in prayer guide 12, page 217. Today persistently pray the four prayers listed. Focus special attention on one home-mission area and one continent or country.
2. As you have your quiet time, complete the Daily Master Communication Guide in the margin on page 181.

# Day 4
# Missionary Needs

*Today's Learning Goal*
You will understand some personal and work needs of missionaries and will demonstrate sensitivity to those needs.

## Get to Know Missionaries
The best way to pray for a missionary's needs is to pray for specific needs of which you are aware. Now that you have demonstrated your willingness to pray for missions, you may want to stay informed about specific missionaries. Here are some ways you can do that.

• Attend missions conferences at which missionaries will speak. Take notes about their work and their expressed or implied needs.
• Adopt a missionary family. Study about its place of service. Keep in touch with the family through letters, cards, and maybe even an occasional phone call. Discover ways you can perform real ministries to the family. However, do not consume its valuable time by just asking for information.
• Many missionaries have a newsletter they mail to friends and interested supporters. Get on the mailing list, but also find out how you can help share the expense of the newsletter.
• Read books and magazine articles about contemporary missionaries.[1] Keep a prayer list for particular missionaries you learn about.
• Read newspapers (both secular and church-related) and watch for news items about missionaries. List needs on your prayer list for which you can pray.

Select one of these ways to keep informed about missionaries' specific needs. What will you commit to do to learn more about a missionary's needs so that you can pray specifically?

## Personal Needs

Without clear information from the field, you can only imagine what missionaries need. The categories in today's lesson are not prayer requests but areas of need from which you can form more specific prayer requests.

> ### PERSONAL NEEDS
> 1. Language and culture
> 2. Health and safety
> 3. Children and aging parents
> 4. Spiritual growth and emotional well-being

Missionaries have personal needs that, if not met, may impede their work. One of the first needs is to learn to communicate effectively in another language. Along with language skills, missionaries communicate more effectively if they learn the culture of their new country. Many missionaries have found prayer to be the only way they can master these difficulties. Sometimes their living conditions are difficult, if not hazardous. They need prayer for what they eat. They need to be able to travel, and often transportation is difficult at best. Missionaries would be grateful if we prayed for an adequate home in which they could live. The various frustrations and disappointments missionaries must grapple with provide an endless list. Often they must bear their burdens without other human help. Your prayers are the significant provision God has made on earth to help meet all of their needs.

*Your prayers are the significant provision God has made on earth to help meet missionaries' needs.*

 Imagine that you have accepted an appointment as a missionary to a particular country. Try to imagine what you would face as a missionary in that country. In each category below, write concerns you might face.

Language and culture: _____

_____

Health and safety: _____

_____

Children and aging parents: _____

_____

Spiritual growth and emotional well-being: _____

_____

**If you were a missionary in this country, which need do you think would be of greatest concern to you?**

_____

## Daily Master Communication Guide

SCRIPTURE REFERENCE:

_____

_____

*What God said to me:*

_____

_____

_____

_____

_____

_____

_____

*What I said to God:*

_____

_____

_____

_____

_____

_____

_____

### Work Needs

Prayer for missionaries' work is needed in order to get the gospel to the lost, carrying out Jesus' Great Commission. Missionaries and national believers seek to conquer territory controlled by Satan as they build God's kingdom. Their victories require our prayers. Here are some of their work needs:

---

#### WORK NEEDS

1. Cooperative relationships with nationals
2. Professional skills (such as preacher, doctor, agriculturist, accountant, and so forth)
3. Success in witnessing and church planting
4. Effectiveness in discipling believers and nurturing churches

---

 Which general need in the box above relates to each specific need listed below? Write the number of the general need on the line beside each item.

_____ a. A missionary doctor needs to pass his medical exams, written in the Portuguese language, before he can practice medicine.

_____ b. Fifty new converts await help in the villages the missionary visits.

_____ c. A chapel wants to organize into a church this spring.

_____ d. The missionary has been asked to write a book for pastors to use in a discipleship group for new Christians.

_____ e. The missionary is training witnessing teams to visit the lost.

_____ f. National leaders are meeting with the missionary to set priorities for using financial resources for the coming year.

Answers: a. 2, b. 4, c. 3 and/or 4, d. 4, e. 3, f. 1.

### Pray for Missionaries

Many people pray for missionaries on their birthdays. Missionaries depend on intercessory prayers on this special day. Some even save major decisions until this day, because they know many people will be praying. A prayer calendar may be available from your international-missions organization.[2]

 Walking in Fellowship with God Today

1. Read Philippians 4:19 and consider its implications for missionaries. Claim this promise for missionaries.
2. Practice praying for missionaries' needs today. Use "Personal Needs" and "Work Needs" in prayer guide 12, page 217, to stimulate your thoughts. If you know a missionary personally, pray for him or her by name.
3. As you have your quiet time, complete the Daily Master Communication Guide in the margin.

---

[1] An excellent missions magazine is *The Commission*. Write to the International Mission Board of the Southern Baptist Convention; P.O. Box 6767; Richmond, VA 23230-0767; or call 1-800-866-3621.

[2] A missionary prayer calendar is included in *Open Windows*, a quarterly devotional guide. To order WRITE LifeWay Church Resources Customer Service, 127 Ninth Avenue, North, Nashville, TN 37234-0113; FAX (615) 251-5933; PHONE 1-800-458-2772; EMAIL to CustomerService@lifeway.com; or order ONLINE at *www.lifeway.com*.

# Day 5
## Praying for the World

### A Prayer for the World

The Bible is a missionary book from beginning to end. God sent Jonah to pagan Nineveh to proclaim repentance (see Jonah 1:2). The universal reign of the Lord is a favorite theme throughout the Old Testament (see Ps. 22:27; 82:8; 86:9; Isa. 66:23; Hab. 2:14). The universal reign of Jesus will be accomplished only through sending. The psalmist wanted all the earth to fear and praise the one true God. His prayer in Psalm 67 is appropriate for you to pray for the world.

 Read Psalm 67 in the margin and circle the words that express the psalmist's desire for all nations of the earth to know God.

Stop and pray this prayer for all of the nations of the world.

### Prayer Concerns for the World

 As you read this section, underline words and phrases that could be prayer concerns for the nations of the world.

When God views the world, He sees the total picture—the continuing political, economic, social, and religious situations, as well as the changing upheavals of war, revolution, floods, droughts, famines, and similar disasters. We too should be aware of current happenings and should care about these conditions. As much as possible, our prayers should encompass the world. We should pray for changes in nations that have continuing problems, as well as those in crisis situations.

A country's political, social, and economic climate affects the spread of the gospel. Prayers are needed in overcoming continuing problems such as poverty and oppression, which hinder the spread of the gospel and the readiness of people to hear the gospel.

God cares about all of the individuals in a country—those in power, the oppressed, those who are hurting, those who are healing hurts, the rich, the poor, the young, the old, Christians, and non-Christians. We must train ourselves to automatically pray when we hear troubling news about another land.

Information about the situation in God's world comes to us through many channels: radio, television, the Internet, newspapers, movies, books, and magazines. The public media constantly provide us information we should pray about.

The Lord of the harvest may allow news to come our way simply to stimulate our prayer for missions. Often we hear of a government that has started a process to evict missionaries from their country. In other cases, red tape keeps missionaries from obtaining or renewing visas. Various kinds of terrorist groups at times threaten missionaries. The news media alert us to critical situations.

Some Christians feel called to pray for the heads of state in many nations. They ask for their conversions and for God to work through these world leaders to carry out His will in the world. God may impress on you that prayer ministry.

*Today's Learning Goal*
You will recognize God's concern for all people of the world to be saved, and you will demonstrate your agreement with Him by praying for worldwide missions concerns.

*God be merciful unto us, and*
*bless us,*
*and cause His face to shine upon us;*
*That Thy way may be known upon earth,*
*thy saving health among all nations.*
*Let the people praise thee, O God;*
*let all the people praise thee.*
*O let the nations be glad and sing for joy:*
*for thou shalt judge the people righteously,*
*and govern the nations upon earth.*
*Let the peoples praise thee, O God;*
*let all the people praise thee.*
*Then shall the earth yield her increase;*
*and God, even our own God, shall bless us.*
*God shall bless us;*
*and all the ends of the earth shall fear him"* (Ps. 67).

## Daily Master Communication Guide

SCRIPTURE REFERENCE:

_____

_____

### What God said to me:

_____

_____

_____

_____

_____

_____

### What I said to God:

_____

_____

_____

_____

_____

_____

List some of the prayer concerns you underlined.

_____

_____

_____

_____

_____

_____

Become acquainted with your denomination's missions agencies. Try to secure publications of missions agencies. See prayer guide 12 on page 217 for the phone numbers of North American and international missions prayerlines.

Praying for missions functions or ministries is another way to organize prayer for the world. You may pray for the following in a country, in a continent, or worldwide, using a day of the week for each.

---

### MISSIONS FUNCTIONS/MINISTRIES

Day 1: Church development, spiritual awakening, and discipling

Day 2: Church planting, evangelism, and partnership evangelism

Day 3: Leadership training (seminaries, Bible and lay institutes, extension programs)

Day 4: Hospitals, clinics, public health

Day 5: Publication work and literature distribution

Day 6: Mass media (television, radio, films)

Day 7: Student evangelism and youth work

---

Write this week's memory verse(s) on a separate sheet of paper.

### Walking in Fellowship with God Today

1. Turn to "Pray Around the World in a Week" on page 223. Take time to pray around the world today.
2. Recall pictures you have seen of international cities and people. Read Psalm 67 again in prayer guide 12 on page 217 as your prayer. Picture these cities and people knowing the true God.
3. Review the list of prayer concerns you completed in today's lesson and pray for those concerns.
4. As you have your quiet time, complete the Daily Master Communication Guide in the margin.

# ESTABLISHING A MINISTRY OF PRAYER

## New Every Morning

Like many Christians, I was reared in a devout home, went to Christian camps, attended a Christian college, and saw dozens of "revivals." But no one ever told me that revival implies renewal.

In the summer of 1956 I began work on a Ph.D. Early academic success was a thrill, especially when some professors made glowing predictions about a career as a musicologist. During the fall of that year I began to drift toward a new orientation in life: career and success were my goals. I never stopped attending church or actively participating in church, but deep inside I was serving a false god—self.

A student brought me a German Bible and explained that it was of no use to him. I was excited; I enjoyed languages. A few days later I was up early to prepare a rather technical lecture. The lecture proved to be much easier than I had anticipated. It was ready quickly, so I decided to practice German with the new Bible. I chose the first chapter of John. I began reading casually, but the words, so familiar in English but electrifying in another language, captured me. The glory, the magnificence of the person of Christ, was evident in a dimension I had somehow never quite perceived. Day after day I pursued the majesty of John's picture of Christ, with hunger mounting all the time. I was so captivated by the end of it that I decided to read through the entire Bible.

On the morning I read Exodus 3, however, something new happened to me. In the dark of the morning I read about Moses' curious approach to the burning but unburnt bush. The Lord's words were surely for me that morning: "Put off thy shoes from off thy feet, for the place whereon thou standest is holy ground" (v. 5). Sensing that I was in the presence of infinite holiness, I understood quite well how Moses must have felt ("Moses hid his face; for he was afraid to look upon God," v. 6). I knelt. The wonderful, crushing burden of infinite holiness was more than I could bear. Weeping, I faced the choice I had made of my own selfish ends. After that I committed my life to the unconditional lordship of Christ.

A career died that morning; self died, too. Everything was new! A new spring was in my step—new life! New response was in my witness—new power! A new song was in my heart—new joy! That November morning was many years ago. God's faithfulness grew my quiet time from 30 minutes to two or more hours. Oh, the beauty and glory of His Word! I cannot seem to get enough! Each month, each year is new and lovelier than the last.

*New* is one of the Bible's most beautiful words. Even God's compassions are "new every morning" (Lam. 3:23), and I get up in the morning excited about that! The word *growth* implies newness—increasing new life. Daily renewal and constant newness are the normal life for a growing Christian.

### Key Idea
Intercessory prayer is a ministry that unleashes God's power to bring about His Kingdom goals in this world.

### This Week's Learning Goal
You will understand ways individuals and churches can conduct ministries of intercessory prayer, and you will determine how God wants you to participate in the ministry of intercession.

### Verses to Memorize
"The eyes of the Lord run to and fro throughout the whole earth, to shew himself strong in the behalf of them whose heart is perfect toward him" (2 Chron. 16:9).

"Now unto him that is able to do exceeding abundantly above all that we ask or think, according to the power that worketh in us, unto him be glory in the church by Christ Jesus throughout all ages, world without end" (Eph. 3:20-21).

# Day 1
## Your Personal Prayer Ministry

*Today's Learning Goal*
You will understand ways you can develop and enrich your personal ministry of intercessory prayer, and you will demonstrate constancy in prayer.

*"It came to pass in the month Nisan, in the twentieth year of Artaxerxes the king, that wine was before him: and I took up the wine, and gave it unto the king. Now I had not been before time sad in his presence. Wherefore the king said unto me, Why is thy countenance sad, seeing thou art not sick? This is nothing else but sorrow of heart. Then I was very sore afraid, and said unto the king, Let the king live for ever: why should not my countenance be sad, when the city, the place of my fathers' sepulchres, lieth waste, and the gates thereof are consumed with fire? Then the king said unto me, For what dost thou make request? So I prayed to the God of heaven. And I said unto the king, If it please the king, and if thy servant have found favour in thy sight, that thou wouldest send me unto Judah, unto the city of my fathers' sepulchres, that I may build it. And the king said unto me, (the queen also sitting by him,) For how long shall thy journey be? and when wilt thou return? So it pleased the king to send me; and I set him a time" (Neh. 2:1-6).*

 Schedule a time to pray with your prayer partner this week. Write the day and time here.

_____

### Prayer Warriors

The history of the church shows that only a few accept the high calling of a continuous and arduous ministry of intercessory prayer. We usually call these extraordinary pray-ers prayer warriors. Prayer is the major ministry in their lives. Their work is just as important in the body of Christ as any other ministry.

Not all who experience *Disciple's Prayer Life* are called to become prayer warriors. All who study *Disciple's Prayer Life*, however, are equipped to be involved in a ministry of prayer. You need to seek the Lord's guidance about the extent to which He wants you involved in a ministry of prayer. You will most certainly want to continue developing your personal and private ministry of prayer. You may also sense God calling you to involvement in your church's prayer ministry. Today we will examine several concepts that will help enrich your personal ministry.

### Pray Without Ceasing

 As you read the following paragraphs, underline ways you can better fulfill the command "Pray without ceasing" (1 Thess. 5:17).

Praying without ceasing has two dimensions. First, your prayers should be regular and continuous, as stated in "Ask While Abiding in Christ" in week 9. Daniel prayed three times every day (see Dan. 6:10). The members of the church in the Book of Acts "continued stedfastly in … prayers" (Acts 2:42). Paul wrote Timothy, "I have remembrance of thee in my prayers night and day" (2 Tim. 1:3).

By this time you have built into your life a regular, daily quiet time. You practice thanksgiving at mealtime. Brief periods of prayer can also be added at other times of the day.

 For an example of a brief prayer in a tense situation, read Nehemiah 2:1-6 in the margin. When and why did Nehemiah pray?

_____

_____

Nehemiah was burdened by the state of affairs of the remnant of people living in Jerusalem. He prayed to God in detail (see Neh. 1:5-11). His private praying prepared him for continuing in a state of prayer. When the king gave Nehemiah an invitation to make a request, he "prayed to the God of heaven" (Neh. 2:4) and made his request. That had to be a brief prayer. Nehemiah wanted God's will accomplished by the king's response. Nehemiah was a man who prayed without ceasing.

Praying without ceasing also indicates the constant attitude of relating everything in your life to God every hour of the day. Such constancy is one way to recognize God in every department of your life and in every relationship you have. Paul said that he prayed unceasingly for the Roman and the Colossian churches (see Rom. 1:9; Col. 1:9). Anything in your environment can prompt you to acknowledge God. A beautiful landscape calls for praise; God is its Creator. Any small or large blessing should prompt thanksgiving; an attitude of gratitude recognizes God as the source of all good gifts. Sin should bring forth immediate confession. Need in your life should cause you to turn to God immediately.

Your goal is that praying without ceasing will become a habit of maintaining constant awareness of God's presence and of acknowledging that presence by a habit of uninterrupted prayer. Read Proverbs 3:6 in the margin. Every blessing all day long is from Him. Every need is appropriate for His attention. Every demonstration of His qualities deserves praise. Developing this kind of unceasing contact with God may require considerable concentration, but the joy of His presence is the reward of simple obedience to the command to pray without ceasing.

*"In all thy ways acknowledge him"* (Prov. 3:6).

 **List ways you can better follow the command "Pray without ceasing."**

_____

_____

## Fasting and Praying

A discipline that has faded from special prayer efforts but has proved effective in the past is fasting. Jesus practiced fasting (see Matt. 4:2), as did Moses (see Ex. 34:28). Read Matthew 6:16-18 in the margin. Obviously, Jesus assumed that His followers would fast occasionally.

You too may choose to fast from time to time. The value of fasting lies in the concentration of your will on God. In fasting, the will says no to bodily appetites. It affirms that the highest and most worthwhile desires are not physical but spiritual. The will deliberately takes leave of the outer world and directs the mind to God alone. That is why fasting and praying go together.

Fasting is best undertaken when you are free from duties and other cares and can concentrate on prayer. Often it is wise to be alone. Both Moses and Jesus were alone when they fasted. Fasting may be done jointly with a spouse or friend(s), especially if the prayer accompanying it is for a special concern to all involved. Fasting may be undertaken for many kinds of special prayer efforts, such as for a revival, for a need, or simply for the discipline of concentrating on God.

A fast may be partial or complete. A partial fast, for example, may include drinking water or fruit juices but avoiding solid food. A fast may be for any length of time and may include one missed meal or many. Most fasts of more than one meal should begin with the evening meal. Fasting denies the body blood sugar and should not be undertaken if you have any body abnormality or illness, especially diabetes or hypoglycemia. To fast when you will be involved in heavy physical or mental work is not wise, either.

*"When ye fast, be not, as the hypocrites, of a sad countenance: for they disfigure their faces, that they may appear unto men to fast. Verily I say unto you, They have their reward. But thou, when thou fastest, anoint thine head, and wash thy face; that thou appear not unto men to fast, but unto thy Father which is in secret: and thy Father, which seeth in secret, shall reward thee openly" (Matt. 6:16-18).*

## Daily Master Communication Guide

SCRIPTURE REFERENCE:

_____

*What God said to me:*

_____

_____

_____

_____

_____

_____

*What I said to God:*

_____

_____

_____

_____

_____

_____

Jesus instructed us not to allow any outward signs to be seen when we fast. Fasting is not for the knowledge of others. Like all true prayer, fasting is primarily for the Lord.

Jesus was at a very important point when He fasted; He was about to begin His public ministry. When Moses fasted, He was on Mount Sinai for the second receiving of the Ten Commandments. In both cases the fasting provided assistance for prayer at very important junctures for the human race.

 **In which of the following cases would fasting seem appropriate?**
❑ When I need to make a significant decision
❑ When I want to draw closer to the Lord in prayer
❑ When my self-discipline is out of control
❑ When I am preparing for a difficult or important task
❑ When I want to intensify my praying for a particular request

Fasting and praying would be appropriate in any one of those situations. You choose fasting to focus your attention on God in prayer.

### A Specialized Personal Prayer Ministry

Some people, sensing calls from God to pray for specific concerns, have developed specialized ministries of intercession for those concerns. If you feel led to develop a specialized ministry of intercession, you might pray for such concerns as—

+ national leaders;
+ your denomination;
+ missionaries in a particular country;
+ home missionaries in a particular state;
+ missionary evangelists, doctors, or church planters;
+ one missionary family;
+ specific lost persons in the community;
+ unsaved children and youth in the church;
+ local church leaders and volunteer workers;
+ homebound adults;
+ a Bible-study group or department;
+ sick persons in the hospital.

Many more subjects could be the focus of a ministry of intercession.

**Pray and ask God if He has a special ministry of intercession He wants you to participate in. If God has revealed to you a subject for a specialized personal intercessory prayer ministry, write that subject here.**

_____

God wants all of us to pray for these kinds of concerns. Remember that God has a special ministry for each person in the body of Christ. You may be called to a ministry of prayer. Your calling may be in a different area, so do not feel inferior if God does not call you to a special prayer ministry.

### Prayerwalking

Many believers are prayerwalking through the streets of their communities. As they walk, they pray with their eyes open for spiritual awakening in their locales. There is nothing magical about the act of walking, and there is no set pattern for prayerwalking. But walking through the arena of need helps us pray with spontaneity about the ways we expect God to answer our prayers.

Our proximity to the need also helps us draw near to those for whom we pray. Getting close to the community focuses our prayer, encouraging us to pray for specific families and individuals. But we also use prayerwalking to enlarge our vision of the entire community's needs.

Prayerwalking may be done individually or with other believers. As you walk, pray for the persons you see and allow the Holy Spirit to make you sensitive to their needs. Pray scriptural prayers and highlight God's promises as you walk.

*Walking through the arena of need helps us pray with spontaneity about the ways we expect God to answer our prayers.*

 **Plan to try prayerwalking. Write a time and a place here.**

_____

 **Walking in Fellowship with God Today**

1. Walk through your home and pray for the persons in the photographs around your home. When you see a gift someone gave you, pray for the person who gave it to you. Let the newspaper or a television newscast present opportunities to pray for leaders of the world, for victims, and for oppressed people. As you travel today, pray that the churches you pass will honor God and bring praise to His name. If you work outside the home, pray for those who work around you. Let all of the elements in your environment become daily reminders to talk to God about what He is doing and wants to do in the world. Continue to learn to pray without ceasing.

2. As you have your quiet time, complete the Daily Master Communication Guide in the margin on page 190.

## Day 2
## Your Church's Prayer Ministries

In week 7 we looked at ways your church can function as a house of prayer. Turn back to page 104 and review day 4.

 **What are some ways your church currently emphasizes prayer?**

_____

_____

*Today's Learning Goal*
You will understand ways your church can provide opportunities for members to participate in a ministry of prayer.

### Prayer Coordinator

Giving special emphasis to prayer may require much planning and coordination, depending on the church size and the extent of its prayer ministry. A prayer coordinator for the entire church prayer ministry should be appointed or elected. The pastor and the prayer coordinator, along with other persons, prayerfully decide which prayer ministries are most appropriate for the church at that time. The pastor and coordinator then begin informing the church about the prayer ministries, establishing the necessary organization, and enlisting persons to serve.

Sharing responsibilities for different aspects of the prayer ministry will allow your church to do more than if only one person carries that load. Pray for God to call persons to assume responsibility for each special project or emphasis. Recruitment of pray-ers can be done through a pastoral letter, notices in bulletins, personal invitations, surveys, and so forth.

Let's examine a variety of ways your church can involve people in a prayer ministry. The following are examples to help stimulate your thinking.

*Pray for God to call persons to assume responsibility for each special project or emphasis.*

### Special-Project Prayer Teams

*Around the pastor.* The pastor may ask that from two to five deacons pray in his office during services. A group may pray for him in his various responsibilities.

*Around events and projects.* Every activity worth doing is worth praying for. The church should provide teams to pray for activities like mission trips, visitation, Children's Bible Drills, Vacation Bible School, and Christmas and Easter musicals.

### Prayer Services

The midweek service is an important service of prayer. If you call it a prayer meeting, then be sure that prayer is the primary focus of the service. A twilight or evening service (vespers) or a morning service (matins) may be held on any day of the week. In these services the pastor may lead the church together in prayer or divide the congregation into small groups for conversational prayer.

### Prayer in Church-Program Organizations

Prayer should be encouraged in all church-program organizations (Bible study, discipleship training, missions organizations, music groups, and so forth). All group sessions and services should include prayer. In any group session the leader may call for a time of meditation, intercession, praise and thanksgiving, prayer for guidance, or silent prayer.

*All group sessions and services should include prayer.*

### Family Altars

Families should be encouraged to have family devotional times. A simple family altar includes a brief Bible reading and prayer by one or more family members (see week 7, days 2–3).

### Prayer Groups

Some effective prayer groups are men's prayer groups, women's prayer groups, youth prayer groups, and Bible-study groups. These may meet on any schedule they choose. Spontaneous prayer groups should be encouraged in neighborhoods, homes, apartments, and other appropriate settings.

## Prayer Chains

In a prayer chain a contact person calls two members in the chain. Each group leader calls the next group leader in the chain and the first person in his or her group. Each group member then calls the next group member in the chain. Each person should have a chart so that if his contact is not available, he can call the next person and keep the chain going. New groups (columns in the chart) should be added for each eight or so persons in the chain. A new prayer chain could be added for each eight groups enlisted. A prayer-chain list might look like this:

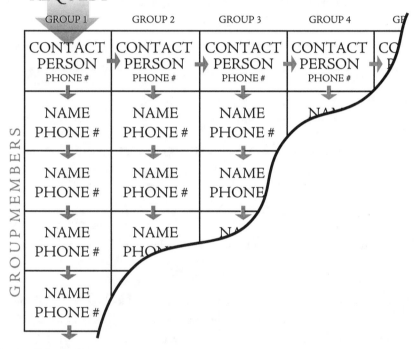

## Prayer Meals

Christians meet together to share a meal and to pray afterward. This could be a special one-time event or a weekly prayer group. For example:

- A group of businesspersons meeting for breakfast
- A group of homemakers meeting for brunch
- A group of fellow employees meeting for lunch
- A group of teens meeting to eat and pray before weekly visitation

## Special Prayer Times

*Prayer alert.* The pastor alerts the congregation to special needs for prayer, such as a referendum on gambling or an unexpected crisis.

*Prayer concert.* The pastor calls for a time of prayer together, with the emphasis on unity in prayer. A particular cause is usually involved, such as world missions and/or spiritual awakening. The International Mission Board of the Southern Baptist Convention challenges churches to set aside time the first Sunday of each month for a concert of prayer for world evangelization.

*Prayer and fasting.* A specified time of praying and abstaining from food is designated by the pastor for the congregation. Participation must be voluntary. It should be held for a very grave matter or for a period of repentance.

*Daily Master Communication Guide*

SCRIPTURE REFERENCE:

_____

*What God said to me:*

_____
_____
_____
_____
_____
_____
_____
_____

*What I said to God:*

_____
_____
_____
_____
_____
_____
_____

*Prayer vigil.* A specified number of hours, usually during the evening or night, is set aside as a watch in which groups or individuals pray continuously.

*Season of prayer.* In a special emphasis on important causes, such as the week of prayer for international, home, or state missions or any major concern, a period of time is set aside for special prayer.

You have talked about, prayed for, and considered your involvement in your church's prayer ministry for several weeks now. What dreams do you have for that ministry? List types of prayer ministries you would like for your church to sponsor. Circle the ones you would like to participate in.

_____     _____

_____     _____

_____     _____

What church member(s) do you think God would like to use to provide sound leadership to your church's overall prayer ministry?

_____

Pray that God will call a person in your church to assume this task.

### Equipping the Church to Pray

Read Ephesians 4:11-13 in the margin and think about the vital role of persons who have gifts for equipping others for the work of ministry. Stop and pray for the equippers in your church.

*"He gave some, apostles; and some, prophets; and some, evangelists; and some, pastors and teachers; for the perfecting of the saints, for the work of the ministry, for the edifying of the body of Christ: till we all come in the unity of the faith, and of the knowledge of the Son of God, unto a perfect man, unto the measure of the stature of the fulness of Christ"* (Eph. 4:11-13).

The pastor and persons in the church's prayer ministry should keep prayer before the people in sermons, in teaching, in newsletter articles, and by example. Each prayer time can be a teaching time by instruction or simply by modeling effective praying.

*Disciple's Prayer Life.* You have experienced *Disciple's Prayer Life* by personal study and group learning. You and others in your prayer group would be the best equipped to lead other groups through a study of the course. Imagine the praying power of a whole congregation that had learned to pray like the great pray-ers of the Bible.

*In God's Presence.* This six-week course will help church members develop a meaningful, daily prayer life centered on confession, praise, worship, thanksgiving, petition, and intercession.[1]

*The Life-Changing Power of Prayer.* This study of the biblical teachings and principles of prayer could be led by the pastor or another equipper. A sound biblical understanding of prayer is vital for believers today.[2]

*Prayer retreats.* Sometimes a concentrated time of study and practice of prayer can best meet the discipleship needs of a group. Schedule a time on a weekend, preferably away from church, where you can spend time learning to pray more effectively. Keep in mind that learning is most effective when practice and modeling are a part of the learning process.

🌿 In the previous paragraphs draw a star beside each type of equipping you have experienced personally. Underline each one your church has offered in the past year to help equip members to pray. Circle the ones you think are most needed to help equip your church's members to pray.

Prayer is God's gift to us all. Every member and every organization should be concerned that your church become a house of prayer. God's work and activity do not have room for attitudes and competition. The church's mission requires a unity of spirit and cooperation that only God can give. Join hands and hearts with all who want to advance prayer in your church. United prayer has exceptional power!

*United prayer has exceptional power.*

🌿 Walking in Fellowship with God Today 🌿

1. Pray for your pastor, church leaders, and others who have an opportunity to advance the cause of prayer in your church. Pray for bold leadership that will encourage united prayer. Pray for persons to be called for special tasks in your church's prayer ministries.
2. As you have your quiet time, complete the Daily Master Communication Guide in the margin on page 193.

---

1 To order *In God's Presence* (item 0-8054-9900-8): WRITE LifeWay Church Resources Customer Service; One LifeWay Plaza; Nashville, TN 37234-0113; FAX order to (615) 251-5933; PHONE 1-800-458-2772; EMAIL to *CustomerService@lifeway.com*; order ONLINE at *www.lifeway.com*; or visit the LifeWay Christian Store serving you.
2 Order *The Life-Changing Power of Prayer* (item 0-6330-1980-1) from one of the sources in footnote 1.

# Day 3
# An Intercessory Prayer Ministry, Part 1

Today's lesson provides a basic pattern for organizing an intercessory prayer ministry in a church. Before you decide that today's lesson is not for you and your church, consider a testimony from history.

*Today's Learning Goal*
You will know the needs and requirements of an intercessory prayer ministry and will demonstrate your commitment to intercessory prayer.

## One Hundred Years of Hourly Intercession
In 1727 24 men and 24 women agreed to pray one hour each, once each day, for God's blessings on their congregation and its witness to the world. Thus, 2 persons were praying at all times. That small group was joined by others through the years, and they carried out what would be a century of hourly intercession by the Moravian Brethren.

This group saw many of their number called to missions—first to Greenland, then to America, and eventually to the ends of the earth. John Wesley joined a Moravian meeting at Aldersgate in London in 1738. Under the preaching that night Wesley felt his "heart strangely warmed." Wesley became a flaming evangelist and was a key figure in the Great Awakening in England and America. The direct and indirect influence of the Moravian Brethren had a profound impact on world missions during that one hundred years of intercessory prayer. It all began with a group of 48 who gave themselves to intercessory prayer.[1] If we are to see a great spiritual awakening in our day, we must give ourselves to united, fervent, and persistent intercessory prayer. How would you like to become a part of a new one-hundred-year prayer meeting?

An intercessory prayer ministry can require a large number of participants and much organization, but it can also be effective with only a few dedicated intercessors. The following information will help you custom-make an intercessory prayer ministry for your church. Plans A, B, and C give suggestions that range from simple to complex. As you read each section, write notes in the margins to indicate what you think would be best for your church. If you already have an intercessory prayer ministry, look for ideas that could enhance your church's ministry.

## Intercessory Prayer Ministry

Churches are rediscovering the principle that intercessory prayer unleashes God's power to accomplish His will on earth. Consequently, many churches are developing organized ministries of intercessory prayer. Intercessory prayer ministry is a program that attempts to maintain continuous prayer in the church for long periods of time. It may involve 24 hours a day, seven days a week, or it may be established for shorter periods. Persons are enlisted to fill each time slot. Normally, they agree to pray for a 1-hour period once each week. The number of persons willing to participate and the facilities available will determine how extensive your intercessory prayer ministry is.

Intercessory prayer is work. The dictionary defines *work* as "sustained physical or mental effort to overcome obstacles and achieve an objective or result." Jesus taught that "men ought always to pray, and not to faint" (Luke 18:1). Intercessory prayer requires concentration, persistence, and faithfulness. It is a vital weapon in spiritual warfare. It overcomes great obstacles. Miraculous results come in answer to intercessory prayer. Yes, intercessory prayer is work!

Some churches have made the mistake of planning a ministry that required more people to pray than they could enlist. Burnout, disappointment, frustration, and guilt feelings have detracted from the joy that should come from such a ministry. If your church is just starting an intercessory prayer ministry, consider starting small with the willing people and resources you have. Then expand your ministry as you get better organized and as answered-prayer reports generate more interest in participation.

## Coordinator

Regardless of the size of your intercessory prayer ministry, a coordinator is helpful. One person or a couple may lead the work of the ministry. The coordinator's primary job is to organize the ministry, enlist participants, provide training, coordinate the day-to-day functioning of the ministry, and report about the ministry to the congregation. The coordinator assigns responsibilities to volunteers and calls on others to assist as needed.

## Organization

*Plan A.* An informal organization suffices when only a few pray-ers and a limited number of hours are involved. Participants work together to see that the ministry functions smoothly.

*Plan B.* As the number of pray-ers and the length of time increase, a coordinator is needed. He or she delegates other responsibilities as needed. A secretary for the prayer ministry is advisable. This person handles updating prayer requests and prayer notebooks, replenishing supplies, and compiling reports for the church.

*Plan C.* An extensive 24-hour intercessory prayer ministry needs a coordinator, at least one secretary, and team captains for each day of the week. Team captains are responsible for making sure that all time slots are filled on their assigned days. They assist with finding alternates and replacing persons who are unable to continue serving. If telephone prayer requests are called in, persons are needed for counseling, special ministry, and follow-up on an on-call basis.

## Who and When

*Plan A.* Use mature Christians and experienced prayer warriors. Volunteers can be received after orientation and training. Make sure that all participants can keep prayer requests confidential. A small group of available participants could conduct the intercessory prayer ministry on a Saturday morning, Sunday afternoon, Friday night, or another time.

*Plan B.* When more participants are available, the intercessory prayer ministry could cover certain hours each day (7:00 a.m. to 9:00 p.m., for instance) or certain days during the week (Friday night through Sunday night, for instance).

*Plan C.* A 24-hour prayer ministry will require a minimum of 168 pray-ers, one for each hour of the week. Having more than one pray-er per hour would allow for joint praying from time to time. A sufficient supply of alternates is also advisable. Alternates are those who may not commit to a weekly assignment but would substitute for persons who must be absent.

## Training

*Plan A.* With a very small group, a general meeting covering basic expectations and procedures may be sufficient. Certainly, additional opportunities for growth in one's prayer life would be helpful. Basic prayer training is a good starting place.

*Plan B. Disciple's Prayer Life* would provide excellent training for pray-ers. Teach the obligations inherent in the intercessory prayer ministry. Establish and maintain high standards of faithfulness, punctuality, and courtesy. Prayer retreats and short-term studies in discipleship training can also provide training opportunities. *A House of Prayer: Prayer Ministries in Your Church* can be used both to organize a prayer ministry and to train participants.[2]

*Plan C.* If you have a telephone in the prayer room, pray-ers should be taught principles of telephone courtesy. Tell them that they must not attempt to counsel on the telephone. Lead them to understand how helpful it will be to others to fill out forms correctly, to notify the prayer coordinator or secretary when they cannot be present so that an alternate can be secured, and to maintain punctuality. Monthly or quarterly meetings can be used for continuing education. Focus training on ways to increase effectiveness and to keep prayer times fresh and exciting.

*Daily Master Communication Guide*

SCRIPTURE REFERENCE:

_____

*What God said to me:*

_____
_____
_____
_____
_____
_____
_____

*What I said to God:*

_____
_____
_____
_____
_____
_____

### Your Church

Tomorrow we will look at more details about developing an intercessory prayer ministry. If your church already has an intercessory prayer ministry, think of ways it could be expanded or improved. If your church does not have an intercessory prayer ministry, think of what God might have your church do to start one.

 On a separate sheet of paper, write your thoughts about the following subjects as they relate to your church's intercessory prayer ministry. Bring this information with you to your group session this week.
- intercessory prayer ministry coordinator
- organization
- who
- when
- training

 Walking in Fellowship with God Today

*An intercessory prayer ministry can be a powerful tool if committed to the Lord.*

1. An intercessory prayer ministry can be a powerful tool if committed to the Lord. Pray for your church, its total ministry of prayer, the intercessory prayer ministry (existing or needed), and prayer warriors in your church. Pray that God will gift and call additional prayer warriors from among your church members. Finally, pray that other members of your *Disciple's Prayer Life* group will discern God's leadership for your church's prayer ministry.
2. As you have your quiet time, complete the Daily Master Communication Guide in the margin on page 197.

---

[1] "Another Century of Intercession," editorial, *Christianity Today*, 18 February 1977, 35.

[2] To order *A House of Prayer* (item 0-7673-9393-7): WRITE LifeWay Church Resources Customer Service, One LifeWay Plaza, Nashville, TN 37234-0113; FAX order to (615) 251-5933; PHONE 1-800-458-2772; EMAIL to *CustomerService@lifeway.com*; ONLINE at *www.lifeway.com*; or visit the LifeWay Christian Store serving you.

## Day 4
## An Intercessory Prayer Ministry, Part 2

Today we will continue examining the details of an intercessory prayer ministry. As you did yesterday, write notes in the margins about applying the following ideas to your church's prayer ministry.

### Where

*Plan A.* In a basic intercessory prayer ministry, pray-ers may pray in their homes.

*Plan B.* A Bible-study room or an empty closet at church may be used as a prayer room while not in use. If possible, a special room should be set aside for the prayer room. Keys to the church would be necessary for those who are assigned hours when the building is locked. Ultimately, the prayer room should have an outside entrance. It should have a lock, and each participant should be given a key or combination number. Women should sign up only for daylight hours.

*If possible, a special room should be set aside for the prayer room.*

*Plan C.* Ideally, a prayer room should have a private, outside entrance. Some churches even build a special prayer chapel or prayer tower.

## Prayer Requests

*Plan A.* If people are not praying in a central location, special prayer requests can be shared by phone at an agreed time each week. Each person should keep a notebook with prayer requests and answers to prayer. If a central location is used, a single notebook or prayer list may be kept for use by pray-ers. Prayer requests may be listed in the church bulletin or newsletter.

*Plan B.* Prayer lists like those in *Disciple's Prayer Life* may be adapted for use. Requests from church members, church staff, church leaders, missionaries, missions periodicals, and other sources may be used. Hospital lists and membership lists with new members identified are also helpful. Pray-ers may also call the two missions prayerlines in prayer guide 12, page 217, for current missions requests.

*Plan C.* Some churches provide a separate telephone line, the number of which is published so that people in the community can call in requests. Sometimes when intercessory prayer ministries become well known, requests come in by phone and mail from people around the world.

*Prayer requests may be listed in the church bulletin or newsletter.*

## Equipment and Supplies

*Plan A.* The simplest prayer ministry should include at least a prayer-request notebook. Pray-ers will want their Bibles and perhaps a hymnal.

*Plan B.* A prayer room should be equipped to assist pray-ers in every way possible. Some or all of the following items should be provided.

+ Kneeling altar or table and chairs
+ The Bible in several translations
+ Books on prayer
+ Charts or records to record attendance
+ Prayer-request forms with space to show answers
+ Prayergrams to write notes to persons prayed for
+ Cards, card files, or notebooks to list continuing prayer concerns and special emphases, such as prayer for Bible-study teachers, discipleship-training leaders, various church officers, emergencies, crusades and conferences, church visitation, the budget, deacons, and other concerns
+ Paper, pencils, and pens

*Plan C.* Additional items for an extensive intercessory prayer ministry could include the following.

+ Card files with color-coded cards to show continuing requests for church members, the lost, illness, missions causes, and so forth
+ Telephone to receive requests
+ A referral list, including counselors and agencies that can provide help for special needs
+ Decorative items such as a stained-glass window, pictures, or Scriptures on the wall
+ Bulletin board to post news of events in the Christian world or world news indicating need of prayer, answers deserving praise and thanksgiving, noteworthy insights, and so on.

*A prayer room should be equipped to assist pray-ers in every way possible.*

## Daily Master Communication Guide

SCRIPTURE REFERENCE:

_____

### What God said to me:

_____

_____

_____

_____

_____

_____

### What I said to God:

_____

_____

_____

_____

_____

_____

## Forms

Develop the following forms or use the ones in *A House of Prayer: Prayer Ministries in Your Church*.[1]

*Pew prayer-request form.* Provide forms in pew racks or in another place in the worship center for persons to record prayer requests. Ask for information such as date; prayer request; person(s) involved; address and phone number, if appropriate; person making the request; and indication as to whether the request should be shared or kept confidential.

*Prayer-request form.* Include the same information. Add blanks for the person's name who received the request, whether the pastor or staff should be notified, and so forth.

*Prayergram.* A prayergram is a postcard. Pray-ers can write prayergrams to persons they pray for as encouragement. Include the church's name and address on the card. Other information could include a famous quotation about prayer, a scriptural prayer promise, and the church's prayer telephone number.

*Alternate-request form.* Use this form for pray-ers to request alternates for their time slots. Include information about how to use the form and indicate to whom to give it. Ask for the date of the request, pray-er's name, date and time an alternate is needed, and signature.

*Answered-prayer form.* This form should be completed when a specific answer to prayer comes. Use it to encourage prayer warriors and, when appropriate, to provide information for sharing with the church. Information should include the request that was answered, person(s) involved in the request and answer, how the Lord answered the request, date of the request, and date of the answer.

*Other forms.* You will need forms for enlisting participants, developing a schedule for the prayer times and pray-ers, recording attendance, and so forth.

## Manual

As your prayer ministry expands, you may want to provide pray-ers a manual that includes—

- a statement of purpose;
- a brief history of the prayer ministry;
- a statement of the commitment pray-ers should make;
- participants' responsibilities;
- a description of how the prayer ministry works;
- procedures to follow;
- a description of resources available and how to use them;
- guidelines to follow, including what to do and what not to do;
- suggestions on how to prepare for prayer times;
- suggestions on how best to use prayer times;
- scriptural promises and prayers;
- sample prayers to pray for the lost, the sick, civil leaders, church leaders, other Christians, missionaries, and so forth;
- inspirational quotations about prayer's effectiveness or an intercessor's role;
- a bibliography of books, tapes, and other materials for individual training;
- a list of participants and alternates with their phone numbers;
- other information unique to your prayer ministry.

### Your Church

 On a separate sheet of paper summarize your thoughts on the following subjects as they relate to your church's prayer ministry.

- • where
- • prayer requests
- • equipment and supplies
- • forms
- • manual

 Walking in Fellowship with God Today

1. By now you should have a good idea of the kind of intercessory prayer ministry you would like to see your church have. On a separate sheet of paper make a prayer list about your church's prayer ministry. Begin praying today for the specific details of your dream about an intercessory prayer ministry.
2. As you have your quiet time, complete the Daily Master Communication Guide in the margin on page 200.

---

[1] To order *A House of Prayer* (item 0-7673-9393-7): WRITE LifeWay Church Resources Customer Service; One LifeWay Plaza; Nashville, TN 37234-0113; FAX order to (615) 251-5933; PHONE 1-800-458-2772; EMAIL to *CustomerService@lifeway.com*; order ONLINE at *www.lifeway.com*; or visit the LifeWay Christian Store serving you.

## Day 5
## Conclusion

### Keep Growing

Our prayer in writing *Disciple's Prayer Life* has been that it *not* become a credential in your life to prove your spirituality. For many people, credentials become stopping places. A college degree, for some people, means the end of study. In the world system, credentials may become the certification for a certain kind of authority.

In the Christ-life, the only certification you have is the life of Christ Himself and His presence within you. *Disciple's Prayer Life* does not earn you the right to say that you have arrived as a prayer warrior. What you do does not make your prayers acceptable to God; they are acceptable because of Christ. You pray in the legal worth of His name. You present to God His moral perfection. You pray in all of His purity and in His mind. His Spirit interprets your prayers to your Heavenly Father.

Growth is the normal life for a Christian. The Christian life is a progression. Read 2 Peter 3:18 in the margin. The implication of continual renewal for your prayer life is obvious: at any point in your pilgrimage your prayer life should never be less than it was before.

Many great persons of prayer experienced a profound renewal at some point in their lives. Their biographies indicate that constant renewing of their minds and spirits became the norm for the rest of their lives. (You might enjoy reading *Deeper Experiences of Famous Christians* by J. Gilchrist Lawson [The Warner Press, 1911, 1972].) Let's examine some other things you can do to continue to grow.

*Today's Learning Goal*
You will demonstrate your commitment to continue growing in your personal fellowship with God.

*"Grow in grace, and in the knowledge of our Lord and Saviour Jesus Christ" (2 Pet. 3:18).*

*Study* The Life-Changing Power of Prayer. Study *The Life-Changing Power of Prayer* in a small group. The study can be spread over a period of time, with participants sharing insights. A teaching guide is included at the back of the book.

*15-month review plan.* Perhaps you realize that many things you have learned in *Disciple's Prayer Life* are still not solidly ingrained in your personal prayer life. *Disciple's Prayer Life* provides 65 daily assignments for "Walking in Fellowship with God Today." By reviewing and practicing one of these assignments for a week at a time, you can thoroughly assimilate the concepts in your praying. You may want to do this by yourself or with a group. If you join a group of *Disciple's Prayer Life* graduates, you can have a guided study for your prayer group for 15 months or more. During the week each group member should focus on the day's material assigned. During the group session, share experiences and discuss new insights that come in practicing prayer. Then spend time praying together.

*Participate in prayer retreats.* A prayer retreat is recommended in the leader guide at the back of your workbook (pp. 228–30). You may have participated in a prayer retreat just prior to this course. Now that you have completed *Disciple's Prayer Life*, attending or leading another retreat will help you experience fresh insights in the company of a new group of fellow believers. Your testimonies from your experiences could also contribute to the experience for others. Consider attending or leading other prayer retreats offered by your church or denomination.

*A prayer retreat helps you experience fresh insights in the company of fellow believers.*

*Learn from the personal prayer lives of great pray-ers.* Biographies of great men and women of prayer can be instructive for you. Many valuable biographies of missionaries, preachers, and other great men and women of God are available. Consider reading one or more of the following books.

+ *Praying Hyde* by Francis McGaw (Bethany Fellowship, 1970)
+ *The Life of David Brainerd, Chiefly Extracted from His Diary,* by President [Jonathan] Edwards (Baker Book House, 1978)
+ *George Mueller of Bristol and His Witness to a Prayer Hearing God* by Arthur T. Pierson (Fleming H. Revell, n.d.)
+ *Answers to Prayer from George Mueller's Narratives,* compiled by A. E. C. Brooks (Moody Press, n.d.)
+ *Rees Howells, Intercessor* by Norman P. Grubb (Christian Literature Crusade, 1973)

## Growth Plans

We often fail to do what we want to do because we do not plan.

Think about your prayer life and prayer ministry. Read through your Daily Master Communication Guides. What has God been saying to you during these 13 weeks? Use a separate sheet of paper if needed.

_____

_____

_____

How do you plan to continue growing in your personal fellowship with God? Write a plan of action and list steps you will take to keep growing.

_____

_____

_____

_____

_____

Be prepared to share your plan in this week's group session. I hope that you mentioned that you will continue to have a daily quiet time. Plan to keep a journal just as you have recorded your communication with God in your Daily Master Communication Guides in this workbook. You can create your own prayer journal by recording in a blank journal or notebook your daily communication with God. You may also want to duplicate and insert in a three-ring notebook the prayer guides on pages 205–17, as well as the prayer articles and charts on pages 218–25. Feel free to photocopy the charts in these sections of your workbook for your personal use in prayer. Another option for your quiet times is to use *Day by Day in God's Kingdom: A Discipleship Journal*, which provides an easy-to-use format for your daily quiet time. This 13-week journal provides room for you to write entries about your Bible reading and prayer five days each week.[1]

## Growing Older and Praying More

Our prayer lives should grow as we grow older. The prayers of the elderly in the Bible indicate that prayer strength should increase as our physical forces diminish. In his dying days Jacob blessed the sons of Joseph (see Gen. 48:20 in the margin). Moses blessed Israel before his death (see Deut. 33:2-3 in the margin). Although He was not elderly at the end of His earthly life, Jesus' greatest recorded prayer is the prayer He prayed the night before He died (see John 17). The Bible pray-ers continued an active prayer life to the ends of their lives. Today retirement should be a time of increasing prayer as people have more time to devote to prayer. God may preserve Christians into old age to use their prayers to accomplish great works in the body of Christ. The later years of life offer many advantages in the prayer life—the fruit of much experience, greater wisdom, and more time to pray.

Do you know elderly persons in your church who would make good prayer warriors? Write their names here.

_____

_____

*"He blessed them that day, saying, In thee shall Israel bless, saying, God make thee as Ephraim and as Manasseh: and he set Ephraim before Manasseh" (Gen. 48:20).*

*"He said, The Lord came from Sinai, and rose up from Seir unto them; he shined forth from mount Paran, and he came with ten thousands of saints: from his right hand went a fiery law for them. Yea, he loved the people; all his saints are in thy hand: and they sat down at thy feet; every one shall receive of thy words" (Deut. 33:2-3).*

*"Let us not be weary in well doing: for in due season we shall reap, if we faint not" (Gal. 6:9).*

*"My beloved brethren, be ye steadfast, unmoveable, always abounding in the work of the Lord, forasmuch as ye know that your labour is not in vain in the Lord" (1 Cor. 15:58).*

Helping senior adults develop prayer ministries and grow as prayer warriors could become a significant ministry of your church. Even homebound members could participate by praying together by phone or on conference calls with other homebound members.

 Pray that God will call someone in your church to lead a ministry of prayer through senior adults. If God places a specific individual on your mind for this task, write his or her name on your temporary daily prayer list (see p. 224).

### Finishing the Course

One of the greatest goals you can set for yourself is to finish the particular work of prayer God has for you. Paul said, "Brethren, I count not myself to have apprehended: but this one thing I do, forgetting those things which are behind, and reaching forth unto those things which are before, I press toward the mark for the prize of the high calling of God in Christ Jesus" (Phil. 3:13-14). Later he expressed the satisfaction "I have fought a good fight, I have finished my course, I have kept the faith" (2 Tim. 4:7). One of the glories of Christ's great prayer in John 17 is His declaration "I have finished the work which thou gavest me to do" (v. 4).

A prayer life that is biblical will continue strong to the end of life. Perhaps at the end of *Disciple's Prayer Life* the greatest prayer that disciples could pray is to ask God to help them finish the course and be able to say to Him when they step into eternity: "I have finished the course. I have finished the work You gave me to do." Paul wrote two words of encouragement that may be helpful to you at this point. Read Galatians 6:9 and 1 Corinthians 15:58 in the margin on page 203.

 Write this week's memory verse(s) on a separate sheet of paper.

> ### A PARTING BLESSING
> "Now unto him that is able to keep you from falling, and to present you faultless before the presence of his glory with exceeding joy, to the only wise God our Savior, be glory and majesty, dominion and power, both now and ever. Amen" (Jude 24-25).
>
> —T. W. Hunt and Catherine Walker

###  Walking in Fellowship with God Today

1. Thank God for the development of your prayer life during the past 13 weeks. Ask Him to help you grow as a Christian and as a prayer warrior for the rest of your life.
2. As you have your quiet time, complete the Daily Master Communication Guide in the margin.

[1]To order *Day by Day in God's Kingdom: A Discipleship Journal* (item 0-7673-2577-X) WRITE LifeWay Church Resources Customer Service, One LifeWay Plaza, Nashville, TN 37234-0113; FAX order to (615) 251-5933; PHONE 1-800-458-2772; EMAIL to *CustomerService@lifeway.com*; ONLINE at *www.lifeway.com*; or visit the LifeWay Christian Store serving you.

# PRAYER GUIDE 1
## Giving God a Reason

*Principle:* A correct basis for our asking gives God a reason for answering our prayer.

*When to apply:* Each time you make a request in prayer
*How to apply:* Ask yourself, *Why should God answer this prayer request?* Then give God a reason to answer.

### REASONS GOD ANSWERS PRAYER

1. The prayer acknowledges God's—
   + honor—God's good name, integrity;
   + character—qualities of God;
   + glory—outshining of God's attributes;
   + sovereignty—supreme power, rank, authority.
2. The prayer is supported by the intercession of Jesus through His priesthood.
3. The prayer is supported by the intercession of the Holy Spirit.
4. The prayer comes from one who is related to God and Christ.
   + Father and child
   + Master and servant

For eight principles of asking, see prayer guide 9, page 214.

| CHARACTER TRAITS OF GOD | | | |
|---|---|---|---|
| Trait | Reference | Trait | Reference |
| Longsuffering | Num. 14:18 | | |
| Merciful, great in mercy | Num. 14:18 | | |
| Forgiving | Num. 14:18 | | |
| | | | |
| | | | |
| | | | |
| | | | |
| | | | |
| | | | |
| | | | |
| | | | |
| | | | |
| | | | |
| | | | |
| | | | |
| | | | |
| | | | |

You may reproduce this chart for your personal use.

## PRAYER-REQUEST LOG

| Request | Basis | Answer |
| --- | --- | --- |
| | | |
| | | |
| | | |
| | | |
| | | |
| | | |
| | | |
| | | |
| | | |
| | | |
| | | |
| | | |
| | | |
| | | |
| | | |
| | | |
| | | |
| | | |
| | | |
| | | |
| | | |
| | | |
| | | |
| | | |
| | | |
| | | |
| | | |
| | | |
| | | |
| | | |
| | | |

You may reproduce this chart for your personal use.

# PRAYER GUIDE 2
## Knowing God

### NAMES OF GOD

1. God (*Elohim*)—Sovereign, Power, Creator
2. Lord (*Adonai*)—Master, Ruler, Owner
3. Jehovah (the self-existing Lord)—eternal, changeless, faithful
4. The Lord our Provider (*Jehovah-Jireh*)
5. The Lord our Healer (*Jehovah-Rophe*)
6. The Lord our Banner (*Jehovah-Nissi*)
7. The Lord who sanctifies (*Jehovah-M'Kaddesh*)
8. The Lord our Peace (*Jehovah-Shalom*)
9. The Lord our Shepherd (*Jehovah-Rohi*)
10. The Lord our Righteousness (*Jehovah-Tsidkenu*)
11. The Lord who is there (*Jehovah-Shammah*)
12. God Almighty (*El-Shaddai*)—powerful and willing to supply

Others:

_____

_____

_____

_____

_____

### NAMES OF JESUS

1. Bread of life
2. Light of the world
3. Door of the sheep
4. Good Shepherd
5. Resurrection and Life
6. Way
7. Truth
8. Life
9. Rabbi
10. Judge
11. High Priest
12. King of kings
13. Lord of lords
14. Friend
15. Brother
16. True Vine

Others:

_____

_____

_____

_____

### THE MAGNIFICAT

Use Luke 1:47-55 as a model prayer of praise and adoration.

1. God is my Savior (v. 47).
2. God has regard for me (v. 48).
3. God is mighty (v. 49).
4. God has done great things for me (v. 49).
5. Holy is His name (v. 49).
6. God has mercy on those who fear Him (v. 50).
7. God demonstrates His strength (v. 51).
8. God scatters the proud (v. 51).
9. God dethrones the mighty (v. 52).
10. God exalts the humble (v. 52).
11. God satisfies the hungry (v. 53).
12. God sends the rich away empty (v. 53).
13. God helps His servant (v. 54).
14. God remembers to be merciful (v. 54).

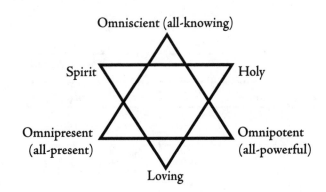

# PRAYER GUIDE 3
## Prayer Identities

*When to use:* When a change in needs, circumstances, or concerns calls for a different prayer relationship with God.
*How to use:* Look for a Bible character with circumstances similar to yours. Reexamine his or her prayer experiences in the Bible. Come to God from a different perspective and engage in an appropriate prayer activity.

| BIBLE PRAY-ERS | | | |
|---|---|---|---|
| **Person** | **Identity** | **Prayer Activity** | **For Him/Her God Was** |
| Cornelius | God-fearer | seeking God | True God |
| Daniel | loyal follower | being faithful (persevering) | Most High God |
| Enoch | companion | walking with God | Companion |
| Abraham | friend of God | talking with God | Friend |
| Jacob | clinger | struggling with God | Blesser |
| Moses | Israel's intercessor | dialogue and arguing | Holy One |
| Gideon | soldier | obedience | Great Commander |
| Hannah | believer | believing in God | Rewarder of faith |
| Elijah | God's prophet | honoring God | The Almighty |
| Elisha | spiritual realist | seeing God's reality | Reality |
| Hezekiah | king of Israel | turning to God | God of Israel |
| Nehemiah | God's servant | supplicating God | Righteous One |
| Isaiah | yearner | waiting on God | Upright One |
| Jeremiah | God's spokesman | being broken before God | Righteousness |
| Ezekiel | God's watchman | watching God | Warner |
| Mary | God's handmaiden | exalting God | Mighty One |
| Peter | pastor | being bold with God | Sovereign, Lord |
| Paul | man filled with strength and knowledge | living with God | Glorious Source |
| John | lover of God | fellowshipping with God | Love |
| Jesus | Son-Servant of God | attending to God's business | Father, Master |

| DAVID'S PRAYER RELATIONSHIPS | | | |
|---|---|---|---|
| **Reference** | **Prayer Identity** | **Prayer Activity** | **God Was to Him** |
| Psalm 18:1-3 | soldier | praising God | Deliverer |
| Psalm 51 | sinner | confessing, repenting | Forgiver |
| Psalm 23 | sheep | adoring God | Shepherd |
| Psalm 7:6,8,11 | fleeing victim | pleading | Judge |
| 1 Chronicles 29:14 | offerer | worshiping | Source of offering |
| 2 Samuel 12:16 | father | praying for child | Lord |
| 2 Samuel 24:17 | king | pleading for subjects | Lord |
| Psalm 103 | worshiper | blessing the Lord | Lord |
| Summary: | uniquely human | acknowledging God | Lord |

# PRAYER GUIDE 4
## Using the Bible in Prayer

### SCRIPTURE'S VALUE IN PRAYER

1. Scripture provides preparation for prayer.
2. Scripture provides guidance.
3. Scripture provides wisdom.
4. Scripture provides subjects for prayer.

### WAYS TO USE SCRIPTURE IN PRAYER

1. Quote a promise as assurance of an answer.
2. Quote a fulfilled promise as a reason for praise.
3. Apply Bible verses to a current situation.
4. Use Bible verses as a prayer or a praise.
5. Use Bible phrases in prayer.

| GOD'S COMMANDS | |
|---|---|
| Reference | Command |
| | |
| | |
| | |
| | |
| | |
| | |
| | |
| | |
| | |
| | |
| | |
| | |
| | |
| | |
| | |
| | |
| | |
| | |
| | |
| | |

You may reproduce this chart for your personal use.

# PRAYER GUIDE 5
## Expressing Gratitude in Prayer

*When to use:* Anytime, always

*How to use:* Use the following ideas to stimulate thoughts about subjects for gratitude and to express gratitude. Keep a list of things for which you want to praise and thank God regularly.

### A CHRISTIAN'S ATTITUDE OF GRATITUDE

Properly expressing gratitude means that you thank God continuously, permanently, and for all things—large and small, "good" and "bad." Gratitude—

1. permeates life;
2. believes that God is good;
3. produces trust;
4. glorifies God.

### GRATITUDE FOR SPIRITUAL BLESSINGS

Thank God for—

1. people who have had a spiritual impact on your life;
2. meaningful spiritual experiences;
3. the advance of the Kingdom.

### WAYS TO EXPRESS GRATITUDE

1. Physical reminders
2. Verbal thanksgivings for—
    + past blessings
    + God's current work in your life
    + future expectations
3. Prayers
4. Songs
5. Testimonies

### MY GRATITUDE TO GOD IN STONE

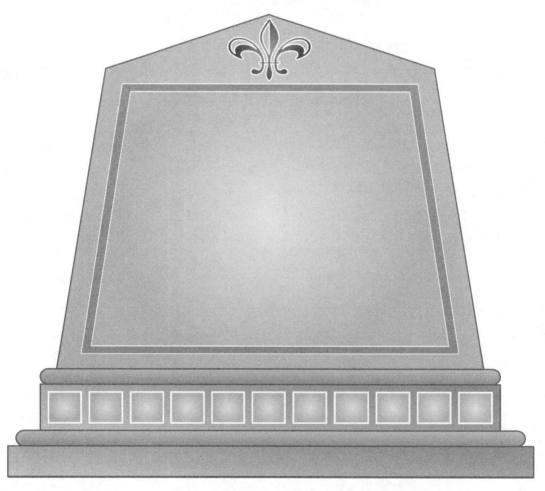

# PRAYER GUIDE 6
## Worshiping God in Prayer

### BIBLE PRAISE WORDS

1. Magnify and exalt
2. Rejoice and exult
3. Ascribe
4. Bless
5. Laud
6. Praise
7. Worship
8. Hallelujah
9. Alleluia
10. Adore
11. Extol
12. Hosanna
13. Glorify
14. Honor

### PSALMS TO USE IN PRAYER

1. Exhortation Psalms: 34, 67, 147, 148, 149, 150
2. Refuge Psalms: 11, 16, 57, 59, 71, 91, 121, 124, 141
3. Contemplation Psalms: 1, 42, 62, 65, 84, 119
4. Majestic Psalms: 8, 19, 24, 29, 48, 50, 76, 93, 97, 113

### WAYS TO WORSHIP

1. Body language
2. Music
3. Offerings
4. Prayer
5. Praise

### HE IS WORTHY

The Lamb is worthy to receive—

1. power;
2. riches;
3. wisdom;
4. strength;
5. honor;
6. glory;
7. blessing.

*Worthy is the Lamb that was slain.*

### REASONS GOD IS WORTHY OF PRAISE

*Qualities showing that God is worthy of praise:* God is infinite, transcendent, unique, wise, and completely perfect.

| Reason | Reference |
|---|---|
|  |  |
|  |  |
|  |  |
|  |  |
|  |  |
|  |  |
|  |  |
|  |  |

You may reproduce this chart for your personal use.

# Prayer Guide 7
## Praying Together

### Reasons to Pray with Others

1. The prayers of others strengthen your praying.
2. Others see factors you may fail to see.

### Tips for a Family-Altar Time

1. The pastor, his wife, and other spiritual leaders in the church should commit their homes to family prayer times to serve as models for others.
2. The husband and the wife can help each other provide spiritual leadership for the family. This is a matter of co-operation, not competition.
3. Elements of the family-altar time can include—
   + reading a Bible passage;
   + sharing opinions and ideas about what you read;
   + talking about your life together;
   + talking about your church;
   + talking about events in the Lord's work that your prayers might touch;
   + talking about family and friends who need prayer;
   + prayer.
4. Do not feel obligated to find solutions to problems discussed.
5. Do not feel that you must appear spiritual or must pray more impressively than another.
6. Pray with great freedom to be yourself.
7. Spend time together in the morning and continue praying for one another throughout the day.
8. If your family altar works best in the evening, sacrifice a television program for the eternal value of time with the Lord. The best time is probably just before bedtime.

### Praying for Missionaries and Believers in Communist Countries

1. Pray that believers—
   + can secure Bibles;
   + will be protected from attack, imprisonment, harassment, embarrassment, and informers;
   + will obtain necessities of life when they are denied jobs;
   + will be given wisdom, guidance, and fruitfulness in their witnessing;
   + will be guided in possible areas of citizenship.
2. Pray for missions and other agencies that attempt to help them.
3. Pray for persons whose names are obtained from newspapers or Christian news reports.
4. Pray that the governments will develop more lenient attitudes to allow freedom to worship and freedom to print and distribute Bibles.

| Subjects to Pray For | | Other Subjects | Reference |
|---|---|---|---|
| 1. Calling of Christian workers | Matthew 9:38 | | |
| 2. Christian fruit | John 15:16 | | |
| 3. Boldness in witnessing | Acts 4:24-31 | | |
| 4. Filling of the Holy Spirit | Acts 8:15 | | |
| 5. Deliverance | Acts 12:5 | | |
| 6. Missionaries | Acts 13:2-5 | | |
| 7. Church leaders | Acts 14:23 | | |
| 8. Reconciliation | 2 Corinthians 5:20 | | |
| 9. Right conduct | 2 Corinthians 13:7 | | |
| 10. All Christians | Ephesians 6:18 | | |
| 11. Love, knowledge, judgment | Philippians 1:9 | | |
| 12. Preservation | 1 Thessalonians 5:23 | | |
| 13. Persons in authority | 1 Timothy 2:1-2 | | |
| 14. Wisdom | James 1:5 | | |
| 15. Healing | James 5:14-16 | | |

You may reproduce this chart for your personal use.

# PRAYER GUIDE 8
## Agreeing with God

*Confess:* to speak the same thing, to agree

### STEPS IN CONFESSING SIN

1. Acknowledge that the sin was committed.
2. Repent or turn from the sin.
3. Accept God's forgiveness.

### REASONS TO BELIEVE THAT SIN IS FORGIVEN

1. Scripture promises forgiveness.
2. Scripture pictures sin as being removed.
3. Christ's blood cleanses the conscience.
4. Forgiven people can forgive others.

### SUBJECTS FOR CONFESSION

1. Confess sin
2. Confess your needs
3. Confess the needs of others
4. Confess your new nature in Christ
5. Confess Jesus as Savior
6. Confess Jesus as Lord
7. Confess the rightness of God's ways
8. Confess truth

### CONFESSING CHRIST

*Peter:* "Thou art the Christ, the Son of the living God" (Matt. 16:16).
*Nathanael:* "Rabbi, thou art the Son of God; thou art the King of Israel" (John 1:49).
*Thomas:* "My Lord and my God" (John 20:28).

### PSALM 51
### A MODEL CONFESSION OF SIN

**Wrongs to Confess**

1. Transgressions (acts of revolt or rebellion, choosing your own way; v. 1)
2. Iniquity (moral crookedness or perversity; v. 2)
3. Sin (to miss the mark, fail to measure up to God's standards; v. 2)
4. Evil (wickedness; v. 4)

**Things to Ask God to Do**

1. Be merciful (v. 1)
2. Blot out the transgression (v. 1)
3. Wash and cleanse (v. 2)
4. Purge (v. 7)
5. Deliver from guilt (v. 14)
6. Open your lips (v. 15)

**Changes to Expect/Request**

1. To know wisdom (v. 6)
2. To be cleansed whiter than snow (v. 7)
3. To hear joy and gladness so that you can rejoice again (v. 8)
4. To receive a clean heart (v. 10)
5. To receive a right spirit (v. 10)
6. To know once again the joy of God's salvation (v. 12)
7. To have a willing spirit (v. 12)

### CONFESSING TO OTHERS

Public confession should be limited to the circle of the offense. It should never endanger anyone else's privacy or reputation.

## BIBLICAL PICTURES OF SIN'S FORGIVENESS

**Micah 7:18-19**

"Thou wilt cast all their sins into the depths of the sea" (Mic. 7:18-19).

**Isaiah 38:17**

"Thou hast cast all my sins behind thy back" (Isa. 38:17).

**Psalm 103:12**

"As far as the east is from the west, so far hath he removed our transgressions from us" (Ps. 103:12).

## GOD INVITES ASKING

*"Ask, and it shall be given you; seek, and ye shall find; knock, and it shall be opened unto you"* (Matt. 7:7).

*"If ye shall ask any thing in my name, I will do it"* (John 14:14).

*"If ye abide in me, and my words abide in you, ye shall ask what ye will, and it shall be done unto you"* (John 15:7).

*"Hitherto have ye asked nothing in my name: ask, and ye shall receive, that your joy may be full"* (John 16:24).

## PRINCIPLES OF ASKING

1. *Ask in the Spirit.* To ask in the Spirit means that every petition proceeds from the mind of the Spirit, not from selfish motives or self-serving ends.
2. *Ask with the mind.* The mind is the instrument by which you are able to form your requests. With the mind you make your requests precise and specific.
3. *Ask in Jesus' name.* When you use Jesus' name, you claim to represent Him and to act like Him. You have His desires, His qualities, His gratitude, and His outlook. When you prepare to make a request in Jesus' name, first ask yourself, *What would Jesus want in this situation?* Let His desires become your desires.
4. *Ask while abiding in Christ.* Prayer is both a means of abiding in Christ and a result of abiding in Christ. To abide in Him, you continue in constant fellowship with Him, you pray without ceasing, and you obediently accept His will and Word for you without objection. As a branch abides in the vine, a Christian abides in Christ.
5. *Ask in faith.*
   + Ask without doubt in your heart.
   + Believe that the things you ask will come to pass.
   + Reflect God's character of constancy.
   + Recognize God's authority and power to answer.
   + Have confidence in God's care and purposes for your life.
   + Claim a Bible promise and hold God to His Word.
6. *Ask in humility.* Humility needs others. Praying in humility recognizes your need of God. Humility submits to God. Pride, arrogance, and independence prevent an attitude of humility. The secret to humility is understanding who God is. Pride always indicates that you have failed to perceive His greatness.
7. *Ask in sincerity.* When you pray in sincerity, your faith leads you to pray genuine, heartfelt prayers. You are so serious about your praying that your prayer is earnest and fervent. Sincere prayer is not put-on, fake, or artificial.
8. *Ask with perseverance. Perseverance* means *persistence, not giving up.* God expects perseverance in order to—
   + make you sure of what God wants;
   + make you sure of what you want;
   + train you to take your eyes off circumstances that may be discouraging;
   + make you focus on Him;
   + prove and establish earnestness;
   + demonstrate real faith.

# PRAYER GUIDE 10
## Dealing with Hindrances and Delays

### WAYS GOD RESPONDS TO PRAYER REQUESTS
1. Yes
2. No
3. Wait
4. Refuses to hear

### STOP SIGNS TO ANSWERED PRAYER

### TWO CAUSES OF UNBELIEF
1. Fearing that God does not want to give
2. Fearing that what you are asking for is too great or too difficult

### OVERCOMING UNBELIEF
1. Concentrate on Christ and His message.
2. Exhort one another daily.
3. Hold on to your confidence in Christ.
4. Pray and fast.

### SIN ROADBLOCKS TO PRAYER

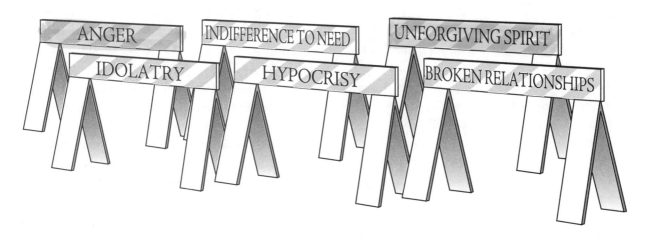

1. *Anger* (see 1 Tim. 2:8): getting angry, losing control of yourself, being vindictive
2. *Idolatry* (see Ezek. 14:3): loving someone or something more than God, an idol of the heart
3. *Indifference to need* (see Prov. 21:13): mistreating or denying help to the needy
4. *Hypocrisy* (see Matt. 6:5): praying to be seen by people rather than by God
5. *Unforgiving spirit* (see Mark 11:25): refusing to forgive someone who has done something against you
6. *Broken relationships* (see Matt. 5:23-24): allowing a broken relationship to continue between you and another

# PRAYER GUIDE 11
## Asking for Yourself and Others

## MODEL PRAYER REQUESTS

### Matthew 6:9-13—the Model Prayer
1. That God's kingdom come and His will be done (v. 10)
2. For daily bread (v. 11)
3. For forgiveness (v. 12)
4. For escape from temptation and deliverance from evil (v. 13)

### John 17
1. Keep them that they may be one (v. 11).
2. Protect them from the evil one (v. 15).
3. Sanctify them; set them apart (v. 17).
4. That Christians be united so that others may believe in Christ (v. 21)
5. That Christians be with Christ so that they can behold His glory (v. 24)

### Ephesians 3:14-19
1. That they be strengthened in the inner man (v. 16)
2. That Christ dwell in their hearts through faith (v. 17)
3. That they be able to know the love of Christ (vv. 18-19)
4. That they be filled with all the fullness of God (vv. 18-19)

### Ephesians 1:15-23
1. For a spirit of wisdom and of revelation in the knowledge of God (v. 17)
2. That the eyes of their understanding be enlightened (v. 18)
3. Know the hope of God's calling (v. 18).
4. Know the glory of His inheritance (v. 18).
5. Know the surpassing greatness of His power (v. 19).

### Colossians 1:9-12
1. That they be filled with the knowledge of God's will (v. 9)
2. That they may walk worthy of the Lord, pleasing Him, being fruitful in good works, increasing in the knowledge of God (v. 10)
3. That they be strengthened with all power, attaining steadfastness and patience with joyfulness (v. 11)

### Philippians 1:9-11
1. That their love may abound in all knowledge and judgment (v. 9)
2. That they may approve the things that are excellent (v. 10)
3. Be sincere and blameless (v. 10).
4. That they be filled with the fruits of righteousness (v. 11)

### INTERCEDE FOR THESE
1. Friends and acquaintances
2. Enemies
3. Civil authorities
4. Your nation
5. The sick
6. Others

### FIVE STEPS IN PRAYING FOR THE LOST
1. Cultivate a genuine concern and love for the lost.
2. Discover specific persons in your circles of relationship who are lost.
3. Pray appropriately and in detail for these specific persons:
   - "Lord, bring effective witnesses, including me, across their paths."
   - "Savior, arrange circumstances in their lives so that the details of their lives will point them to Christ."
   - "Lord, send Your Holy Spirit in great power to convict them of their sin and lostness."
   - "Father, cause them to understand through Your Holy Spirit that Jesus is adequate for their salvation from sin."
4. Persist in prayer.
5. Thank God for each step He takes in moving them to salvation.

### BROADEN YOUR VISION FOR THE LOST
1. For God to remind missionaries of their original call as Christ's ambassadors. If you can, name specific missionaries you have met or heard.
2. For God to quicken the hearts of lost persons in the paths of missionaries and to give missionaries sensitivity to the lost in meeting their needs, relating to them, and drawing them to Christ
3. For God to enlarge the evangelistic vision of your own church and to equip witnesses in it
4. For God to give you a greater burden for the lost and skill and sensitivity in witnessing

### PRAYING FOR OTHER CHRISTIANS
1. For unity
2. For preservation and deliverance
3. For sanctification, or holiness

# PRAYER GUIDE 12
## Praying for Missions

### PRAYING FOR LABORERS

1. Pray for the youth and adults of your church to be sensitive to the call of the Holy Spirit to missionary service.
2. Pray for your children to be called into the harvest.
3. Pray for college and seminary students to learn God's specific plans for their lives.
4. Pray for evangelists and pastors God may call to places of greater need.
5. Pray about your involvement in the harvest.

### PAUL'S *A* TO *F* PRAYER REQUESTS

Acceptance by coworkers—other believers (see Rom. 15:31b)

Boldness in witnessing (see Eph. 6:19)

Clarity in communicating (see Col. 4:4)

Deliverance from evil (see Rom. 15:31a)

Extension of the ministry (see Col. 4:2-3)

Fruitfulness in spiritual endeavors (see 2 Thess. 3:1)

### PRAYERS BASED ON MISSIONS IMPERATIVES

1. Pray that the lost will hear the gospel.
2. Pray that the lost will repent and believe.
3. Pray that missionaries will go. For instance:
   + Church planters who can help start new churches and disciple believers
   + Evangelists who can preach the gospel
   + Teachers who can help train others to spread the gospel
   + Christian groups in other cultures and nations who can develop and send missionaries to their own people around the world
   + Bible translators who can help provide the Bible in a language people can read and understand
4. Pray that God will be glorified.

### PERSONAL NEEDS

1. Language and culture
2. Health and safety
3. Children and aging parents
4. Spiritual growth and emotional well-being

### WORK NEEDS

1. Cooperative relationships with nationals
2. Professional skills (such as preacher, doctor, agriculturist, accountant, and so forth)
3. Success in witnessing and church planting
4. Effectiveness in discipling believers and nurturing churches

### MISSIONS FUNCTIONS/MINISTRIES

1. Church development, spiritual awakening, and discipling
2. Church planting, evangelism, and partnership evangelism
3. Leadership training (seminaries, Bible and lay institutes, extension programs)
4. Hospitals, clinics, public health
5. Publication work and literature distribution
6. Mass media (television, radio, films)
7. Student evangelism and youth work

### PSALM 67

God be merciful unto us, and bless us,
and cause His face to shine upon us;
That thy way may be known upon earth,
thy saving health among all nations.
Let the people praise thee, O God;
let all the people praise thee.
O let the nations be glad and sing for joy:
for thou shalt judge the people righteously,
and govern the nations upon earth.
Let the peoples praise thee, O God;
let all the people praise thee.
Then shall the earth yield her increase;
and God, even our own God, shall bless us.
God shall bless us;
and all the ends of the earth shall fear Him.

### NORTH AMERICAN MISSIONS INTERCESSORY PRAYERLINE
1-800-554-PRAY

### INTERNATIONAL MISSIONS PRAYERLINE
1-800-395-PRAY

# How to Memorize Scripture

1. Choose a verse that speaks to your need or, if the verse is assigned, discover how it meets a particular life need.
2. Understand the verse. Read the verse in relation to its context. Read the verse in various translations.
3. Record memory verses on a cassette tape so that you can listen to them. Leave a space after each verse so that you can practice quoting it. Then record the verse a second time so that you can hear it again after you have quoted it.
4. Locate and underline the verse in your Bible so that you can see where it is on the page.
5. Write the verse on a card, including the Scripture reference and the topic it addresses. This allows you to relate the verse to a particular subject so that you can find it when a need arises.
6. Place the written verse in prominent places so that you can review it while you do other tasks. Put it over the kitchen sink, on the bathroom mirror, on the dashboard for reviewing at stop lights, and on the refrigerator.
7. Commit the verse to memory. Divide it into natural, meaningful phrases and learn it word by word. If you learn it word-perfect in the beginning, it will be set in your memory, will be easier to review, will give you boldness when you are tempted, and will convince the person with whom you are sharing that he or she can trust your word.
8. Review, review, review. This is the most important secret of Scripture memorization. Review a new verse at least once a day for six weeks. Review the verse weekly for the next six weeks and then monthly for the rest of your life.
9. Use these activities to set a verse in your mind: see it in pictorial form; sing it, making up your own tune; pray it back to God; do it by making it a part of your life; and use it as often as possible.
10. Have someone check your memorization. Or write the verse from memory and then check it yourself, using your Bible.
11. Make Scripture memorization fun. Make a game of remembering verses with your family and friends. One game is to cite a reference to someone before the person can cite it to you. For instance, if you cite John 15:5, the other person must quote it. If the other person says the reference first, you must quote it.
12. Set a goal for the number of verses you will memorize each week. Do not try to learn too many verses so fast that you do not have time for daily review, which is essential to memorizing Scripture.[1]

---

[1]Adapted from Avery T. Willis, Jr., *MasterLife 1: The Disciple's Cross* (Nashville: LifeWay Press, 1996), 112.

# How to Have a Quiet Time

Spending time with Christ each day will keep Him at the center of your life. If you have not been having a quiet time, begin by setting aside at least 15 minutes each day. If you keep this appointment, you will be blessed in many ways.

## Keys to Success

1. Make a personal quiet time the top priority of your day.
   - Select a time that fits your schedule. Usually, morning is preferable, but you may need to choose another time.
2. Prepare the night before.
   - If your quiet time is in the morning, set your alarm. If it is difficult for you to wake up, plan to exercise, bathe, dress, and eat before your quiet time.
   - Select a place where you can be alone. Gather materials, such as your Bible, a notebook, and a pen or a pencil, and put them in the place selected so that you will not waste time in the morning.

---

3. Develop a balanced plan of Bible reading and prayer.
   - Pray for guidance during your quiet time.
   - Follow a systematic plan to read your Bible. You may want to follow the one provided in *Day by Day in God's Kingdom: A Discipleship Journal*.[1]
   - Make notes of what God says to you through His Word. During this course you should record notes in the Daily Master Communication Guide in the margin of each day's material. After this course you may develop your own prayer journal or use *Day by Day in God's Kingdom: A Discipleship Journal*.
   - Pray in response to the Scriptures you have read.
   - As you pray, use various components of prayer. For example, using the acronym ACTS—adoration, confession, thanksgiving, supplication—helps you remember the components.
4. Be persistent until you are consistent.
   - Strive for consistency rather than for length of time spent. Try to have a few minutes of quiet time every day rather than long devotional periods every other day.
   - Expect interruptions. Satan tries to prevent you from spending time with God. He fears even the weakest Christians who are on their knees. Plan around interruptions rather than being frustrated by them.
5. Focus on the Person you are meeting rather than on the habit of having the quiet time. If you scheduled a meeting with the person you admire most, you would not allow anything to stand in your way. Meeting God is even more important. He created you with a capacity for fellowship with Him, and He saved you to bring about that fellowship.[2]

## Communicate with the Master

1. Praise God for being your Lord.
2. Deny yourself by confessing your sins and by surrendering your will, mind, and emotions to the Master.
3. Take up your cross daily by making yourself available for the Master's use.
4. List questions for which you need answers, matters for which you need guidance, weaknesses for which you need strength, or any other concern about which you wish to communicate with God.
5. Expect God to speak to you about matters on which He places priority and about which He is ready to reveal His will.

## Listen to God Speak to You

1. Read the Bible systematically. Read through an entire book of the Bible, more or less a chapter a day. Balance your choice of books by reading different types of writings in the Bible.
2. Listen to God speak in one of the four areas for which the Bible states it is to be used: teaching—teaching the faith, rebuking—correcting error, correcting—resetting the direction of a person's life, and training—training a person in right living (see 2 Tim. 3:16-17). As you read the Bible, review these four areas until you automatically recognize when God is speaking in these ways.
3. Mark words, phrases, and verses that appeal to you. In the margin you may want to place *M* beside verses you want to memorize, *T* beside verses with significant teachings for your life, *C* for correcting life's course, *R* for rebuke, or *I* for instruction in right living. Periodically review verses you have marked in a category.
4. Summarize what God has said to you through the Scripture. During this course you should record notes in the Daily Master Communication Guide in the margin of each day's material. After this course you may develop your own prayer journal or use *Day by Day in God's Kingdom: A Discipleship Journal*. Review what you record. See whether a pattern emerges.
5. Pray about what God has said to you. Use the Daily Master Communication Guide format to write what you say to God. If you use this plan regularly, it will become second nature to you as you talk with God. Later, as you review your notes, you will see patterns in what God has communicated to you over a period of time.[3]

---

[1] *Day by Day in God's Kingdom: A Discipleship Journal* provides Scriptures, memory verses, and room to record what you experience in your quiet time. To order item 0-7673-2577-X: WRITE LifeWay Church Resources Customer Service, One LifeWay Plaza, Nashville, TN 37234-0113; FAX order to (615) 251-5933; PHONE 1-800-458-2772; EMAIL to *CustomerService@lifeway.com*; ONLINE at *www.lifeway.com*; or visit the LifeWay Christian Store serving you.
[2] Adapted from Avery T. Willis, Jr., *MasterLife 1: The Disciple's Cross* (Nashville: LifeWay Press, 1996), 19–20.
[3] Adapted from Avery T. Willis, Jr., *MasterLife 3: The Disciple's Victory* (Nashville: LifeWay Press, 1996), 25–26.

# BIBLE PROMISES

## Collecting Bible Promises

Bible promises are extremely valuable to anyone making requests of God. The promises tell us what to expect of God, and they give us necessary conditions for positive answers. Promises need to be found, marked, recorded, memorized, and used.

1. Watch for promises in your regular Bible reading, devotional books, sermons, and the testimonies of others. See the promises listed below in "Some Bible Prayer Promises."
2. Mark promises in your Bible by underlining or by using a chosen symbol or color.
3. Record promises on the chart on page 221 or in a prayer journal.
4. Memorize promises and try to recall them throughout the day.
5. Most importantly, use Bible promises in your prayers.

## Using Bible Promises in Prayer

As you face a particular circumstance, God often brings to your mind a promise, or you will notice something in your Bible reading that you feel is a word from God related to your need. Study the promise in its scriptural context to learn (1) to whom the promise applies and (2) conditions tied to the promise.

Be careful to claim promises that apply to your need. As you pray, allow the promise to guide you in what you should ask. Remembering what God has promised will help you trust God for His best answer for your prayer. Using Bible promises will help you pray in faith. As you face your need, remember the promise and include it in the wording of your prayer. For example:

*Promise:* "There hath no temptation taken you but such as is common to man: but God is faithful, who will not suffer you to be tempted above that ye are able; but will with the temptation also make a way to escape, that ye may be able to bear it" (1 Cor. 10:13).

*Prayer:* "Lord, I am facing a temptation that is difficult for me to resist. Your Word states that You will not allow me to be tempted beyond my ability to resist. You have also promised me a way to escape so that I can bear it. Guide me to know and follow the escape plan You have for me."

## Some Bible Prayer Promises

1. "If my people, which are called by my name, shall humble themselves, and pray, and seek my face, and turn from their wicked ways; then will I hear from heaven, and will forgive their sin, and will heal their land" (2 Chron. 7:14).
2. "It shall come to pass, that before they call, I will answer; and while they are yet speaking, I will hear" (Isa. 65:24).
3. "Call unto me, and I will answer thee, and shew thee great and mighty things which thou knowest not" (Jer. 33:3).
4. "If two of you shall agree on earth as touching any thing that they shall ask, it shall be done for them of my Father which is in heaven. For where two or three are gathered together in my name, there am I in the midst of them" (Matt. 18:19-20).
5. "All things, whatsoever ye shall ask in prayer, believing, ye shall receive" (Matt. 21:22).
6. "What things soever ye desire, when ye pray, believe that ye receive them, and ye shall have them" (Mark 11:24).
7. "If ye shall ask any thing in my name, I will do it" (John 14:14).
8. "If ye abide in me, and my words abide in you, ye shall ask what ye will, and it shall be done unto you" (John 15:7).
9. "Hitherto have ye asked nothing in my name: ask, and ye shall receive, that your joy may be full" (John 16:24).
10. "Be careful for nothing; but in every thing by prayer and supplication with thanksgiving let your requests be made known unto God. And the peace of God, which passeth all understanding, shall keep your hearts and minds through Christ Jesus" (Phil. 4:6-7).
11. "Confess your faults one to another, and pray one for another, that ye may be healed. The effectual fervent prayer of a righteous man availeth much" (Jas. 5:16).
12. "This is the confidence that we have in him, that, if we ask any thing according to his will, he heareth us. And if we know that he hear us, whatsoever we ask, we know that we have the petitions that we desired of him" (1 John 5:14-15).

| BIBLE PROMISES | | |
|---|---|---|
| Reference | Promise | Conditions |
| | | |
| | | |
| | | |
| | | |
| | | |
| | | |
| | | |
| | | |
| | | |
| | | |
| | | |
| | | |
| | | |
| | | |
| | | |
| | | |
| | | |
| | | |
| | | |
| | | |
| | | |
| | | |
| | | |
| | | |
| | | |
| | | |
| | | |
| | | |
| | | |
| | | |
| | | |
| | | |

You may reproduce this chart for your personal use.

# PRAISE AND THANKSGIVING LIST

*"Devote yourselves to prayer, keeping alert in it with an attitude of thanksgiving"* (Col. 4:2, NASB).

| Praise/Thanksgiving | Scripture | Blessings Received |
|---|---|---|
| | | |
| | | |
| | | |
| | | |
| | | |
| | | |
| | | |
| | | |
| | | |
| | | |
| | | |
| | | |
| | | |
| | | |
| | | |
| | | |
| | | |
| | | |
| | | |
| | | |

You may reproduce this chart for your personal use.

# DAILY INTERCESSION

## Daily Prayer Requests

Listing prayer requests helps you remember what you requested and reminds you to continue the prayer until God answers it or changes your asking. This process aids you in praying with your mind.

You need two basic categories for daily intercession:

*Permanent daily intercession.* On this list record requests you want to pray for every day on a permanent basis. Using copies of "Daily Prayer List" on page 224, design your own list, including subjects related to your family members, your work, your church, and so forth. Do not make it too long. Use the list as a tool for praying intelligently and efficiently, but do not become a slave to the list.

*Temporary daily intercession.* These requests are concerns you want to pray for daily but only temporarily—items that change frequently, such as persons who are ill, a special upcoming event or project, or a lost person. You may pray for these requests over a long period of time. Nevertheless, the request is of a temporary rather than a permanent nature.

## Ask Specifically

In intercessory prayer both a request mentioned to others and the prayer prayed should be specific. In intercession you are requesting change. Use an action verb in your intercessory prayer to express what you believe God wants to change in attitudes, persons, or situations. Use words such as *convert, save, heal, guide, provide, increase, call, restrain,* and similar words that indicate change. Being specific about the changes you are praying for helps you improve your asking.

Avoid generalities such as "Bless the hospital work" and "Be with our pastor." Jesus has already promised to "be with" believers (see Matt. 28:20). Pray what you mean and mean what you pray. Listing events, people, and agencies in prayer without requesting anything for them is not praying specifically. Describing conditions to God is not asking. When you ask specifically, you can recognize when God answers. That enables you to give specific thanksgiving for His answer.

# WEEKLY INTERCESSION

## Weekly Prayer Requests

Prayer lists can grow to the point that they overwhelm you if you pray for each request each day. Keeping a set of weekly prayer lists will help. By dividing subjects and requests into seven lists, one for each day of the week, you can better manage a large number and variety of requests.

You may want to develop your own lists, using a separate sheet of paper for each day of the week. If you prefer, use copies of "Weekly Prayer List," page 225. Add subjects to each day's list to suit your prayer patterns. For instance, you might pray for the lost during a special time on Sunday morning before church. You might want to divide personal requests among the days of the week. Whatever approach you use, balance the number of requests for any given day so that you do not become overwhelmed and quit praying.

## Pray Around the World in a Week

Your burden for missions may require that you spend more than one day a week in prayer for missions. You may use a prayer calendar to pray for missionaries on their birthdays.[1] Or focus your prayers on missions and world evangelization by using a map to pray around the world in a week.

You may want to pray like this for the missions work taking place on each continent: Sunday—North America, Monday—South and Central America, Tuesday—Africa, Wednesday—Europe and the Middle East, Thursday—Asia, Friday—Australia and the sea islands, Saturday—world evangelization. You may want to start a prayer list for each day. As you study missions work in a particular country, record special requests on the appropriate day's list. For instance, if you learned about a need for a new church in an urban area of Venezuela, you would record that request on your list for Monday. Then as you prayed for the work in South America, you could pray specifically for this need.

---

[1] A missionary prayer calendar is included in *Open Windows*, a quarterly devotional guide. To order: WRITE LifeWay Church Resources Customer Service, One LifeWay Plaza, Nashville, TN 37234-0113; FAX order to (615) 251-5933; PHONE 1-800-458-2772; EMAIL to *CustomerService@lifeway.com*; ONLINE at *www.lifeway.com*; or visit the LifeWay Christian Store serving you.

| DAILY PRAYER LIST | | | | |
|---|---|---|---|---|
| Request | Date | Bible Promise | Answer | Date |
|  |  |  |  |  |
|  |  |  |  |  |
|  |  |  |  |  |
|  |  |  |  |  |
|  |  |  |  |  |
|  |  |  |  |  |
|  |  |  |  |  |
|  |  |  |  |  |
|  |  |  |  |  |
|  |  |  |  |  |
|  |  |  |  |  |
|  |  |  |  |  |
|  |  |  |  |  |
|  |  |  |  |  |
|  |  |  |  |  |
|  |  |  |  |  |
|  |  |  |  |  |
|  |  |  |  |  |
|  |  |  |  |  |
|  |  |  |  |  |
|  |  |  |  |  |
|  |  |  |  |  |
|  |  |  |  |  |
|  |  |  |  |  |

You may reproduce this chart for your personal use.

# WEEKLY PRAYER LIST

Day: _____

Subjects: _____

_____

_____

Continents: _____

| Request | Date | Answer | Date |
|---------|------|--------|------|
|  |  |  |  |
|  |  |  |  |
|  |  |  |  |
|  |  |  |  |
|  |  |  |  |
|  |  |  |  |
|  |  |  |  |
|  |  |  |  |
|  |  |  |  |
|  |  |  |  |
|  |  |  |  |
|  |  |  |  |
|  |  |  |  |
|  |  |  |  |
|  |  |  |  |
|  |  |  |  |
|  |  |  |  |

You may reproduce this chart for your personal use.

# LEADER GUIDE

**Overview of** *Disciple's Prayer Life*

*Disciple's Prayer Life* is a 13-week course that guides Christians to develop an intimate and effective prayer life. It also provides guidance for developing or improving individual and churchwide prayer ministries.

*Disciple's Prayer Life* consists of two elements: individual study and small-group sessions. The workbook is a self-study, interactive tool for guiding individual study. One characteristic of *Disciple's Prayer Life* that makes it different from most books on prayer is that it guides learners to practice the principles of prayer daily. In this way, the concepts have tremendous life-changing potential. Learners must do more than just read the book. They must complete the learning activities on a daily basis. This must be done if the goal of changed prayer lives is to be achieved.

Each week's material is divided into five days of study. This helps learners pace the study, and it enhances learning by helping learners digest one idea before moving to another subject. Learners should be encouraged to complete each week's study one day at a time.

Small-group sessions bring together the individual study with an opportunity to discuss and share insights in a group setting. Praying together in a small group allows participants to further develop their skills in prayer. Each small-group session is designed for one to two hours.

**Planning for** *Disciple's Prayer Life*

Check the box beside each item as you complete the following planning activities.

❑ Study "Introduction to *Disciple's Prayer Life*," beginning on page 6, to familiarize yourself with the course.

❑ Read "Prayer-Retreat Plans" on pages 228–30.

❑ Enlist participants by using the suggestions in "Prayer-Retreat Plans." If you do not use the retreat, enlist participants through personal invitation or through the normal process your church uses to invite participation. Be sure to make clear the demands of the course. Participants need to be ready to commit themselves to daily study, the daily practice of prayer, and attendance at weekly group sessions.

The weekly session material is designed for a group of 6 to 8 persons. It can be adapted to be used by 2 to 5 if no other participants are available. To allow for maximal individual participation in the group sessions, do not attempt to lead a group of more than 10. Eight is ideal.

❑ Determine the session schedule. Select one of the following schedules, but remain flexible and change later if you need to.

a. *1 hour.* This plan is a minimal time for the group session. Use the minimal time allotments listed in "During the Session."

b. *1½ to 2 hours.* This plan allows more time for sharing and praying. Many groups may find this the most satisfying amount of time to process learning and pray. Adapt the time allotments in "During the Session" to align with your agenda.

❑ Arrange the meeting place and time. Consider the following options.

a. *Sunday evening at church.* Many groups will choose to meet during the discipleship-training time. The length of your sessions (1, 1½, or 2 hours) will determine when the session must begin. A small classroom that comfortably handles a group of eight is adequate. Try not to meet in a large room. You want to cultivate a sense of intimacy within the group. This may be an ideal time and place since child care may be provided by the ongoing discipleship-training activities.

b. *Weekday or evening in a home.* Some groups prefer the informal atmosphere of a home for their sessions. Using the same home each week is the best approach for avoiding confusion about the location. However, you may want to rotate the meeting place among several homes. Some groups may choose a mid-morning or mid-afternoon hour. They could occasionally include a covered-dish luncheon before or after the session. Others prefer or require an evening hour.

c. *Before work.* If your group selects this option, allow for ample time for the session and for getting to work on time.

d. *Saturday morning.* This time allows for a variety of locations: church, a home, a community room, a private dining room at a local restaurant (include a light breakfast before or after), and so forth.

❑ Secure resources. Participants should pay for their own materials unless the church decides to pay a portion of the expense. You may want to provide scholarships for persons who cannot afford the materials. Order materials at least six weeks in advance. WRITE LifeWay Church Resources Customer Service, One LifeWay Plaza, Nashville, TN 37234-0113; FAX order to (615) 251-5933; PHONE 1-800-458-2772; EMAIL to *CustomerService@lifeway.com*; order ONLINE at *www.lifeway.com*; or visit the LifeWay Christian Store serving you.

a. *Disciple's Prayer Life* (item 0-7673-2611-3). Each participant will need a copy of this workbook.

b. *The Life-Changing Power of Prayer* by T. W. Hunt (0-6330-1980-1). Each participant will need a copy of this book.

c. Extra Bibles, pencils, and blank paper.

d. Optional: separate copies of the prayer guides on pages 205–17. Providing extra copies will greatly assist participants as they complete their daily assignments and practice praying. Keep in mind that these materials are copyrighted. They may be duplicated *only* for the personal use of persons who have purchased copies of *Disciple's Prayer Life* workbook.

❑ Secure additional materials. Read "Before the Session" for each session in this leader guide. Make a list of materials you will need for the entire study. Order the resources that are not readily available from your church.

❑ Plan to keep accurate records. Enrollment and attendance in *Disciple's Prayer Life* should be counted in your discipleship-training program. Keeping records will also help you determine who is eligible for Christian Growth Study Plan diplomas at the end of the study. Persons missing any sessions should complete makeup assignments to qualify for diplomas (see p. 243).

## Leadership Suggestions

1. Facilitate the group session. You may feel inadequate to be a "teacher" on the subject of prayer. Keep in mind that participants should have spent several hours during the week with their personal tutors—their *Disciple's Prayer Life* workbooks and the Holy Spirit. Your primary role in the group session is to help participants share insights, ask questions, share victories and frustrations, review basic teachings, and practice praying. Consider yourself a lead learner rather than a prayer expert.

2. Pray humbly and privately for great spiritual growth in your life. Endeavor to exemplify in your attitudes and prayers the teachings presented in *Disciple's Prayer Life*. Your model of being a learner and a faithful pray-er will challenge group members to be the same.

3. In reporting answers to questions about personal experiences or habits, give yours first to help others feel free to share. In quoting memory verses, quote yours first as a pattern for others to follow. In discussing factual questions, however, the answers should come from the members first.

4. If the prayers in the group do not seem to follow the biblical pattern or the prayer skill being taught, open a discussion afterward about how that prayer time could have been improved. Jesus Himself analyzed prayer and spoke against its faults. He pointed out "vain repetitions" in Matthew 6:7. Do not hesitate to lovingly correct poor habits or unhealthy practices.

5. Affirm the good praying habits you notice. *Disciple's Prayer Life* should help eliminate poor prayer patterns and strengthen good ones.

6. Study the following instructions for group praying. Use a variety of types of group praying during the sessions.

## Intercession in a Group

When leading a group to participate in intercessory prayer, suggest that an individual pray for only one subject related to his or her prayer and leave other topics for others to mention in their prayers. This opens the way for more members to pray. It also enables participants to pay better attention to others' prayers rather than continually revise their own mental lists of items they could pray for. Encourage members to pray several different times rather than to pray one long prayer for several needs.

In receiving prayer requests from the group, guard against using the prayer time for long, unnecessary descriptions of a situation. Avoid receiving too many requests before stopping to take the requests to the Lord in prayer. If too many requests are shared, people tend to pray, "Lord, You have heard all of the things we have talked about, and we want You to meet these needs." We need to make our prayers specific so that we and the Lord know what we expect Him to do in each case.

If requests keep consuming too much time, consider—
+ limiting requests to only one type of need;
+ asking participants to share their requests by praying for the need;
+ allotting a specific time for requests and sticking to it;
+ allowing only one- or two-sentence requests.

## Sentence Prayers

Praying a sentence prayer is an easy way to learn to pray. A simple way to start is to provide part of a structured sentence that each person completes. The group is given the first part of the sentence, which each person is to repeat. Then each individual completes the prayer with his or her own word or words. For example, each person says, "God, I thank You for …" and completes the sentence.

This pattern can be used in praying for missions advance. Individuals supply the name of a country needing the gospel: "I pray that the lost people in the country of _____ will hear the gospel of Jesus" or "I pray for the Christians in _____ to be bold in witnessing."

When time is limited, use sentence prayers. The leader needs to state the length of prayer used, the subjects covered, and how the prayer time will close.

## Conversational Prayer

Conversational prayer is a group talking to God as in normal conversations. It is characterized by the following.
1. Short two- or three-sentence prayers are used.
2. One subject at a time is prayed for. Several members add their prayers on that topic before anyone brings a new prayer need to God.
3. As in conversation, no order is prescribed for who will pray, how many times a person talks, or for how long.
4. I and my are used instead of we and us, especially when a person is expressing a personal confession or need.
5. Formal terms such as *Dear Heavenly Father* are not used unless by the first person praying, who wants to welcome God and acknowledge His presence.
6. Conversation continues as long as the group desires or time permits.
7. *Amen* and *In Jesus' name* are not used during the middle of the conversation with God. The person closing the time of prayer acknowledges that the prayer conversation was made possible through Jesus' name.

# Prayer-Retreat Plans

This retreat is designed to teach biblical principles of praying through instruction and practice. It can stand alone as a means of equipping Christians to pray more effectively or can be used to introduce *Disciple's Prayer Life*. The final session of the retreat is designed to enlist participants in a detailed study of the course. A group should be established for each eight persons who sign up for the course.

This retreat plan includes content for five hours of study and praying. Customize your retreat schedule by adding breaks, meals, recreation, and so forth. Extending the retreat over a two-day period (Friday night and Saturday or two weeknights, for example) will allow for greater assimilation of the content into life.

## BEFORE THE RETREAT

While preparing for the retreat, pray for God's guidance. Enlist others in the church to pray for the event with you. If the size of the retreat dictates, you may want to establish some work groups to prepare for publicity, lodging, meals, breaks, recreation, program, and so forth. You or the assigned work group should complete the following preparatory activities.
1. Decide on the date, time, and place for the retreat. Reserve and set up the retreat area. The room should be set up for groups of eight (at tables if possible).
2. Enlist participants. This retreat should be open to all church members interested in learning to pray more effectively. Retreat participants will not be obligated to join a *Disciple's Prayer Life* group, although they will be invited to do so. Each should bring a Bible, pencil, and notepad.
3. Provide extra Bibles, pencils, paper, name tags, and markers.
4. Provide for child care if needed.
5. Prepare and display a large poster that lists the week titles from *Disciple's Prayer Life*. Prepare an arrow that can point to the week to be studied each session. Save this poster for use each week of the study.
6. Read "During the Retreat" and list each content area to be dealt with. You will need to study each area before the retreat. If time permits, study all 13 weeks of *Disciple's Prayer Life*. Prepare to guide each activity. If you desire, enlist others to prepare some of the content presentations to increase variety and interest.
7. Make a separate list of additional resources you may need to conduct the activities. Secure these resources. The retreat requires a minimum of additional resources.
8. Develop an agenda based on your schedule. Add breaks, meals, and recreation according to your preferences. Reserve approximately half of each session for prayer by the group even if you do not complete the study activities.
9. Depending on your plans and schedule, you may want to provide *Disciple's Prayer Life* workbooks to sell to those who plan to join a *Disciple's Prayer Life* group. In this way they can begin studying week 1 immediately.

## DURING THE RETREAT

**Getting Acquainted** (15 mins.)
1. Divide into groups of eight. Explain that these groups will

stay together for the duration of the retreat. Make sure that each person has a name tag.

2. Ask each person to share his or her name, family status, and earliest fond memory related to prayer.

3. Introduce retreat leaders. Briefly overview the retreat agenda. Begin with an opening prayer inviting the Lord to teach participants to pray more effectively.

## Session 1: Knowing and Praising God (45 mins.)

1. Provide a five-minute lecture on the names of God (week 2, day 1) and what they mean to someone who approaches God in prayer. As you discuss each name, write it on a chalkboard, on an overhead cel, or on poster board.

2. Draw the Star of David (week 2, days 3–4). Add the six words describing God and give a brief definition of each.

3. Conduct a Bible search for names of Jesus by assigning and reading the Scriptures from week 2, day 5 that reveal His various names. Ask small groups to discuss how these names affect their relationships with Jesus in prayer.

4. Ask small groups to reflect on the One to whom we pray. Ask them to pray sentence prayers of praise to God for who He is. Each prayer should contain only one trait or name, but each person may pray several times.

5. Conclude the session by examining Mary's Magnificat in Luke 1:47-55. Invite someone to pray this prayer of adoration to God for the group.

## Session 2: Personal Fellowship with God (60 mins.)

1. Introduce the concepts of a personal prayer identity, main prayer activity, and relationship with God by conducting Bible studies of Cornelius and Daniel (week 3, day 2).

2. Summarize "The Lord Is My Professor" on page 35. Share your own 23rd Psalm. Give instructions and invite participants to write their own psalms.

3. After most have finished, ask small-group members to share their psalms with one another.

4. Illustrate from David's life how we can select an identity according to need (week 3, day 3).

5. Ask everyone to spend time in silent prayer, walking in personal fellowship with God through their prayer identities and using their main prayer activities.

## Session 3: Principles of Asking (60 mins.)

1. Introduce the four reasons God answers prayer (week 1, days 2-5). Give special attention to the material on

acknowledging God. Guide a brief Bible study of prayers that illustrate this basis for prayer.

2. Name and describe the eight principles of asking (week 9).

3. Divide small groups into groups of four. Ask these groups to pray together and acknowledge God's sovereignty, character, glory, and honor. Ask them to give thanks for the privilege of prayer and to ask for the development of proper attitudes in their lives.

4. Guide a Bible study of the three stop signs to prayer (week 10, day 1) and the six roadblocks to answered prayer (week 10, day 2).

5. Discuss the meaning of *confession* and the necessity of agreeing with God. Point out that confession is not only for sin but also for confessing needs, confessing Jesus as Lord and Savior, and confessing truth.

6. Ask participants to turn to Psalm 51 and pray the psalm privately.

7. Conclude the session by asking persons to confess truths they know from Scripture. Quote together Psalm 67:3.

## Session 4: Praying for Missions (60 mins.)

1. Quickly mention the variety of needs we can pray about for missions. (Use the lists in prayer guide 12.) Ask members to take notes as you describe ways they can pray.

2. Distribute to each group missions magazines, newsletters, local newspapers, denominational newsletters, and other resources with missions news. Ask each participant to locate one or more specific persons or needs to pray for.

3. Ask small groups to share with one another missions concerns they discovered. Ask one person to lead a prayer for each concern as it is mentioned.

4. Assign a continent and a group of states to each group. Ask each small group to brainstorm the kinds of missions needs that probably exist in the assigned areas.

5. Ask groups to pray Paul's A to F prayers in prayer guide 12 for the assigned areas and the Christians and missionaries in those areas.

6. Conclude the session by reading Matthew 9:35-38. Divide into pairs and pray that God will call from your church laborers for the harvest. Pray for specific individuals who come to mind.

## Session 5: Invitation to *Disciple's Prayer Life* (60 mins.)

1. Display the week-titles poster. Using the prayer guides as needed, give a brief overview of each week.

2. Describe the characteristics and demands of a LIFE course. Give illustrations from *Disciple's Prayer Life* as appropriate.

3. Display and describe the features of the workbook that will aid in developing an intimate and effective prayer life.

4. Summarize the contents of week 13, giving special attention to the variety of prayer ministries individuals and churches can become involved in.

5. Ask someone to read or summarize "One Hundred Years of Hourly Intercession" (week 13, day 3, p. 195).

6. Invite participants to join a *Disciple's Prayer Life* group to develop a more intimate and effective prayer life. Give details of the group sessions and how to enroll.

7. Assure members that they will be expected to pray only when they want to.

8. Ask everyone to stand and join hands. Call on someone to lead in a closing prayer of commitment that all participants will help make their church a house of prayer.

### AFTER THE RETREAT

1. Follow up with those who have enrolled for *Disciple's Prayer Life*. Make sure that they understand what they need to do to prepare for session 1.

2. Begin preparation for session 1.

# Developing a Life of Prayer

### BEFORE THE SESSION

❑ Carefully study week 1 and complete all of the learning activities.

❑ Display the week-titles poster you prepared for the prayer retreat, with the arrow pointing to week 1.

❑ Review the three assignments participants should bring to the session (see item 5 below).

❑ Read "During the Session." Secure necessary materials and be prepared to guide each activity.

❑ Prepare or enlist a member to give a three-minute overview of week 2.

❑ Pray for each group member.

### DURING THE SESSION

**1. Arrival Activity** (10–15 mins.)
As group members arrive, ask them to think about why they have decided to participate in *Disciple's Prayer Life*. You may want to provide light refreshments. When everyone is present, spend time getting better acquainted. Share about such things as family, job, salvation experience, hobbies, and so forth. Ask each member to share why he or she has decided to study *Disciple's Prayer Life*.

**2. Highlights and Opening Prayer** (7 mins.)
Pray a brief prayer acknowledging the Holy Spirit's presence as your Teacher. Pray, "Lord, teach us to pray." Give members an opportunity to share highlights or new insights from their week's study. Share one of your own as a model for sharing. Since this is a new group, do not be discouraged if members are hesitant to share. They will become more open in time.

**3. Check Memory Verses** (3 mins.)
Divide into pairs and ask each person to check the partner's memory verse(s) for this week. Keep in mind that some may choose to memorize only one verse each week. Encourage members to memorize verses word for word and to review often.

**4. Review Introduction** (10 mins.)
+ Call attention to the distinctive features of *Disciple's Prayer Life* as a LIFE course (pp. 6–7).
+ Summarize the requirements for a Christian Growth Study Plan diploma (p. 244).
+ Emphasize the importance of a daily quiet time. Encourage members to record their communication with

God in the Daily Master Communication Guide in the margin of each day's material.

- Encourage members to use the prayer guides daily in their prayer times. Each week members should regularly review the prayer guides for the current and previous weeks of study. By doing so, they will learn to use the concepts and principles more effectively in their prayers.
- Answer any questions members may have.

**5. Reasons God Answers Prayer** (20–30 mins.)

Ask members to recall the four reasons God answers prayer. Ask them to turn to prayer guide 1 (p. 205). Review the four reasons by completing the following.

- On page 14 members were to answer two questions about how sharing a prayer request could take away from or give to God the glory for the answer. Ask them to share their answers in groups of four. Then ask them to pray in their small groups prayers of praise, acknowledging God for who He is.
- On page 18 members were asked to respond to questions about the intercession of Jesus and the Holy Spirit. Ask members to share their responses in the same groups of four and to conclude with a prayer of thanksgiving for the intercessory work of Jesus and the Holy Spirit.
- On page 19 members were asked to compare and contrast God with a human father. Ask volunteers to share responses with the large group. Discuss ways children and servants can approach God in prayer as Father and as Master (review the final paragraphs in day 5).

**6.** *Disciple's Prayer Life* **Covenant** (5 mins.)

Ask everyone to turn to the *Disciple's Prayer Life* covenant on page 9. Allow members to add to, reword, or adjust the covenant according to consensus. Members should record changes on their own copies of the covenant. Allow a brief time of silent prayer. Then ask members who are willing to make the covenant to sign their names on their copies. Give group members time to sign one another's covenant. This will remind them to support one another throughout the course.

**7. Preview Week 2** (3 min.)

Call on the person enlisted to preview week 2.

**8. Closing Prayer** (2 min.)

Stand in a circle and join hands. Lead the group in a prayer of commitment to God and to one another during this study.

## AFTER THE SESSION

1. Evaluate each activity and determine ways to improve participation in future sessions.
2. Report attendance.
3. Begin preparation for the next session.
4. Due to the nature of the course, new members should not be added after session 2. Next week will be the last opportunity to join the group.

# SESSION 2

# Knowing God

## BEFORE THE SESSION

❑ Carefully study week 2 and complete all of the learning activities.

❑ Display the week-titles poster with the arrow pointing to week 2.

❑ Provide for two groups of four with chairs close enough that members can share intimately with one another during small-group times. You may want to arrange a separate circle for large-group times.

❑ Read "During the Session." Secure necessary materials and be prepared to guide each activity.

❑ On poster board or on a large sheet of paper, draw the Star of David. Draw six blank lines, one at each point of the star. Display the poster and provide a marker to add the six qualities of God.

❑ Prepare or enlist a member to give a three-minute overview of week 3.

❑ Pray for each group member.

## DURING THE SESSION

**1. Arrival Activity** (10 mins.)

Instruct members to skim through Psalms and identify characteristics, qualities, or names of God. Ask members to add these to the appropriate lists in prayer guides 1 and 2 (pp. 205 and 207). Allow members time to share their findings with one another.

**2. Highlights and Opening Prayer** (12 mins.)

Give members an opportunity to share special highlights or new insights from their week's study. Open with prayers of adoration and praise. Ask members to mention a character trait of God or to call Him by one of His names and then to speak a word of praise or adoration. Continue by allowing each member to pray as many different times as desired.

**3. Check Memory Verses** (3 mins.)

Divide into pairs and ask each person to check the partner's memory verse(s) for this week. Review verses from last week.

**4. Small-Group Processing** (20–30 mins.)

Divide into groups of four and follow these instructions.

- Ask members to turn to page 25 and share their feelings and thoughts about the God of creation's desiring fellowship with them.
- Ask members to turn to pages 27–28 and discuss how they would pray for Mary, William, Lenzie, and Patrick in light of God's omniscience.
- Ask members to turn to page 29 and share the Bible events they listed that testified to God's power.
- Ask members to turn to pages 32–33 and discuss the meanings of Jesus' names and how those aspects of Jesus' character would be helpful in prayer.

**5. Small-Group Praying** (5 mins.)

In the same small groups of four, ask members to pray for special concerns or needs. Ask them to give special attention to offering their prayers through Jesus and basing their requests on a special aspect of Jesus' character.

**6. Large-Group Quiz** (2 mins.)

Return to the large group. Call attention to the Star of David you prepared and fill in the blanks as members call out the six qualities of God.

**7. Mary's Magnificat** (3 mins.)

Ask volunteers to share how meaningful and useful Mary's prayer has been as a model for their praise and adoration. Ask members to turn to prayer guide 2 (p. 207). Using the list of praise statements from the Magnificat, spend time in prayer, praising and adoring God for who He is and what He has done. Allow members to pray sentence prayers.

**8. Preview Week 3** (3 mins.)

Call on the person enlisted to preview week 3.

**9. Closing Prayer** (2–7 mins.)

Join hands in a circle. Ask each member to pray silently that the person on the right will develop a much greater knowledge of God during the next week. Close the way you began: in prayer, praising God aloud for who He is.

### AFTER THE SESSION

1. Evaluate each activity and determine ways to improve participation in future sessions.
2. Report attendance.
3. Begin preparation for the next session.

4. You might want to plan something special midway through the course. Begin thinking about a special event before or after session 7. Consider one of the following.

- A half-day prayer retreat. Schedule time in an informal setting like a home or a state park. Use prayer guides and prayer charts to review and practice the principles of prayer the group has learned. Include time for informal fellowship to help the group get better acquainted.
- A covered-dish meal. Allow additional time for special prayer together for your church as a house of prayer.
- A special prayer breakfast with time devoted to praying together.

## SESSION 3

# Walking in Personal Fellowship with God

### BEFORE THE SESSION

❑ Carefully study week 3 and complete all of the learning activities.

❑ Display the week-titles poster with the arrow pointing to week 3.

❑ Carefully review prayer guide 3 (p. 208). Try to write an application for each relationship described. This way you will be able to help others who are having trouble understanding how to use the guide in their prayer times.

❑ Read "During the Session." Secure necessary materials and be prepared to guide each activity.

❑ Prepare or enlist a member to give a three-minute overview of week 4.

❑ Pray for each group member.

### DURING THE SESSION

**1. Arrival Activity** (12–17 mins.)

As members arrive, greet each warmly. Collect the 23rd Psalms written for day 1 (p. 37, one per person) and mix them up. Read them one at a time and allow the group to guess whose psalm you have read. After guesses have been made, ask the author to make a brief statement about why he or she selected that particular prayer identity.

If any members have written more than one psalm, give them an opportunity to share the additional psalm with the group.

**2. Highlights and Opening Prayer** (7 mins.)

Give members an opportunity to share special highlights or new insights from their week's study. Call on a member to lead in an opening prayer of thanksgiving for the privilege of having a personal relationship with God.

**3. Check Memory Verses** (3 mins.)

Divide into pairs and ask each person to check the partner's memory verse(s) for this week. Review verses from previous weeks. Ask a volunteer to share a brief testimony about how Scripture memorization is helping him or her grow spiritually. Someone else might want to share how one of the verses has been especially meaningful this week.

**4. Small-Group Sharing** (10–15 mins.)

Divide into groups of four and ask members to share the following with their small groups.

- The paragraph describing ways their prayer lives are affected by their primary relationships with God ("Describe Yourself," p. 39).
- The wonderful physical traits described on page 43.
- The natural abilities they listed on page 44.
- Prayers of praise and thanksgiving (p. 44).

**5. Small-Group Praise and Thanksgiving** (5–10 mins.)

Ask the same small groups to use sentence prayers of praise and thanksgiving for the many good gifts God has given.

**6. Large-Group Discussion** (10 mins.)

Lead a discussion about how the charts in prayer guide 3 (p. 208) can be used in prayer times. Make sure everyone understands that circumstances and needs may dictate the use of different prayer identities and prayer activities. Give some of the combinations from the charts and ask members to suggest circumstances and needs for which those relationships with God would be helpful in prayer.

**7. Personal Prayer** (5 mins.)

Ask each member to select one of the relationships with God described in prayer guide 3, based on his or her current needs. Ask members to kneel and simultaneously pray aloud. This may be a new experience for some. Encourage members not to hesitate to pray, for God rejoices when His children offer their prayers to Him. He can hear even when we all pray at once.

**8. Preview Week 4** (3 mins.)

Call on the person enlisted to preview week 4.

**9. Closing Prayer** (5 mins.)

Divide into groups of four. Ask them to huddle together like a football squad and to pray for one another's personal walk with God.

1. Evaluate each activity and determine ways to improve participation in future sessions. Think about each group member and ask yourself: *Is this person hesitant to participate? Does he or she seem to be prepared? Does he or she need a special word of encouragement this week?* Write or call group members who may need special help or a word of encouragement.
2. Report attendance.
3. Begin preparation for the next session.
4. Discuss with some or all group members ideas for the special event to precede or follow week 7. Decide what type of activity you will plan.

## SESSION 4

# Using the Bible in Prayer

### BEFORE THE SESSION

☐ Carefully study week 4 and complete all of the learning activities.

☐ Display the week-titles poster with the arrow pointing to week 4.

☐ Read "During the Session." Secure necessary materials and be prepared to guide each activity.

☐ Provide a chalkboard and chalk or paper and a marker.

☐ Prepare to teach the group to pray conversationally. See the instructions in "Conversational Prayer" on page 228.

☐ Study the case studies in activity 5 below and prepare your answers in case members have difficulty.

☐ Prepare or enlist a member to give a three-minute overview of week 5.

☐ On a poster board or large sheet of paper write Psalm 139:23-24 for use in the closing prayer.

☐ Pray for each group member.

### DURING THE SESSION

**1. Arrival Activity** (5–10 mins.)

As members arrive, ask them to share with one another the Bible promises they discovered during the week. If they have few, encourage them to search their Bibles for other promises. Activities like this permit members to expand their prayer lists, providing greater resources for their prayer times.

**2. Highlights and Opening Prayer** (7 mins.)

Give members an opportunity to share special highlights or

new insights from their week's study. Read the Bible promise in Jeremiah 33:3. Claim this promise in prayer, asking God to reveal great truths to members as they search His Word.

**3. Check Memory Verses** (3 mins.)

Call out references of memory verses from previous weeks and ask volunteers to recite the verses. Divide into pairs and ask each person to check the partner's memory verse(s) for this week.

**4. Scripture's Value in Prayer** (10 mins.)

On a chalkboard or paper write the words *holy, trustworthy, enlightening, true*. Ask members to explain how each quality of Scripture makes the Bible a valuable tool for prayer.

Ask members to describe the various ways the Bible can be used in prayer. Make sure that they mention the five ways identified in prayer guide 4 (p. 209).

**5. Case Studies** (10–15 mins.)

Read each of the following case studies. Ask members to discuss ways the person in each case study could use the Bible to help himself or herself in prayer. Ask members to suggest specific Scriptures that would be helpful.

• Martin is a very busy business executive. When he takes time to pray in the mornings before leaving home, he has difficulty focusing on anything other than the work demands facing him. Consequently, he spends most of his prayer time praying for guidance and help for the day. How could Martin use the Bible to expand his prayer concerns and prayer life?

• Angie is praying. She has asked God to forgive her for a sin she committed. She has been weak in resisting temptation; she has asked for forgiveness for this type of sin many times before. Can Scripture help her gain victory over this besetting sin? How?

• Chun Ho is concerned about his church's spiritual health. He believes that a spirit of apathy and self-satisfaction prevents the church from doing what God wants it to do. He is not sure how to pray effectively for his church or what to ask for. Could the Bible help him with this prayer concern? How?

**6. Agree or Disagree** (5 mins.)

*Disciple's Prayer Life* suggests that a command in Scripture is also a promise. Ask members to state whether they agree or disagree with that statement. After discussion help members understand that a command is indeed a promise. Encourage members to record Bible promises on the chart "Bible Promises" on page 221.

**7. Scriptural Praying** (10–15 mins.)

Divide into groups of four and pray for current needs and concerns. Encourage members to pray conversationally. Ask them to use Scripture in prayer by doing such things as quoting promises or using Bible phrases in their prayers.

**8. Preview Week 5** (3 mins.)

Call on the person enlisted to preview week 5.

**9. Closing Prayer** (7 mins.)

Display the poster with Psalm 139:23-24. Ask the group to read this passage in unison to begin your closing prayer time. Give members an opportunity to pray thoughts related to God's leadership "in the way everlasting."

### AFTER THE SESSION

1. Evaluate each activity and determine ways to improve participation in future sessions.
2. Report attendance.
3. Begin preparation for the next session.

## SESSION 5

# Expressing Gratitude in Prayer

### BEFORE THE SESSION

❑ Carefully study week 5 and complete all of the learning activities.

❑ Display the week-titles poster with the arrow pointing to week 5.

❑ Read "During the Session." Secure necessary materials and be prepared to guide each activity.

❑ Provide two poster boards or large sheets of paper and markers. Lay or display them where members can write on them.

❑ Set up chairs according to the diagram in the adjacent column. Make sure that the inner circle faces outward and the outer circle faces inward.

❑ Prepare or enlist a member to give a three-minute overview of week 6.

❑ Pray for each group member.

### DURING THE SESSION

**1. Arrival Activity** (5 mins.)

Ask members to write on the posters as many things as possible for which they are thankful. Ask them to include important things as well as things they often take for granted.

**2. Highlights and Opening Prayer** (7–12 mins.)

Give members an opportunity to share special highlights or new insights from their week's study. Use a litany approach for your opening prayer. Calling attention to the posters made during the arrival activity, ask members to begin each verse of the prayer by saying, "For …" and then mentioning one thing for which they are thankful. After the item is mentioned, call for the whole group to respond with the refrain "We give You thanks, O God our Father." Continue by alternating between the individual statement and the group response.

**3. Check Memory Verses** (3 mins.)

Divide into pairs and ask each person to check the partner's memory verse(s) for this week.

**4. Rotation Sharing** (15–20 mins.)

Divide into two groups. Ask one group to sit in a tight circle facing outward. Ask members of the other group to sit opposite the members already seated, creating a circle facing inward.

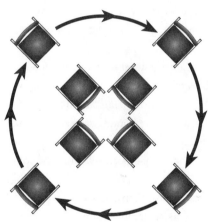

Ask pairs to share the information called for in item a below. Then rotate the outer circle clockwise so that each person has a new partner. Then ask partners to share item b. Rotate again. Continue this process until all items have been shared.

a. Ask members to look at their list of "bad" things God may have used in a special way for their good (p. 69).

b. Ask members to show or describe the four mental pictures they drew or described in day 2 (p. 70).

c. Ask members to retrieve their devotional outlines about continuous gratitude (p. 72).

d. Ask members to share "My Gratitude to God in Stone" in prayer guide 5 (p. 210).

e. Ask members to share their verbal thanksgivings on page 74.

**5. Family Praise Histories** (15–20 mins.)

Return to the large group. Ask members to share their family praise histories. Discuss ways these have been meaningful to families. Ask members to suggest ways and times praise histories could be used as meaningful family celebrations of God's goodness.

**6. Prayer Time** (10 mins.)

Suggest that the group spend this prayer time expressing gratitude to God for the many ways He has blessed them. Ask each member to mention only one item at a time. Allow members to pray as many different times as time allows. Close the prayer time by thanking God for what He is doing in this *Disciple's Prayer Life* group.

**7. Preview Week 6** (3 mins.)

Call on the person enlisted to preview week 6.

**8. Closing Prayer** (2 mins.)

Ask members to join hands and to sing the Doxology as the closing prayer.

### AFTER THE SESSION

1. Evaluate each activity and determine ways to improve participation in future sessions. If any members had not prepared their families' praise histories, encourage them to keep working. If family circumstances make this assignment difficult, ask them to prepare personal praise histories.

2. Report attendance.

3. Begin preparation for the next session.

## SESSION 6

# Worshiping God in Prayer

### BEFORE THE SESSION

❑ Carefully study week 6 and complete all of the learning activities.

❑ Display the week-titles poster with the arrow pointing to week 6.

❑ Read "During the Session." Secure necessary materials and be prepared to guide each activity.

❑ Borrow enough church hymnals for each member to use one.

❑ Make sure that you have all arrangements finalized for the special activity you planned before or after week 7. Enlist members as needed to make any last-minute preparations.

❑ Prepare or enlist a member to give a three-minute overview of week 7.
❑ Pray for each group member.

## DURING THE SESSION

**1. Arrival Activity** (10–15 mins.)

Ask members to look through the hymnals to find favorite hymns that help them worship God in spirit. Give each one an opportunity to read one stanza of the hymn selected. Select one or two hymns to sing together.

**2. Highlights and Opening Prayer** (7–12 mins.)

Give members an opportunity to share special highlights or insights from their week's study. Review the list of Bible praise words in prayer guide 6 (p. 211). Ask members to use these praise words as you pray a series of sentence prayers. Make this a truly worshipful experience.

**3. Check Memory Verses** (3 mins.)

Divide into pairs and ask each person to check the partner's memory verse(s) for this week. Review verses from previous weeks.

**4. Contrasting Worship** (20 mins.)

Divide into two groups. Ask one group to review and discuss worship in the flesh. Ask the other group to review and discuss worship in spirit and truth. Ask both groups to list examples of their assigned types of worship. Ask them to suggest ways to improve personal and corporate worship in spirit and truth. After groups have completed their studying, call for reports. Call on one member to pray for your pastor and others involved in leading public worship in your church.

**5. Exhorting Psalms** (5 mins.)

Ask members to turn to the exhorting psalms they wrote (p. 91). Ask several volunteers to read their psalms to the group. Join hands. Call on one member to lead the group in a prayer of praise. Rather than saying, "Amen," close by having everyone say in unison: "Father, we glorify and magnify Your holy and righteous name. You are worthy to be praised!" Practice the closing before beginning the prayer.

**6. Preview Week 7** (3 mins.)

Call on the person enlisted to preview week 7. Announce the schedule for the special event planned for before or after week 7.

**7. Closing Prayer** (12–17 mins.)

Focus the closing prayer on worshiping God in prayer, using Scripture and Bible praise words. Tell members that they may keep their eyes open and use their Bibles or prayer guides as they form and offer their prayers.

## AFTER THE SESSION

1. Evaluate each activity and determine ways to improve participation in future sessions.
2. Report attendance.
3. Begin preparation for the next session.

# SESSION 7

# Praying Together

## BEFORE THE SESSION

❑ Carefully study week 7 and complete all of the learning activities.
❑ Display the week-titles poster with the arrow pointing to week 7.
❑ Read "During the Session." Secure necessary materials and be prepared to guide each activity. If you have planned a special event for this week's session, adapt this agenda by expanding the length of the activities and adding activities you have chosen.
❑ Secure and display at least one copy each of *Bible Express, More, Adventure, essential connection, Living with Teenagers, Open Windows,* and *HomeLife.* All of these have helps for personal and family worship times. Each has a different format and/or target audience. If your church does not have these, they may be ordered from the sources listed on page 227.
❑ Provide paper for listing evidence in activity 4 below.
❑ Prepare or enlist a member to give a three-minute overview of week 8.
❑ Pray for each group member.

## DURING THE SESSION

**1. Arrival Activity** (5 mins.)

As members arrive, allow time for them to examine the periodicals you have displayed. If you do not have the periodicals, extend your prayer time by five minutes.

**2. Highlights and Opening Prayer** (12–17 mins.)

Give members an opportunity to share special highlights or insights from their week's study. Ask members to use conversational prayer to pray for unity in their homes and church. Pray that this unity will bring God such glory that many will come to Christ for salvation.

**3. Check Memory Verses** (3 mins.)

Divide into pairs and ask each person to check the partner's memory verse(s) for this week.

**4. Power in Unity** (20 mins.)

Read the last sentence on page 95. Distribute paper. Ask members to review week 7 and to list evidence that supports this principle for united prayer. Discuss the evidence. Give members an opportunity to share evidence from their own experiences that supports this principle.

Ask members to share briefly their experiences praying with their prayer partners and/or small group this week. Ask for sentence prayers for an increase in united praying in your church.

**5. Family and Church Prayer** (15–25 mins.)

Ask each member to share (1) how the group can pray for his or her family's devotional time and (2) thoughts about how he or she senses God leading to involvement in a prayer ministry—personal or church. After someone shares these items, call on a member to lead the group in praying for this person. Repeat this process for each group member.

**6. Preview Week 8** (3 mins.)

Call on the person enlisted to preview week 8.

**7. Closing Prayer** (2 mins.)

Call on a member to pray that God will use church leaders and group members to help your church become more of a house of prayer.

### AFTER THE SESSION

1. Evaluate each activity and determine ways to improve participation in future sessions.
2. Relate to your pastor or your church's prayer coordinator ways your group members are sensing God's leadership toward involvement in a prayer ministry. Make a prayer list based on the thoughts shared during the session. Pray for these concerns in the coming weeks. Watch for opportunities to nurture or create opportunities to develop a more extensive prayer ministry in your church.
3. Report attendance.
4. Begin preparation for the next session.
5. Find on page 202 the list of books recommended for further reading. Check their availability at your church or community library. If you locate some of them, check them out. Enlist members to read them before session 13 and to prepare brief book reports on the persons' prayer lives. Renew the books as necessary so that members will have time to finish reading.

# Agreeing with God

### BEFORE THE SESSION

❑ Carefully study week 8 and complete all of the learning activities.

❑ Display the week-titles poster with the arrow pointing to week 8.

❑ Read "During the Session." Secure materials and be prepared to guide each activity.

❑ Provide a chalkboard and chalk or paper and markers.

❑ Prepare or enlist a member to give a three-minute overview of week 9.

❑ Pray for each group member.

### DURING THE SESSION

**1. Arrival Activity** (10 mins.)

As members arrive, encourage them to find places by themselves in the meeting room. Instruct them to pray Psalm 51 and to confess their sins.

**2. Highlights** (12 mins.)

Ask members to gather as a group. Ask a volunteer for a definition of *confession* and write it on the chalkboard. Ask members to list four kinds of confession they studied this week (see p. 111). Write these on the chalkboard. Give members an opportunity to share special highlights or new insights from their week's study. Ask a couple of volunteers to share their experiences of confessing Christ as Savior.

**3. Check Memory Verses** (3 mins.)

Divide into pairs and ask each person to check the partner's memory verse(s) for this week.

**4. Certain Forgiveness** (15–20 mins.)

Give members an opportunity to share with the group their pictures of forgiveness on page 116. Show and explain your own as a model for sharing. Write the word *forgiveness* on the chalkboard. Ask what life would be like without forgiveness. Discuss responses. Divide into two groups. Ask groups to discuss ways they would help someone who felt that his or her sins were unforgivable (p. 118).

**5. Public Confession** (5–10 mins.)

Ask members to discuss the principle for public confession (p. 120): "Public confession should be limited to the circle of the offense. It should never endanger anyone else's privacy or reputation." Ask them to identify problems that can arise if this principle is not followed.

**6. New Nature** (5 mins.)

Divide into groups of four. Ask members to spend the allotted time confessing their new nature in prayer.

**7. Preview Week 9** (3 mins.)

Call on the person enlisted to preview week 9.

**8. Closing Prayer** (7–12 mins.)

Ask members to turn to their lists of truths about God and His ways that they prepared in day 5 (p. 124). After they review their lists, call for sentence prayers. Ask members to confess truths to God one at a time. Allow members to pray as many times as they wish.

### AFTER THE SESSION

1. Evaluate each activity and determine ways to improve participation in future sessions.
2. Report attendance.
3. Begin preparation for the next session.
4. Plan for extra group time in the next two weeks so that your group can make plans for a prayer retreat after the course. Call members and notify them of the extended time. During this time plan the following.
   + Retreat time, place, and agenda
   + Child care if needed
   + Refreshments, meals, breaks, and so forth
   + Recreation time if desired
   + Transportation and lodging

     Plan for a meaningful time of prayer, fellowship, and celebration. Plan to have prayer times, using conversational prayer on a variety of subjects. Create variety by praying in pairs, in small groups, and as a large group. Review activities in the introductory prayer retreat and the other 12 sessions. Select activities that were particularly meaningful to your group and plan to repeat them. Delegate responsibilities to members.

     If your church has other *Disciple's Prayer Life* groups, discuss with other leaders the possibility of having a combined retreat for all participants.

## SESSION 9

# Applying the Principles of Asking

### BEFORE THE SESSION

❑ Carefully study week 9 and complete all of the learning activities.

❑ Display the week-titles poster with the arrow pointing to week 9.

❑ Read "During the Session." Secure materials and be prepared to guide each activity.

❑ Prepare copies of the team assignment in the adjacent column.

❑ Provide a table with chairs for the arrival activity.

❑ Prepare or enlist a member to give a three-minute overview of week 10.

❑ Pray for each group member.

### DURING THE SESSION

**1. Arrival Activity** (15–20 mins.)

Direct members to the table provided. Ask them to share their lists from Matthew 5—7 and John 14—17 (p. 127). This sharing will help members expand their lists of commands and promises from these passages more quickly. In addition, some may be able to share fresh insights that others overlooked. Point out that studying these passages should be a lifelong process.

**2. Highlights and Opening Prayer** (7 mins.)

Give members an opportunity to share other special highlights or new insights from their week's study. Ask for volunteers to share about their experiences with their prayer partners. Call on one member to lead the opening prayer.

**3. Check Memory Verses** (3 mins.)

Divide into pairs and ask each person to check the partner's memory verse(s) for this week. Review verses from previous weeks.

**4. Applying the Principles** (20–30 mins.)

Divide into pairs. Assign each pair at least one principle of asking. Most, if not all, pairs should have two principles assigned to them. Ask members to review the content in week 9 for their assigned principles. Ask each team to prepare to share with the large group the following responses to its assignment. Give each team a copy of the following form.

> **Team Assignment**
> + A brief, clear statement of the principle
> + An illustration of how the principle is applied
> + A description of forces or attitudes that oppose the principle (for example, Spirit vs. flesh, humility vs. pride)
> + Ways a Christian can nurture or cultivate the habit of applying the principle to all asking
> + Things a Christian may do that would violate the principle

After teams have finished their research, call for reports. Discuss any principles or issues that are not clear.

**5. Preview Week 9** (3 mins.)

Call on the person enlisted to preview week 9.

**6. Closing Prayer** (12 mins.)

Divide into pairs. Ask each person to share with his or her partner the greatest need for growth related to the principles of asking. Ask pairs to kneel together and to pray for the needs shared. Ask those who finish to move to another room so that they will not disturb those still praying.

### AFTER THE SESSION

1. Evaluate each activity and determine ways to improve participation in future sessions.
2. Report attendance.
3. Begin preparation for the next session.
4. Continue making preparations for the prayer retreat to follow the course.

## SESSION 10

# Dealing with Hindrances and Delays

### BEFORE THE SESSION

❑ Carefully study week 10 and complete all of the learning activities.

❑ Display the week-titles poster with the arrow pointing to week 10.

❑ Read "During the Session." Secure materials and be prepared to guide each activity.

❑ Using construction paper and a marker, draw the three stop signs and six roadblocks pictured on pages 143 and 146. Draw each item on a separate sheet.

❑ Provide blank paper and pencils.

❑ Prepare or enlist a member to give a three-minute overview of week 11.

❑ Pray for each group member.

### DURING THE SESSION

**1. Arrival Activity** (25–35 mins.)

As members arrive, give each person one of the stop signs or roadblocks you drew and a blank sheet of paper. Ask each member to write a case study that illustrates a prayer that God refuses to answer or delays in answering because of the stop sign or roadblock assigned. Ask members not to use in their case studies the corresponding word or phrase on the sign, because the rest of the group will try to guess the reason for the unanswered prayer. After everyone has finished, collect the signs and the case studies. Mix up the case studies and give one case study to each individual. Lay the signs and roadblocks on the floor in the middle of the group. Ask each member to read his or her assigned case study. Instruct the group to identify the stop sign or roadblock that hinders or delays answer to the prayer. Discuss differences of opinion.

**2. Highlights and Opening Prayer** (12 mins.)

Give members an opportunity to share special highlights or new insights from their week's study. Divide into groups of three or four. Ask each member to identify without explanation the one roadblock that seems to be his or her greatest hindrance to effective praying. Have members pray conversationally for one another to gain victory in the areas identified.

**3. Check Memory Verses** (3 mins.)

Divide into pairs and ask each person to check the partner's memory verse(s) for the week.

**4. Opposites** (10 mins.)

Collect all of the signs you made. Hold up the stop signs one at a time. Ask members to brainstorm in rapid-fire order words that are opposites of the stop signs to answered prayer. Do the same for each roadblock. Discuss ways Christians can best overcome these barriers to spiritual growth and effective praying.

**5. Preview Week 11** (3 mins.)

Call on the person enlisted to preview week 11.

**6. Closing Prayer** (7–12 mins.)

Ask members to turn to prayer guide 8 (p. 213). Using the model requests from Psalm 51, spend time praying silently and then aloud for the kind of changes in our lives that lead to effective and powerful praying.

### AFTER THE SESSION

1. Evaluate each activity and determine ways to improve participation in future sessions. During the week call two or three group members and share words of encouragement. Remind them of your prayers. Ask if they have specific concerns about which you can pray with them this week. Pray with them over the phone.
2. Report attendance.
3. Begin preparation for the next session.
4. By this time you should have made the basic plans for the retreat. If not, try to finalize the basic plans and

agenda this week. Ask group members to help with the details.

5. Begin praying now about what God may want you to do at the conclusion of this course. Should you continue with this group as an ongoing group? Should you get involved in another aspect of your church's prayer ministry? Should you begin planning another semester of *Disciple's Prayer Life* with a new group? Seek God's will in these matters.

## SESSION 11

# Asking for Yourself and Others

### BEFORE THE SESSION

❑ Carefully study week 11 and complete all of the learning activities.

❑ Display the week-titles poster with the arrow pointing to week 11.

❑ Read "During the Session." Secure materials and be prepared to guide each activity.

❑ Provide paper or three-by-five-inch cards.

❑ Prepare or enlist a member to give a three-minute overview of week 12.

❑ Pray for each group member.

### DURING THE SESSION

**1. Arrival Activity** (5 mins.)
As members arrive, give each a sheet of paper or a three-by-five-inch card. Ask members to write their greatest personal prayer requests in the following areas: (1) spiritual growth, (2) family, (3) work/school or other, and (4) personal. Ask them to hold their lists for use later in the session.

**2. Highlights and Opening Prayer** (7 mins.)
Give members an opportunity to share special highlights or new insights from their week's study. Ask members to find the prayers they wrote this week for the sanctification of a Christian brother or sister (p. 172). Divide into pairs. Ask each person to select one group of model prayer requests in prayer guide 11 (p. 216). Ask each one to pray the re-quests for his or her partner and then to pray for his or her sanctification.

**3. Check Memory Verses** (3 mins.)
With members remaining in pairs, ask each person to check the partner's memory verse(s) for this week.

**4. Spiritual Awakening** (15–20 mins.)
Ask members to return to the large group and to share their lists of requests for spiritual awakening (p. 166). Discuss the unity of Christians and the changes each member visualized in day 5. Pray conversationally for the unity of Christians and for spiritual awakening in your nation.

**5. Agree or Disagree** (5 mins.)
Ask members to turn to page 164. Discuss the thoughts written about the power and goal of intercessory prayer. Call on one member to lead in prayer for the increase of intercessory prayer in your church.

**6. Preview Week 12** (3 mins.)
Call on the person enlisted to preview week 12.

**7. Closing Prayer** (22–32 mins.)
Ask members to share their responses to the arrival activity. Pray for one another, using conversational prayer. Focusing on one person at a time, allow everyone to pray for that person before moving to pray for another person in the group. Encourage members to be specific in their prayers. Close the session by singing together "The Bond of Love" or "Blest Be the Tie."

### AFTER THE SESSION

1. Evaluate each activity and determine ways to improve participation in future sessions.

2. During the week call two or three more group members and share words of encouragement. Remind them of your prayers. Ask if they have specific concerns about which you can pray with them this week. Pray with them over the phone.

3. Report attendance.

4. Begin preparation for the next session.

## SESSION 12

# Praying for Missions

### BEFORE THE SESSION

❑ Carefully study week 12 and complete all of the learning activities.

❑ Display the week-titles poster with the arrow pointing to week 12.

❑ Read "During the Session." Secure materials, including a globe or world map, and be prepared to guide each activity.

- ❑ Secure copies of missions periodicals, lists of missions prayer requests, a missionary prayer calendar, denominational publications, and other resources that provide information about missions needs at home and abroad. If your church does not have copies, order them or borrow some from neighbor churches.
- ❑ Bring your Scripture-memory cards for use in the memory drill.
- ❑ Talk to the pastor or a long-time church member to learn how many members of your church have responded to God's call to missions and other full-time Christian ministries.
- ❑ Prepare or enlist a member to give a three-minute overview of week 13.
- ❑ Pray for each group member.

### DURING THE SESSION

**1. Arrival Activity** (15–20 mins.)
As members arrive, ask them to browse through the missions resources provided and select one special missions need for which the group can pray. Ask them to prepare to share with the group brief details about that need. When everyone has found an item to share, call for members to share the needs they discovered. Share yours first as a model of brevity. After each need has been shared, ask for a volunteer to pray for that need. Continue until all needs have been prayed for.

**2. Highlights of the Week** (3 mins.)
Give members an opportunity to share highlights or new insights from their week's study.

**3. Check Memory Verses** (7–12 mins.)
Divide into pairs and ask each person to check the partner's memory verse(s) for this week. For review and fun, conduct a memory-verse drill. Divide into two teams. Alternating between the two teams, ask for memory verses to be quoted. Expect verses to be quoted word for word. Anyone on the team may recite the verse. Award one point for a correct quotation. Subtract one point for each incorrect quotation. At the conclusion of the drill, state that everyone who memorizes God's Word is a winner, for "thy word have I hid in mine heart, that I might not sin against thee" (Ps. 119:11).

**4. Pray for Sending** (10 mins.)
Share with the group your church's record of persons responding to God's call to missions and other full-time Christian work. Ask members to suggest reasons for the good or poor response. Briefly evaluate the activity of laypersons in your church in sharing the gospel with the lost in your community and around the world. Call on one member to lead the group in a prayer for God to call forth laborers from your church into the harvest.

**5. Breakthrough Praying** (10 mins.)
Ask members to turn to "Missions Imperatives" and "Prayers Based on Missions Imperatives," page 179. Briefly discuss the need for intercessory prayer if a breakthrough is to happen in reaching our world for Christ. Ask members to pray sentence prayers for the needs and goals of world evangelization.

**6. Preview Week 13** (5 mins.)
Call on the person enlisted to preview week 13. Discuss details about the prayer retreat to follow the study.

**7. Closing Prayer** (10–15 mins.)
Place a globe or world map on the floor. Ask members to kneel in a close circle around it. Instruct members to pray sentence prayers for world evangelization through missions efforts. Encourage members to pray for only one subject at a time, but remind them that they may pray more than one time.

### AFTER THE SESSION

1. Evaluate each activity and determine ways to improve participation in future sessions.
2. Report attendance.
3. Begin preparation for the next session. Make sure that all last-minute details for the prayer retreat are taken care of this week. Call those responsible for various parts of the retreat to make sure that they have done their jobs.
4. Spend extra time this week praying for group members. Ask God to guide each member to understand how he or she can best become involved in a ministry of prayer.

## SESSION 13

# Establishing a Ministry of Prayer

### BEFORE THE SESSION

- ❑ Carefully study week 13 and complete all of the learning activities.
- ❑ Display the week-titles poster with the arrow pointing to week 13.
- ❑ Read "During the Session." Secure materials and be prepared to guide each activity.
- ❑ If you plan to have a retreat after the course ends, have all final details ready to announce to members.
- ❑ Provide paper and pencils.

□ Secure information about all upcoming opportunities for discipleship training. Prepare to encourage members to get involved in an ongoing program of discipleship training.
□ Pray for each group member.

### DURING THE SESSION

**1. Arrival Activity** (10 mins.)
As members arrive, give each a sheet of paper and ask each to write an evaluation of the course. Ask for comments on the workbook, the homework requirements, the group sessions, the leader, and so forth. Ask members to identify the most meaningful part of the course. Ask them to identify anything they would suggest changing in a future study of *Disciple's Prayer Life*. Ask members to complete the Christian Growth Study Plan form on page 243 and to turn it in to you.

**2. Highlights and Opening Prayer** (8 mins.)
Give members an opportunity to share special highlights of the course. Sing the Doxology as an opening prayer of praise.

**3. Check Memory Verses** (7 mins.)
Divide into pairs and ask each person to check the partner's memory verse(s) for this week. Review all of the verses memorized during the course.

**4. Prayer Ministry** (15–20 mins.)
Return to the large group. Discuss each individual's dreams and plans for involvement in a prayer ministry. Decide on any steps that need to be taken to establish or improve your church's intercessory prayer ministry. Record responses to share with appropriate persons.

**5. Commissioning and Blessing** (20 mins.)
Ask each member, one at a time, to kneel in the center of the group and to share his or her ministry or growth goal or greatest personal need. Then ask that person to call on one member to lead a prayer for this concern. Ask the pray-er to place his or her hands on the person kneeling and to pray for the concern shared. Follow this pattern for each member.

Challenge each person to continue growing spiritually by participating in an ongoing program of discipleship training. Share with the group upcoming opportunities in your church. Discuss some of the options on page 194.

**6. Retreat** (3 mins.)
Announce final retreat plans and encourage members to attend.

**7. Closing Prayer** (10 mins.)
Stand close together in a circle and lock arms. Pray sentence prayers of praise and thanksgiving for what God has done during the course.

### AFTER THE SESSION

1. Evaluate each activity. Write a report on the study for reference the next time you lead a group through *Disciple's Prayer Life*.

2. Report attendance. Give final enrollment and attendance figures for use on the Annual Church Profile.

3. Complete and mail all Christian Growth Study Plan forms. Make sure that each person receives the *Disciple's Prayer Life* diploma when it arrives. If possible, award the diplomas during a worship service.

4. Follow up with each group member soon after the course has concluded to make sure that each is following through on personal-growth plans. Guide each into meaningful participation in a prayer ministry.

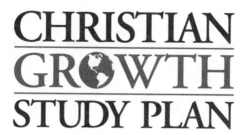

# CHRISTIAN GROWTH STUDY PLAN

*Preparing Christians to Serve*

In the **Christian Growth Study Plan** (formerly the Church Study Course) this workbook, *Disciple's Prayer Life: Walking in Fellowship with God*, is a resource for course credit in the subject area Prayer in the Christian Growth category of diploma plans. To receive credit, read the workbook; complete the learning activities; attend group sessions; show your work to your pastor, a staff member, or a church leader; and complete the following information. This page may be duplicated. Send the completed page to:

**Christian Growth Study Plan**
**One LifeWay Plaza**
**Nashville, TN 37234-0117**
**Fax: (615)251-5067; email:** *cgspnet@lifeway.com*
For information about the Christian Growth Study Plan, refer to the *Christian Growth Study Plan Catalog*. It is located online at *www.lifeway.com/cgsp*. If you do not have access to the Internet, contact the Christian Growth Study Plan office, 1-800-968-5519, for the specific plan you need for your ministry.

## Disciple's Prayer Life: Walking in Fellowship with God
### Course Number CG-0001

### PARTICIPANT INFORMATION

| Social Security Number (USA ONLY-optional) | Personal CGSP Number* | Date of Birth (MONTH, DAY, YEAR) |
|---|---|---|

| Name (First, Middle, Last) | Home Phone |
|---|---|

| Address (Street, Route, or P.O. Box) | City, State, or Province | Zip/Postal Code |
|---|---|---|

### CHURCH INFORMATION

| Church Name |
|---|

| Address (Street, Route, or P.O. Box) | City, State, or Province | Zip/Postal Code |
|---|---|---|

### CHANGE REQUEST ONLY

| ☐ Former Name |
|---|

| ☐ Former Address | City, State, or Province | Zip/Postal Code |
|---|---|---|

| ☐ Former Church | City, State, or Province | Zip/Postal Code |
|---|---|---|

| Signature of Pastor, Conference Leader, or Other Church Leader | Date |
|---|---|

*New participants are requested but not required to give SS# and date of birth. Existing participants, please give CGSP# when using SS# for the first time. Thereafter, only one ID# is required. **Mail to:** Christian Growth Study Plan, One LifeWay Plaza, Nashville, TN 37234-0117. Fax: (615)251-5067.

Rev. 10-01

**Week 1**

Delight thyself also in the LORD; and he shall give thee the desires of thine heart.
*Psalm 37:4, KJV*

**Week 2**

That which we have seen and heard declare we unto you, that ye also may have fellowship with us: and truly our fellowship is with the Father, and with his Son Jesus Christ.
*1 John 1:3, KJV*

**Week 3**

My voice shalt thou hear in the morning, O LORD; in the morning will I direct my prayer unto thee, and will look up.
*Psalm 5:3, KJV*

**Week 4**

I will hasten my word to perform it.
*Jeremiah 1:12, KJV*

**Week 5**

I will praise thee, O Lord my God, with all my heart: and I will glorify thy name for evermore.
*Psalm 86:12, KJV*

**Week 6**

Thou art worthy, O Lord, to receive glory and honour and power: for thou hast created all things and for thy pleasure they are and were created.
*Revelation 4:11, KJV*

**Week 7**

If my people, which are called by my name, shall humble themselves, and pray, and seek my face, and turn from their wicked ways; then will I hear from heaven, and will forgive their sin, and will heal their land.
*2 Chronicles 7:14, KJV*

**Week 1**

This is the confidence that we have in him, that, if we ask any thing according to his will, he heareth us.
*1 John 5:14, KJV*

**Week 2**

Now therefore, I pray thee, if I have found grace in thy sight, shew me now thy way, that I may know thee, that I may find grace in thy sight: and consider that this nation is thy people.
*Exodus 33:13, KJV*

**Week 3**

O God, thou art my God; early will I seek thee: my soul thirsteth for thee, my flesh longeth for thee in a dry and thirsty land, where no water is.
*Psalm 63:1, KJV*

**Week 4**

If ye abide in me, and my words abide in you, ye shall ask what ye will, and it shall be done unto you.
*John 15:7, KJV*

**Week 5**

In every thing give thanks: for this is the will of God in Christ Jesus concerning you.
*1 Thessalonians 5:18, KJV*

**Week 6**

God is a Spirit: and they that worship him must worship him in spirit and in truth.
*John 4:24, KJV*

**Week 7**

Again I say unto you, that if two of you shall agree on earth as touching any thing that they shall ask, it shall be done for them of my Father which is in heaven. For where two or three are gathered together in my name, there am I in the midst of them.
*Matthew 18:19-20, KJV*

## Week 1

This is the confidence we have in approaching God: that if we ask anything according to his will, he hears us.
*1 John 5:14, NIV*

## Week 2

If you are pleased with me, teach me your ways so I may know you and continue to find favor with you. Remember that this nation is your people.
*Exodus 33:13, NIV*

## Week 3

O God, you are my God,
    earnestly I seek you;
my soul thirsts for you,
    my body longs for you,
in a dry and weary land
    where there is no water.
*Psalm 63:1, NIV*

## Week 4

If you remain in me and my words remain in you, ask whatever you wish, and it will be given you.
*John 15:7, NIV*

## Week 5

Give thanks in all circumstances, for this is God's will for you in Christ Jesus.
*1 Thessalonians 5:18, NIV*

## Week 6

God is spirit, and his worshipers must worship in spirit and in truth.
*John 4:24, NIV*

## Week 7

Again, I tell you that if two of you on earth agree about anything you ask for, it will be done for you by my Father in heaven. For where two or three come together in my name, there am I with them.
*Matthew 18:19-20, NIV*

## Week 1

Delight yourself in the LORD
    and he will give you the desires of your heart.
*Psalm 37:4, NIV*

## Week 2

We proclaim to you what we have seen and heard, so that you also may have fellowship with us. And our fellowship is with the Father and with his Son, Jesus Christ.
*1 John 1:3, NIV*

## Week 3

In the morning, O LORD, you hear my voice;
    in the morning I lay my requests before you
    and wait in expectation.
*Psalm 5:3, NIV*

## Week 4

I am watching to see that my word is fulfilled.
*Jeremiah 1:12, NIV*

## Week 5

I will praise you, O LORD my God, with all my heart;
    I will glorify your name forever.
*Psalm 86:12, NIV*

## Week 6

You are worthy, our LORD and God,
    to receive glory and honor and power,
for you created all things,
    and by your will they were created
    and have their being.
*Revelation 4:11, NIV*

## Week 7

If my people, who are called by my name, will humble themselves and pray and seek my face and turn from their wicked ways, then will I hear from heaven and will forgive their sin and will heal their land.
*2 Chronicles 7:14, NIV*

### Week 8

If we confess our sins, he is faithful and just to forgive us our sins, and to cleanse us from all unrighteousness.
*1 John 1:9, KJV*

### Week 9

Call unto me, and I will answer thee, and shew thee great and mighty things, which thou knowest not.
*Jeremiah 33:3, KJV*

### Week 10

If I regard iniquity in my heart, the Lord will not hear me.
*Psalm 66:18, KJV*

### Week 11

Be careful for nothing; but in every thing by prayer and supplication with thanksgiving let your requests be made known unto God.
*Philippians 4:6, KJV*

### Week 12

The harvest truly is plenteous, but the labourers are few; pray ye therefore the Lord of the harvest, that he will send forth labourers into his harvest.
*Matthew 9:37-38, KJV*

### Week 13

The eyes of the LORD run to and fro throughout the whole earth, to shew himself strong in the behalf of them whose heart is perfect toward him.
*2 Chronicles 16:9, KJV*

### Week 8

At the name of Jesus every knee should bow, of things in heaven, and things in earth, and things under the earth; and that every tongue should confess that Jesus Christ is LORD, to the glory of God the Father.
*Philippians 2:10-11, KJV*

### Week 9

If ye shall ask any thing in my name, I will do it.
*John 14:14, KJV*

### Week 10

Ye ask, and receive not, because ye ask amiss, that ye may consume it upon your lusts.
*James 4:3, KJV*

### Week 11

Our Father which art in heaven, Hallowed be thy name. Thy Kingdom come. Thy will be done in earth, as it is in heaven. Give us this day our daily bread. And forgive us our debts, as we forgive our debtors. And lead us not into temptation, but deliver us from evil: for thine is the kingdom, and the power, and the glory, for ever.
*Matthew 6:9-13, KJV*

### Week 12

Finally, brethren, pray for us, that the word of the LORD may have free course, and be glorified, even as it is with you.
*2 Thessalonians 3:1, KJV*

### Week 13

Now unto him that is able to do exceeding abundantly above all that we ask or think, according to the power that worketh in us, unto him be glory in the church by Christ Jesus throughout all ages, world without end.
*Ephesians 3:20-21, KJV*

**Week 8**

At the name of Jesus every knee should bow,
   in heaven and on earth and under the earth,
and every tongue confess that Jesus Christ is Lord,
   to the glory of God the Father.
*Philippians 2:10-11, NIV*

**Week 9**

You may ask me for anything in my name, and I will
do it.
*John 14:14, NIV*

**Week 10**

When you ask, you do not receive, because you ask
with wrong motives, that you may spend what you
get on your pleasures.
*James 4:3, NIV*

**Week 11**

Our Father in heaven, hallowed be your name, your
kingdom come, your will be done on earth as it is in
heaven. Give us today our daily bread. Forgive us our
debts, as we also have forgiven our debtors. And lead us
not into temptation, but deliver us from the evil one.
*Matthew 6:9-13, NIV*

**Week 12**

Finally, brothers, pray for us that the message of the
Lord may spread rapidly and be honored, just as it
was with you.
*2 Thessalonians 3:1, NIV*

**Week 13**

Now to him who is able to do immeasurably more
than all we ask or imagine, according to his power that
is at work within us, to him be glory in the church and
in Christ Jesus throughout all generations, for ever
and ever!
*Ephesians 3:20-21, NIV*

**Week 8**

If we confess our sins, he is faithful and just and
will forgive us our sins and purify us from all
unrighteousness.
*1 John 1:9, NIV*

**Week 9**

Call to me and I will answer you and tell you great and
unsearchable things you do not know.
*Jeremiah 33:3, NIV*

**Week 10**

If I had cherished sin in my heart,
   the Lord would not have listened.
*Psalm 66:18, NIV*

**Week 11**

Do not be anxious about anything, but in everything,
by prayer and petition, with thanksgiving, present your
requests to God.
*Philippians 4:6, NIV*

**Week 12**

The harvest is plentiful but the workers are few. Ask
the Lord of the harvest, therefore, to send out workers
into his harvest field.
*Matthew 9:37-38, NIV*

**Week 13**

The eyes of the LORD range throughout the earth to
strengthen those whose hearts are fully committed
to him.
*2 Chronicles 16:9, NIV*